FAIRFIELD COUNTY, SOUTH CAROLINA MINUTES OF THE COUNTY COURT

1785-1799

By

BRENT H. HOLCOMB, C.A.L.S.

This volume was reproduced from
An 1981 edition located in the
Publisher's private library,
Greenville, South Carolina

Please direct all correspondence and orders to:

www.southernhistoricalpress.com
or
SOUTHERN HISTORICAL PRESS, Inc.
PO BOX 1267
375 West Broad Street
Greenville, SC   29601
southernhistoricalpress@gmail.com

Originally published: Easley, SC. 1981
Copyrighted 1981 by:
The Rev. Silas Emmett Lucas, Jr.
Greenville, SC
ISBN #0-89308-212-0
All rights Reserved.
Printed in the United States of America

Andrew Mc.Dowell	John Stinson. R. C.
Willm Boyd. R. C.	James Neilly.
John Cameron	Francis Mc. Daniel
James McMillin	Saml. Arnot
Robt Phillips Ju^r.	Andrew Cameron
John Elliot	John Porter
Saml Beatty	Norris Weaver
Danl Wottan	John Maybin
Saml. Caldwell	Christ^r Huffman
John Cork.	Joseph Cameron
Wm. Neilson	John Atcheson.
Lewis Owens.	Benjn. Mc.Graw
Adam Free.	Saml Proctor

The Court proceeded to Elect a Sheriff, where upon Casting up the Votes, it appeared that William Boyd Gent. was duly Elected.

The Court then proceeded to Elect a Coroner when upon Casting up the Votes it appeared that Burr Harrison Esq.r was duly Elected.

The Rates of Taverns for provisions, Forrage and Liquors were then ascertained and are as follows Viz.

Tavern Rates

Jamaica Rum when carried away @ p quart	2^s/4^d
West India D^o. -- @ p quart	2/
Taffia ---- D^o ---- @ p quart	1/2
Jamaica Rum when drank in grog at the Tavern at p Half pint	9^d
West India D^o @ p Half pint	7^d
Taftia D^o. ----D^o. @ D^o.	4^d
Good Peach Brandy -----D^o. @ D^o.	7^d
Good Whiskey ----- D^o. @ D^o.	4^d
Loaf Sugar used for half a pint of Liquor	2^d
Brown Sugar D^o. -----------D^o.	1^d
French Brandy for Half a pint	9^d
Gin --------- for D^o.	9^d

Tavern Rates Continued

	L. s. d.
Madeira Wine ------ p Bottle -----	0. 4. 8.
Vidonia Wine ------ p D^o ----------	- 4. 8.
Port Wine ----------p D^o. ----------	- 4. 8.
Madeira or Port Wine by the Quart ------	- 3. 6.
All other inferior Wines by the Quart --	- 2. 4.
Bottled Porter ----- p Bottle ----------	2. -
Draft D^o. ---- p Bottle ---------------	- 1. 4.
Bottled Bristol Cyder p, D^d ----------	2. -
Draft Cyder ---- p Quart ---------------	0. 9^d

Meals of Good Healthy Provisions

Breakfast	@ 8^d
Dinner	@ 1^s/2^d
Supper	@ 8^d.

All bespoke Dinners where a Bill of Fare is given, the Parties agree on the Price.

Lodgings One Night On

A Featherbed with Clean Linnen   6^d
A Mattress with D^o.   4^d
For Stabling a Horse one Night on corn blades or good hay   8^d
Fort two Quarts of Indian Corn on three Quarts of Oats   4^d
For one night in a good pasture   3^d

A Bill of Sale for Sundries from John Hathcock to Thos Parrot Senr was regularly proven in Court by Willm Cato and Smith Ogilvie.

Thomas Parrot Senr petitioned the Court for a Licence to retail Spiritous Liquors.

Ordered, That the prayer of his Petiton be Granted.
The Court adjourned to Ten o'Clock tomorrow morning.

John Winn
Richard Winn
Jno Buchanan
James Craig

Wednesday 27th. July 1785.

The Court met according to adjournment and Appointed the following persons Overseers on the following Roads Viz.

The Ridge Road to Charleston

	Overseers.
From the County Line near Lee's Old place, to) Cockralls)	John McDaniel
From Cockeralls to the Court House)	Moses Cockeralls
From the Court House to Cedar Creek)	William Robinson
From Cedar Creek to the Round Top or County Line))	Richard Taylor
On the now blazed Road to Camden to be cut thirty feet wide	
From Thomas Hill to the Wolf Pit)	John Adam Arick.
From the Wolf pit to the County Line)	Roland Williamson.
On the new blazed Road to Congaree to be cut thirty feet wide.	
From the Blazes below Thomas Hills to Cedar Creek))	Samuel McKinney
From Cedar Creek to the County Line)	John Swilla
On the Road from Winnsborough to Liles's For to be cut thirty feet Wide	
From Winnsborough to Col. Jno Winn's)	Richard Gldney [Gladney]

From Colo Winn's to Ederingtons Road)	Thomas Watts
From Ederington's road to Lisle's Ford)	Elijah Majors
From the County Line Sandy River,) to Alcorns Old Place)	Eleazer Moberly.
From Col. Winn's Mill Road to Thomas Nelsons)	William Hughes
From Thomas Nelson opposite to Daniel Wootans)	John Ogilvie.
From Daniel Wootans to Joseph Gibson's Senr)	Daniel Wootans
From Joseph Gibsons to Little River)	Jacob Frazer
From Little River to Cedar Creek)	John Turnepseed

Road to Shirers Ferry

From Lee's old place to Hills Creeks)	John Lee
From Hill's Creek to Little River)	Thomas Shannon
From Little River to the forks of the) Congaree Road)	Henry Rogers
From the Forks of the Congaree Road to) Shirer's Ferry)	John Cooke

The Road from James Alcorns to the County Line towards Sandy River.
Francis Coleman

The old Road From Winnsborough to Camden

From the Charleston Road to Wateree Creek)	Larkin Cardin.
From Wateree Creek to Dutchmans Creek)	William Cason.
From Dutchman's Creek to Tolersons Old place)	Zachariah Nettles
From Tolersons old place to the County Line)	Thomas Muse

Rockey Mount Road

From the Fork of the Old Camden & Rockey Mount) Road to James Loves)	James Love
From James Loves to the Moutain Gap)	Thomas Stone.
From the Moutain Gap to the County Line)	Macaijah Picket

Constables appointed
      The Court proceeded to the appointment of Constables when

Thos Parrot Senr	Daniel Wooton
Francis Kirkland	Nathl Harven
Willm Owens	Larkin Cardin
Willm Gray	Leonard Hill
Edwd Mc.Graw	John Mills
Willm Kirkland	Moses Hollis
son of John	
James Johnston	James Simmons
Samuel Luckey	

      were duly appointed and the oath of office administred to Thomas
Parrot Senr
      Francis Kirkland and James Johnston.
Tavern Senr
Jas. Lewis

James Lewis petitioned the Court for a Tavern Licence

Ordered that the prayer of his petition be Granted.

Licence to
Sam: Caldwell
    Samuel Caldwell petitioned the Court for a Tavern Licence.
Ordered That the prayer of his Petition be Granted.

On Motion Ordered That Licences granted this Sitting of the Court, do continue but Six months and that the Clerk do receive Thirty Shillings Lawful Money for each of them to be detained in his Hands untill the Court shall give him further directions.

On Motion Ordered

Overseers to
appoint
warners.
    That the several Overseers of the Road shall appoint their own Warners, who shall be Liable to the same penalties (for non performance) as if they had been appointed in Court.

Court
House
    The Court then proceed to appoint the place for erecting the Court House and Goal when it was unamimously agreed that Winnsborough being the most Central part in the County the Building should be erected there.

The court then adjourned to the fourth Monday in October next.

                  John Winn
                  Richard Winn
                  Jn° Buchanan
                  James Craig.

Monday. 24th October 1785.

The Court met according to Adjournment.

Nelson
Young
    A Writ of Attachment Granted by John Buchanan Esqr to Thomas Nelson again to Isaac Young for Fifty Bushels of Corn, was returned (regularly Served) to the Court.

Whereupon Isaac Young appeared and produced Rebeccah Elliot formerly wife to Daniel Gowen deceased from whom the said Young rented a tract lf Land and had engaged to pay her and her present Husband John Elliot, the Rent of Fifty five Bushels of Corn.

The said Rebeccah Elliot Satisfied the Court that her former Husband purchased the said Land and that had been Seventeen years in possession of the same.

Judgment.

It appears to the Court that the plaintiff had no Cause of Action against the Defendant as the said Rebeccah Elliot had never given up possession of the said Land for which the plaintiff demanded Rent.
Therefore ordered to pay Costs.

Wooten
Const.
    Daniel Wooton was Qualified to serve as Constable for this County.
Adjourned till tomorrow at Eleven o'Clock

                  John Winn
                  Jn° Buchanan
                  Richard Winn

Tuesday 25th. October 1785.

The Court met according to Adjournment.

License to J. McDonald	A Petition from Mc.John McDonald was read, Praying for a License to keep a Tavern.
	Ordered that the prayer of the Petition be Granted.
L. Cardin Const.	Larkin Cardin took the Oath of a Constable.
J. Winn to Wm. Durphey	John Winn Esqr acknowledged in open Court the Signing Sealing and Delivery of Titles by way of Lease and release to William Durphey for Two Lots of Land No. 133 (one Hundred and thirty three) and No. 71 (Seventy one) in the Town of Winnsborough.
D^d to J. Milling	Also to John Milling for Eight Acres of Land adjoining the same Town and for the following Lotts therein Viz. No. 156. 157. 164. 165. 160. 161. 168. and No. 169.
D^o to D. Evans	Also to David Evans for the Lotts No. 176 & No. 184. in the Town aforesaid.
D^o to J. Hayes	Also to John Hays for the Lot No. 5 in the Town aofresaid.
R. Winn to T. Baker	Genl. Richard Winn acknowledged the Signing Sealing and Delivery of Titles by way of Lease and Release to a Tract of Land on the Head of Jackson's Creek containing thirty two Acres more or less to Thomas Baker Esquire
Coleman to D. Evans	Kador Coleman acknowledged in open Court the having Signed Sealed and Delivered Titles by way of Lease and Release to David Evans for One Hundred and Fifty Acres of Land on the Wateree Creek (originally Granted to George Roden.)
	Susannah Coleman (wife of the said Kador Coleman) appeared in open Court and did renounce Relinquish and Resign all her right of Dower in the above Tract of One Hundred and fifty acres so conveyed by her Husband to the said David Evans.
Downey to Black	Margaret Downey and James Black appeared in Court, and requested the Justices to determine upon a matter in Dispute, depending between them concerning their property in a certain Chestnut Sorrel Mare, But neither part being provided with sufficient Evidence the Court thought proper to order the matter to be left to Arbitration, When Margaret Downey named Capt. John Gray, and James Black, named John Stormond as Arbitrators.
	Ordered That the aforesaid John Gray and John Stormont, Do meet at Samuel Caldwells on Monday the 31st Instant and there Enquire into the Matter upon the Oaths of such Evidences as may be produced; and to finally determine all matters between the parties, But if they cannot agree they are to chose an Umpire, and to send their Umpirage on Award to the Clerks Office at Winnsborough

| W. Boyd Sheriff | William Boyd, who was appointed Sheriff, appeared in Court and took the Oath of Allegiance and Fidelity to the state, also his Oath of Office, after giving Bond according to Law. |

R. Craig U. Sher.   Wm Boyd proposed Mr. Robert Craig as his under sheriff, who received the approbation of the Court and took his Oath of Office.

J. Bell D. Sher.   Mr. Boyd also proposed Mr. John Bell as Deputy Sheriff, who received the approbation of the Court and took his Oath of Office.

Thomas Parrot requested Leave of the Court to resign his Office of Constable which was Granted.

Overseer   Victor Neely was appointed Overseer of the road from Daniel Wooton's to Ewings old place in the room of Daniel Wooton.

Overseer   William Frazier was appointed Overseer of the Highway, in the room of Jacob Frazier deceased.

The Court then adjourned until tomorrow at 11 o'Clock.

John Winn
Richard Winn
Jno. Buchanan

The Court met according to Adjournment.

J. Winn to H. Milling   John Winn Esquire acknowledged in open Cour the Having Signed Sealed and Delivered Titles by way of Lease and Release to Hugh Milling Esquire for one Lot No. 48 (Forty Eight) in the Town of Winnsborough.

D^o to J. Quarrel   Also to Joseph Quarrel for one Lot No. 4 (four) in the Town aforesaid.

D^o to A. Redmond   Also to Andrew Redmond for one Lot No. 49 (forty nine) in the said Town.

D^o to J. & H. Milling   Also for Messrs. John and Hugh Milling for Lotts No. 50. (fifty) and No. (one Hundred and two in the Town aforesaid.

D^o to J. Buchanan   Also to John Buchanan Esquire for Four Lotts No. 140 (one Hundred and forty) 141. (one Hundred and forty one) 61. (Sixty one) and No. 62 (Sixty two). in the Town aofresaid.

D^o to J. Baker   Also to Thomas Baker Esquire for Twenty Acres of land more or less Bounded by Land of the said Thomas Baker John Winn Stephen Draytons and John Vanderhorts and nearly adjoining the Town of Winnsborough.

To Wm. Humphreys   Also to William Humphreys for Four Lotts No. 65. (Sixty five) 64 (Sixty four) No. 137 (one hundred and Thirty Seven) and No. 138. (one Hundred and thirty Eight) in the said Town of Winnsborough.

Overseers   The Court proceeded to appoint Overseers to repair the Road from Hutchesons Mill to Cedar Creek, Vix. From Hutchisons Mill to Mill Creek Capt. Edward Martin. From Mill Creek to the Gross road from Col. Kirklands to McGraw's Mill. Robert Raab. From thence to join Shavers Road. John Alston.

Penelop & P. Winn renounced dower.   Mrs. Penelope Winn Wife of John Winn Esqr. and Mrs. Priscilla Winn, Wife to General Richard Winn, both came into open Court and did then and there Renounce relinquish and resign all and Singular their Rights of Dower to all and every of the Several Lots of Land in Town of

6

Winnsborough, Togerther with all and Singular the Lands known by the
Name of the Winnsborough Lands amounting in measure to Two Thousand
Two Hundred Acres more or less.

Caldwell   Samuel Caldwell petitioned the Court for Leave to return
Lis.^C Deliv^d his Tavern Licence and to take up his Bond, he assigns good
up   reasons for his request therefore the prayer of his
           petition was Granted

J. Quarrel   Joseph Quarrel petitioned the Court for a licence to retail
Licence   Spirituous Liquors.   Granted.
Liquors

T. Baker &   The Court proceeded to nominate Two Justices in the
J. Pearson   room of Henry Hampton and Phillip Pearson Esquires.
Chosen Just^s When Capt. Thomas Baker and John Pearson were Chosen.

    Capt. Gray having declined acting as an Arbitrator for Mrs. Downing
Saml. Caldwell is appointed in his room.

The Court adjourned to the Fourth Monday in January next.

John Winn
Richard Winn
Jno Buchanan

January Term 1786.

The Court met according to Adjournment.

Present the Honble
John Winn
Richard Winn
John Buchanan
James Craig
William Kirkland

    Jacob Brown Esqr produced a Licence from the Honble Henry Pendleton
Adams Burke and John F. Grink Esqr permitting him to practice as an
Atty in any of the Courts of Law or Equity within this State.

    The Court Proceeded to the Drawing Jurors for next Term which are
as follows Viz.

Grand Jurors

Capt. John Cook	Robert Reid
Minor Winn	Moses Cockral
Isaac Love	John Lee
Richard Taylor	William Daniel
Robert Martin	John King
Jacob Bethney	Joseph Kirkland
John Robertson L R	Hugh Young
Benjⁿ Dove	Rowland Williamson
Willm McGraw	
John Pearson.	
W^m Mc.Morris Senr	
William Douhe	

Petit Jurors

John Atckison	Robert Mansell
John Mc.Comb	James Mobley
Willm. Neilson	James Davies
Saml. Caldwell	Joseph Cameron
Richd Woodward	Michael Henning
Robert Ewing	John Elliot

Richd Gladney　　　　　Alex.^r Mc.Kean
John McKinney　　　　　 Willm. McCright
James Russell Junr　　 Alex.^r Robertson Junr

William Martin　　　　　John Dodds
James Mc.Mullin　　　　 John Porter
John Cameron　　　　　 Willm. Wilson
William Boyd　　　　　　And.^w Mc.Dowell
John Cork.　　　　　　　Robt Phillips Junr
Joseph Chapman　　　　　Thomas Parrot Junr

The following Persons drawn to serve as Grand Jurors, appeared, and were Sworn Viz.

John McDaniel　　　　　James Brown
Wm. Dorch　　　　　　　C. D. Bradford
John Alston　　　　　　Henry Hunter F.
Isaac Love　　　　　　 Binoni Holly
Richard-Tayler [stricken]　　James Hart
Wm. Mc.Morris　　　　　John Woodward
Edwd. Martin
Willm. Cason

Col. Hunter appointed foreman.

The Court appointed Jacob Brown Esqr Attorney for the County.

Daniel Brown Esqr produced a Licence from the Honble Henry Pendleton Adams Burke and John F. Grimke Esqr permitting him to practice as an Attorney in any of the Courts of Law or Equity within this State.

The following persons were drawn by Serve as Petit Jurors Viz.

Andrew McDonnell　　　 John Porter
John Elliot　　　　　　Chris.^t Huffman
John Cook　　　　　　　Joseph Cameron
Wm. Nelson　　　　　　 John Atcheson
James Neely　　　　　　John McClarkin
Francis Mc.Daniel　　　Francis McDonald
Saml Arnot　　　　　 appointed Foreman

Pet. & Gr.^d Jurors   Upon the Petit Jurors being called over the above Persons answered to their names. Ordered that proper Notice be taken of the Defaulters of both Grand and Petit Jurors.

Ordered that a Road be laid out from or near Nicholas Thompsons old Place to Widow Dukes

Overseer John King

Road ord.^d   Ordered that a Road be laid out from Stark's Ferry to join in the most conventient Place the Road from Widow Duke's to Nicholas Thompson's Old Place.

Overseer Thomas Stone

J. Winn to J. Woodward   Col: John Winn acknowledged in open Court to have Signed and Sealed a Conveyance Lease and Release unto John Woodward of the Lotts No. 145, 146, 56. 57. and 85. in the Town of Winnsborough.

B. Moberley to Ed: Moberley   Moses Hill and Thomas Holsey appeared in open Court and made Oath that they saw Benjamin Moberley Sign Seal and Deliver Titles by Lease and Release unto Edward Moberley of a tract of Two Hundred Acres of Land which was Granted to the said Benjamin the 26. August 1774. Also that they saw the said Benjamin Moberley Execute Titles of likes nature to John Moberly for One Hundred and fifty Acres Granted to William Moberly by

8

Patent dated 4th March 1760 and they Subscribed their names as Evidence thereto both the above Deeds.

Adjourned till tomorrow at 10 o'Clock.

> John Winn
> Richd Winn
> Jno. Buchanan
> James Craig
> William Kirkland

January Term 1786. Janry 24th.

The Court met According to Adjournment

> Present
> John Winn
> Richard Winn
> John Buchanan
> James Craig
> Willm Kirkland

Upon Petition

Licence to Quarrel	Ordered that Joseph Quarrel do receive a Licence to keep a Tavern for one year.

D^o to J. McDaniel	Ordered that John McDaniel do receive a licence to keep a Tavern for one year.

Barnet
to
Rabb
    Charles Daniel Bradford and Daniel Cockran appeared in Court and being duly Sworn Saith on Oath That they were present and did see William Barnet Deliver and acknowledge as his Act and Deed Titles by Lease and Release to Wm. Rabb of a Plantation containg Two Hundred and fifty Acres Situate on Little River Granted the said Barnet 4th. March 1760.

C. Daniel Bradford also made Oath that he did see Agnes Barnet his wife of the said William Sign Seal and Deliver the same.

M. Pearson
to
Wm. Pearson
    John Pearson Esqr appeared in open Court and being duly sowrn made Oath that he saw Mary Pearson Sign Seal and deliver a certain deed purporting to be a Deed of Gift to William Pearson and Phillip Pearson of certain negro Boys therein named.

W. Rabb
to
Wm. Pearson
    William Raab appeared in open Court and ackowledged the Signing Sealing and delivery of Titles by way of Lease and Release to William Pearson of One Hundred Acres of Land on Broad and Little River

Lis^c to
Jas. Austin
    Ordered that James Austin do receive a Licence to Sell by the gallon Spirituous Liquors for one year and do pay half price of a Tavern Licence.

Isaac Love Vs Edward Maynard - Case

I. Love
vs
Ed: Maynard
    The Parties came into Court and chose Charles Picket, Moses Knighter to arbitrate the matter and make a return to the next Court, and their award to be a Rule of Court.

Isaac Love vs Edward Maynard, Same and Petition, the same order.

A. Gladden
Vs
Jas. Rainey
    Ann Gladden vs Jas. Rainey & Ch^s Lewis The Defend^t James Rainey came into Court and confessed Judgment for L 23. 9. 4. & Costs.

Downey   Margaret Downey vs Hugh Smith Petn.
  vs   The matter was heard and Judgment for Defendant.
H. Smith

Jno Gray   John Gray vs Jane Phillips Case.
  vs
Jane Phillips
                          Jury Sworn

        Andrew McDoul   Saml Arnot
        John Elliot   John Porter
        John Cork.   Christ^{r} Huffman
        Wm. Neilson   John McClurkin
        James Neely   Jos. Cameron
        Fra^{s} McDaniel For: Morris Weaver

We find for
the plaintiff
and assis his
Damage at Twenty
one pounds 15^{s}/   The above Cause brought to Trial by Consent.

Licence to   Robert Parrot petitioned to have his Licence continued.
R. Parrot   Ordered that his Petition be granted.

Petition for   A Petition from the Inhabitants of the East End of the
Justices   County of Fairfield was presented Complaining that they
                have no Person to Administer Justice in that Quarter.
The Justices promised that on the next Vacancy or the Expiration of
their Commissions they would procure or recommend a person to be
nominated from among the Petitioners.

B. Pope   Barnaby Pope vs William Scott
  vs   James Andrew (as Garnishee, sworn properly in hands to
Wm. Scot.   be L4.15^{s}

        Joshua Badger as Garnishee Sworn (as property in his Hands
    to be L 2. 3. 6.

        The court adjourned till tomorrow at 10 o'Clock.

                            John Winn
                            Jno. Buchanan
                            Richd Winn
                            James Craig
                            Willm Kirkland

                January Term 1786. 25th January
        Met according to Adjourn^{m}
                            Present
                            John Winn
                            Richard Winn
                            John Buchanan
                            William Kirkland
                            James Craig

John Winn   John Winn Esqr appeared in open Court and acknowledged the
   to   Signing Sealing and Delivery of a Sett of Titles by way
M. Winn   of Lease and Release to Minor Winn Esqr of Lots No. 64
                No. 115. No. 96. 80. 82. 129. 130. 131. 135 & No. 69.
in the Village of Winnsborough

to Rob: Also to Robert Ellison for Lotts No. 43. 44. 39. & 38. in
Ellison   the Village of Winnsboro.

to Benj: Also to Benjamin Street for Lot No. 24 in the same Village
Street

to Wm: Owens   Also to William Owens for Lot No. 47. in the same Village.

                                10

Laughan   Samuel Laughan appeared in open Court and acknowledged the
   to   Signing Sealing and delivery of a Sett of Titles to John
J. Wilson   Wilson of Three Hundred and Ten Acres of Land on a Branch
                 of Bear Creek.

Jo: Kennedy   William Wright and Morris Weaver appeared in open Court
   to   and being duly sworn Made Oath that they Saw Joseph
J. Milling   Kennedy Sign Seal and deliver a Sett of Titles to John
                 Milling Esqr of One Hundred acres of Land Situate on a
Spring of Waggoners Creek.

Rt. Ellison   Henry Hunter and John Woodward appeared in open Court and
   to   being duly Sworn made Oath that they Saw Robert Ellison
H. Milling   Sign Seal and deliver a Set of Titles by way of Lease &
                 Release to Hugh Milling Esqr of Two Hundred acres of
Land on a Branch of Jacksons Creek.

Wm. Graves   Hugh Milling and David Evans appeared in open Court and
   to   being duly Sworn made Oath that they saw William Graves
Jos: Owens   Sign Seal & deliver a Sett of Titles by way of Lease
                 and Release to Joseph Owens of Five Hundred and forty
acres of Land on Dutchman's Creek.

J. McDown   John Milling and James McCown appeared in open court and
   to   being duly Sworn made Oath That they Saw James McKown Sign
H. McCown   Seal and Deliver to Hugh McKown a Set of Titles by way of
                 Lease and Release for Three hundred and fifty Acres of
Land on Bowers Mill Creek.

Rosborough   Alexander Rosbororough vs John Hicks.
   to   Trial being brought on as Consent. Defend^r acknowledged
Hicks   Judgment for L 12. 5. & Costs.

J. Milling   John Milling vs Saml Beaty. At. Capt. John Gray as
   vs   Garnishee appeared and Satisfied pet. wherefore he with-
S. Beaty   draws his Suit. Capt. John Gray paying Costs.

     Ordered that the Docket be called over.

     Jas. Johnston vs John Richmond. Case Issue Joined.

     Thomas Meredith vs Wm. Graves. Slander Issue Joined.

     Thomas Meredith vs James Graves. Slander Issue Joined.

     Thomas Meredith vs Hugh Means. Slander Judgm^t by Default.

     James Hart vs John Hunter Debt. Judgm^t by Default

     John Miller vs Moses Hollis. Issue Joined

     Thos. Johnston vs Saml Armstrong. Debt confessed Judgment for
principal Interest and Costs of Suit L 11. 14. 4.

Jas. Dodds)
   vs   ) Plt. called and failed to appear in order to prosecute.
John Jarvis) Was non Suited.

Robert Bailey)
   vs   ) Judgment for Plt. for L 1. 17. 6 & Costs
Robert Alcorn)
John Jarvis   )

John & Letitia)
Hutchison   ) John Winn as Garnishee upon Oath Saith He Gave Rich^d
   vs   ) Walker a Bond near the beginning of the year 1782. for
Richd Walker) L 300 worth & upwards as he believes which Bond he
                  has not yet paid.

11

Judgm^t by default ag^n the Dflt. and Costs.

Rober$_t$ Ellison vs. John Phillips.
Judgm^t by default.

Wm. Sibley vs James Owens. Jud^t by Default

Robert Ellison)	
vs)	Default as to Aldridge & Mattocks
McKenzie Mattocks)	
George Lot)	Issue Joined as to Lot.
Isaac Aldridge)	

Isaac Love vs. John Absint.
Discontinued at Plt's. request. He paying costs.

Joel Wilson vs Edwd. Sims.
Discontinued at Plts. request, he paying Costs

Isaac Love vs Mark Fortune.
Judgment by Default

John McCaw
  to
D. McCright.
John Ellison and Margaret McCright appeared in open
Court and being duly Sworn upon Oath Saith that they
Saw John McCaw Signed Sealed & delivered unto David
McCright a Sett of Titles by way of Lease and Release
for One Hundred Acres on a spring branch of Jacksons
Creek.

Road   Petition was presented for a road from Harbot Ferry to Hancocks
road at the Presbyterian Meeting House. Ordered that the
Prayer for the Petition be granted.

David George appointed overseer.

J. Gray
  vs
J. Phillips
Appeal.
John Gray vs Jane Phillips

Upon motion of the defts. Atty. an appeal was granted.

Road   Upon petition
        Granted A Road from Hancocks ferry to Little
River Road, Saml. Simmons overseer.

Adjourned to tomorrow at 10 o'Clock.

John Winn
Richard Winn
Jno. Buchanan
James Craig
William Kirkland

January Term 1786.
25th January 1786.
met according to adjournment

Present
John Winn   John Buchanan
Richard Winn   James Craig
William Kirkland

Thomas Johnston vs James Wilson Judgmt. by default

Licences to)
A:Durphey)   William Duffey Petitioned to obtain a Licence to keep
Jas.McCright)   a Tavern Ordered that the Prayer of the Petition be
John Lee)   Granted.

12

James McCright Petitioned for Store Licence to sell by the gallon. Ordered that the same be granted.

John Lee Petitioned for a Tavern Licence. Ordered that the same be granted.

Huffman
vs
Kinnerly

David Evans and David Read Evans appeared in open Court and being duly Sworn made Oath that they Saw Christopher Huffman and Margaret his Wife Sign Seal and Deliver a Sett of Titles to John Kinnerley of One Hundred Acres of Land on a Branch of Rockey Creek.

J. Winn
to
D. McCreight

John Winn Esquire appeared in open Court and acknowledged the Signing Sealing and delivery fo a Sett of Titles to David McCright of Two Lots of Land No. 139 & No. 63. in the Village of Winnsborough.

Ordered that the Road between 25 mile Creek and Thomas Hill be repaired, and the Old Overseers continued.

Wm. Duggins
to
J. Milling

John Milling appeared in Court and made Oath that the Titles to a tract of Land on Little River known by Duggins Old Place containing Two Hundred Acres more or Less, conveyed to him by William Duggins were destroyed during the Troubles. The said William Duggins now appeared in Court and acknowledged a new Sett of Titles for the same Land.

Ordered that William Owens be discharged from Serving the Office of Constable.

Ordered to proceed in calling over the Docket.

Willm Graves vs Richd Taylor.
Judgment by Default.

Alexander Miller vs James McCown
Discontinued Plt to pay Costs

Alex^r Miller vs James Owens
Judgm^t by Default.

William Rogers vs Daniel Goyin
Issue Joined.

Hugh Randal vs Andrew Spradley
Continued

Jesse Perry vs Wm. Dande
Nonsuited.

Hugh Randal vs Matw. McCright
Nonsuit.

James Norton vs Ch^r Picket
Issue Joined

Robert Ellison vs Wm. Phillips
Judgm^t Default.

Richd. Winn vs John McCown
Judgm^t confessed part.

James Gray vs Fra^s Ederington
Issue Joined.

Willm Graves vs Jas. Owens
Issue Joined

William Graves vs John Hunter
Default.

George Watts vs Dicksey Ward
Default.

Isaac Love vs Thos. Stark
Issue Joined

Isaac Love. vs. Thos. Meredith
Mackenzie Issue as to Meredith
& Mattocks, Wm. Bryant Mattocks.
Default as to Bryant.

Gardwin Ford & Magdalm his Wife
vs
Sarah Witterspoon & Robt. McConnell
Judgm^t by Default.

James Rutland vs Charles Gurk
Issue Joined

James McCollock vs Wm. Raab
Judgm^t for L 4. 17. 102 and
Costs.

William Lewis vs James Hunt
Issue Joined

Wm. McMorris vs Thos. Johnston
Judgment confessed for L 5. 5.
6. & Costs.

Wm. McMorris vs Jas. Neely
Issue Joined

John Milling vs Saml Beatty
withdrawn at Defts. Costs

William Rogers vs John Richmond
Issue Joined

George Freshle vs Jno Bell &
Datts
Judgm.^t confessed accord.^g to
Specialty

Quinton Craig vs Jas. Pearson
Continued.

Barnaby Pope vs Wm. Scott
Judgm.^t by default.

Philip Shaver vs Willm. Chapman
Willm. Rabb, garnishee Sworn says
he had L 3.11.7. Lawful money
in his Hands at the time of the
service of the Writ.

Darkis Hill vs William Nevit
Nonsuit.

Clerks books to be inspected	Ordered that John and Richard Winn Esquires be and are appointed to inspect the Clerks Books
Jo:Phillips to Th:Holsey	John Phillips and James Phillips appeared in open Court and being duly Sworn made Oath That they saw William Phillips Sign Seal and deliver Titles to Thomas Holsey for a Tract of Land containing Fifty Acres on Little River Waters of Broad River.
Jno. Powell to Jas. Phillips	Thomas Holsel and William Tyner appeared in Court and being duly Sworn made Oath that they Saw John Powell and Margaret his Wife Sign Seal and Deliver a Sett of Titles unto James Phillips for one Hundred acres of land on the middle Fork of Beaver Creek Waters of Broad River.
Thos. Holsey to Mar: Holsey	Edward Holsey and Thomas Holsey appeared in open Court and being duly Sworn made Oath That they Saw Thomas Holsey Sign Seal and deliver a Sett of Titles of one Hundred Acres of Land on the North Branch of Little River to Margaret Holsey.
An:Spradling Dep.^y Ext.^y to Sher Boyd	William Boyd Esqr appointed Andrew Spradling as his Deputy to serve a Writ of Attachment upon the Effects of Charles Spradling Administrator of the Estate and Effects of Charles Spradling Senr. deceased which appointment was approved of by the Court

Adjourned to the Court in Course

John Winn
Richd. Winn
Jno. Buchanan
James Craig
William Kirkland

January Court 1786.   Fairfield County.

We the Grand Jury of the County aforesaid Do make the following presentments.

1st. We present as a grievance the selling Spiritous Liquors contrary to Law by Thomas White. Phillip Shaver. Jacob Bethney. Henry McDonald. William Tyrie. John McMullin.

Informounts.   Jas. Andrews
Frederick Hart.

2ndly. We present as a Grievance for Bastardizing for nine before the date hereof. Ann Neel. Elizabeth Lathan. Elizabeth Hollis. and Mrs. Gladdin on the Wateree. Mary. Bell. Firraby Broom. & a free Negro M Porter.

3d. We present as a grievance that a Hundred of Weights and measures are not provided and put into the hands of the Clerk of the County.

4th. We present as a grievance the not Erecting a Court House Goal and Stocks as directed by the Law.

5th. We present as a grievance the Distressed Situation of Indigent Persons who by reason of Old Age & Infirmities are not capable of supporting themselves.

6. We present as a Grievance the great necessity of having some Legal mode immediately entered upon or Established for the regular Support of Orphans and poor children who no Trustees or Guardians.

7. We present as a grievance the want of Direction posts set up at Forks or Cross roads in this County.

8. We present as a grievance the Priviledges daily taken by the Inhabitants of this County in Hunting through and about their neighbors plantations without Lease or approbation particularly on the Sabboth.

9. We the Grand Jurors of the Court aforesaid recommend the Several persons informed against in Clause the first to the mercy of the said Court.

Henry Hunter foreman.

John McDonald	Willm. Cason
Edwd. Martin	James Hart
Wm. McMorris	Benoni Hollis
James Brown	John Woodward
Isaac Love	William Douh
John Love	Jno. Pearson

Fairfield Court

May Term

Monday 8th May 1786.

The Justices Present

Rich.d Winn Esqr	Minor Winn Esqr
William Kirkland	James Craig
Isaac Love	John Turner.

The Court proceeded to Ballot for the Grand and Petit Jury for the next Term when the following Persons were drawn viz.

Grand Jurors.

Edward Martin	Moses Cockrell
C. D. Bradford	Robert Hancock
Jno. Woodward	Rowland Williamson
James Kincaid	James Thomas
Hugh Young	Robert Martin Junr. Wateres
John Pearson	James Russell Junr.
William Daniel	Phillip Raiford
David McGraw	Capt. John Cook.
Areomanus Lisles	William Rabb
William Cason.	Moses Knighton

Robt. Rabb

Petit Jurors

Adam Free	Joseph Cameron
Simon Cameron	Jop Chapman
Robert Ewing	James Dodds
William Watson	Francis McDonald
John Finley	Michael Hanning
Wm. Faris	Lewis Owens
Chas. Montgomery	John Culp
Robert Phillips Junr.	Hugh Montgomery

15

James Neely	Wm. Beard
Saml. Caldwell	John Brown
George Seigler	James Moutie
Jno. Dodds	James McMullin
Willm. Ewing	John McCowal
James McGraw	Sam. Gladney
Thos. Maple	John Mayburn.

The following Gentlemen drawn to Serve as Grand Jurors at last Court now appeared and was Sworn. Viz.

William Daniel	William Dorch
Jacob Bethney	Robert Reid
Moses Cockrell	Capt Jno. Cooke
William McMorris Senr.	John King
Robert Martin.	

A Sufficient number of the Grand Jurors having neglected to attend the following Gentlemen were drawn from the Tallies and Ordered to be immediately Summon^d to attend at this Court. Viz.

William Owens	Thomas Baker Esqr
William Robertson	William McCreight
David McCreight	William Durphey

Sc:Fa:
vs Defaultors
with Grand &
p: Jury
Ordered that a Seire Facias issue against those persons who were summoned to attend as Grand Jurors at this Court and have failed to appear to Show Cause why they should not be fined agreeable to act of assembly viz.

~~John Robertson~~ LR [stricken]	Jas: Kirkland
John Peirson	Rowland Williamson
Wm. McGraw	
~~John Cox-(?)~~ [stricken]	

Ordered that the same process issue against Defaulters on the Petit Jury List Viz.

Henry Beaumont Esquire appeared in Court and produced his Licence properly authenticated to practice as an Attorney within this State, which was approved and permitted to practice in this Court.

The following Persons drawn to serve as Petit Jurors now appeared

State
vs
Keel.
Bast.dy
State of S. C. vs Frederick Keel. Bastardy. Susannah Kish Sworn Says she is now Eight months or thereabouts gone with child, and that Frederick Keel is the Father of it.

On Motion by Daniel Brown Defts Att^y Ordered to be over until next Court and That the said Frederick Keel do enter into Recognization the Sum of L 20 and his Secruity in the Sum of Ten pounds to appear at the next Setting of the Court.

Upon which the said Frederick Keel signed his recognizance for L 20 and Edward Moberly his Security in the Sum of L 10 and

Susannah Kisk Signed her Recognizance for L 20. to prosecute.

Adj^d to 10. o'Clock tomorrow

Richard Winn
M. Winn
James Craig
John Turner
Wm. Kirkland
Isaac Love.

Tuesday May 9th 1786.

The Court met according to adjournment

Present

Richd. Winn Esq.   Minor Winn Esq.
William Kirkland   John Turner
Isaac Love.   James Craig

Js. Turner   James and Sarah Turner appeared in open Court and
to   acknowledged the Signing Sealing and delivery of a
M. Cockrell   Sett of Titles of One Hundred Acres of Land Situate
              on Small Branch of Little River to Moses Cockril.

John Turner   John Turner appeared in open Court and acknowledged the
to   Signing Sealing and delivering to John Lee a Sett of
John Lee   Titles for one Hundred Acres on a Small Branch of Little
              River.

Th. Woodward William Robertson and John Woodward appeared in open
to   Court and being duly Sworn made Oath That they Saw
Robt. Rabb   Thomas Woodward Sign Seal and deliver a Sett of Titles to
              Robert Rabb for Three Hundred Acres of Land Situate on
              Mill Creek in Craven County.

Jas. Rutland James Rutland appeared in open Court and acknowledged
to   the Signing Sealing and Delivery of a Sett of Titles to
Rob. Rabb   Robert Rabb for one Hundred Acres of Land on Mill Creek
              in Craven County.

The following gentlemen drawn to serve as grand jurors now appeared
and were sworn in and received a charge from the Bench. Mr. John
Cooke was appointed their foreman.

John Cook   John King
Robert Martin   William Owens
Jacob Bethney   William Robinson
William McMorris   William Durphey
Robert Reid   John Robertson
Moses Cockril   David McCreight
John Lee   William Daniel

H. Evans an   Adam Estwit presented a Petition requesting that Henry
apprentice   Evans an Infant Orphan may be bound as an Apprentice to
              Him for the Term of Seven or till he attains the age of
              Twenty one.

              The prayer of the petition was granted.

State   State vs James Tate. Isam Fair Wm. Alexander Francis Kirkland
vs   sworn and sent to the grand jury and returned a true Bill.
Tate.

The following Petit Jurors appeared to their names Viz.

Alexr. Robertson Junr.   Jas. Russell Junr.
Jas. McMullin   Jas. Davis
Jos. Chapman   Jos. Cameron
Saml. Caldwell   John Elliot
Richd Gladney   John McKinney
Robt. Ewing   Alexr McKaino.

B. May   Benjamin May vs Bryant Riley. Debt the Defendant appeared
vs   and confessed Judgment for L 54. 10. including Principal
B. Riley Interest and Costs.

T. Meredith   Thomas Meredith vs William Graves Slander. being called
vs   on. the above Petit Jurors were impanelled and Sworn to
Wm. Graves   try the same. John McKinney appointed Foreman who

17

returned their Verdict "We find for the Defendant"

Mat. Hails
apprentice
Morris Weaver presented a Petition requesting that an
infant of the name of Mathew Hails (whom he has long
supported) be bound to Him.

Ordered that the said infant Mathew Hails be bound to the good
Petition Morris till he attains the age of Eighteen to be found by him
in good wholesome Provisions and raiment and one year and a half's
Schooling. and at the Expiration of his Servitude to deliver hime one
good Suit of Cloathing.

Wm. Adair
Apprentice
William Pedian presented a Petition requesting that a son
of Widow Catherine Blair (who has lived with him for some-
time) may with the consent of his said Mother be bound
an apprentice to him.

Ordered that the said Willm. Adair be bound to his Petitioner to
learn the Weaving Trade till he attains the age of Nineteen finding him
in wholesome provisions and good raiment and a good Suit of Cloaths at
the Expiration of his apprenticeship. and a years Education in his
apprenticeship.

State
vs
J. Tate
The State vs James Tate. for a Suspecion of Theft was now
brought to a Hearing when the Defendant pleaded not Guilty.
and put himself upon his County.

The following Jurors were then impanneled & Sworn to try the same
Viz.

Alexander Robertson Junr.	Jas. Russell
James McMullin	Jas. Davis
Joseph Chapman	Jos: Cameron
Samuel Caldwell	John Elliot
Richard Gladney	John McKinney
Robert Ewing	Alexander McKaihe

Evidences Examined for the State, Shadrack Jacobs. Isam Fair.
Wm. Alexander and Francis Kirkland.

For the Defendant Jas: McDaniel John McDaniel. Nedy Moberly.

The evidences having been fully Examined and the Facts thoroughly
investigated. The Jury withdrew and brought in their Verdict.
Not Guilty.

Jno. Cooper
Appointed
Thomas Parrot presented a Petition Requesting that John
Cooper a poor Orphan of the Age of Eleven years be bound
Apprentice to him till he arrives at the Age of Eighteen.

Ordered That the Prayer of the above Petition be Granted and that
the said petition fixed the said Orphan in good provisions and decent
raiment during his apprenticeship and that he shall give him one years
Schooling & one Suit of cloathes at the Expiration.

Jos: Cooper
Apprentice
James Davis Presented a petition requesting that Joseph
Cooper a poor boy be bound as an apprentice to him untill
he attains the Age of Eighteen.

Ordered that the Prayer of the above Petition be granted and that
the said Petitioner find the said poor boy in good Provisions and decent
raiment during his apprenticeship and that he shall be given one years
Schooling & one suit of cloaths at the expiration of his time.

Ann Cooper
Apprentice
William McTeyrie presented a Petition requesting That
Amy Cooper a poor girl of Four years of Age be bound
as an apprentice to him until she attains the age of
Sixteen.

18

Ordered that the Prayer of the above Petition be granted and that the said Petitioner find the said Apprentice in good provisions and decent raiment during her said Apprenticeship and that He give her one years Schooling and one Suit of Cloaths at the Expiration of her time.

Adj^d to 10. O'Clock tomorrow morning

> Richard Winn
> James Craig
> Wm. Kirkland
> M. Winn
> John Turner
> Isaac Love

Wednesday 10th May 1786.

The Court met according to adjournment

Present

Richard Winn	Minor Winn	)
John Turner	William Kirkland	) Esquires
Isaac Love	James Craig	)

Jno. Winn
to
Jos. Quarrel

David Evans and William Durphey appeared in open Court and being duly Sworn made Oath that they Saw John Winn Esquire Sign Seal and deliver Titles to Lot No. 187 containing one half acre in the Village of Winnsborough for the Uses and purposes therein mentioned.

Geo:Lot
to
Jas.Neely

David Evans and John Milling appeared in open Court and being duly Sworn made Oath That they Saw George Lot Sign Seal and Deliver to James Neely a Sett of Titles for one hundred Acres of Land on Mill Creek for the Uses and purposes therein mentioned.

Serle Lewis
to
Jas. Lewis

Charles Lewis and William Lewis appeared in open Court and being duly Sworn made Oath That they Saw Serle Lewis Sign Seal and deliver to Jas. Lewis a Sett of Titles to Four Hundred Acres of Land on Taylors Creek for the uses and purposes therein mentioned.

John Hutchison
Taylor to
Step: Noland

John Steveman and Hugh McKown appeared in open Court and being duly Sworn made Oath that they Saw John Hutchinson Taylor Sign Seal and deliver a Set of Titles to Stephen Noland for one Hundred and Fifty Acres of Land on Little River for the Uses and purposes therein mentioned.

Wm. Meyers.
vs
Jas. Rabb

William Meyers vs James Rabb detimne The Court took the matter up and having Examined Evidence are of Opinion That William Myers has fully proved the Horse found in the possession of James Rabb to be his property therefore.

Order that James Rabb deliver up to the said William Meyers the said Horse and pay the Costs of Suit.

Zachariah Nettles was Sworn in as a Constable.

Wm. Bell's
petition

William Bell Presented a Petition Setting forth that he some years past married a Widow with three Small Children and with difficulty raised them up to be of some Assistance he being old and unable to Labor That some neighbors now endeavor to draw them away from the Petitioner therefore Prays that the Court may impower him to keep the children.

Ordered that the Petitioner do keep the Children untill the Court make further Provision for the said Orphans.

```
Jas. Johnston)
   vs       )   James Johnston vs John Richmond detinue Issue being
Jno. Richmond)   joined, the Cause was called on and the following Jurors
                 impannelled to try the same Viz.
```

Jno. McKinney foreman	James Russell
Jas. McMullin	Jas: Cameron
Joseph Chapman	John Elliot
Saml Caldwell	Alex^r McKaine
Robert Ewing	John Porter
Andrew McDowl	Alexr. Robertson

    The jury find for the Plaintiff and assign his Damage at Four
Pounds Sterling

```
Jno. Stedman      James Turner and Alexr. Robinson appeared in open
   to             Court and being duly Sworn made Oath that they saw
Alex. Robinson    John Stedman Sign Seal and deliver a Sett of Titles
                  to Alexander Robinson Junr. of Four Hundred Acres of
Land on a branch of Little River for the Uses and purposes therein
mentioned
```

```
Ford & als        Gardner Ford & Magdaline his Wife vs Sarah Witherspoon
   vs             and Robert McCombs
Witherspoon       Discontinued at Defendants Costs
& ots
```

```
Meredith          Thomas Meredith vs James Graves
   vs             Discontinued at the plaintiffs Costs.
J^s Graves
```

```
Miller            John Miller vs Moses Hollis Trover.  Issue Joined the
   vs             Cause was called on and the following Jurors impannelled
Hollis            to try the same Viz.
```

John McKinney F.	James Russell
James McMullin	Joseph Cameron
Joseph Chapman	John Elliot
Saml Caldwell	Alex^r McKaine
Robert Ewing	John Porter
Andrew McDowl	Alex^r Robertson

    Robert Harper & Hugh Knox were Examined as Evidences for the
plaintiff. and Charles Picket, Charles Lewis and J. Hollis for the
Defendants. The Chairman having Summ'd up the Evidence the Jury with
draw and brough in their Verdict for the Plaintiff and assign his
Damages at Six pounds five shillings.

```
Smith & A         John Johnston came into Court and made Oath that he
   to             was present and saw John Smith Jun^r and Mary his
Moses Cockril     wife Sign Seal and Deliver Titles by way of Lease
                  and Release to Moses Cockrill for Two Hundred and
Fifty Acres of Land on a Branch of Little and the Wateree Creek and did
also See Babel Hooton & Stephen Terry Sign their names as Evidences.
And the said Terry having already proved the said Titles by Oath before
William Brown Esquire as appears on the release and he and the other
Evidence Babel Hooton being both dead the Court admitted the proof
made and ordered the same to be recorded.
```

```
Lewis    William Lewis vs James Hunt.  Case by Petition Charles Picket
  vs     and Mrs. Lewis were examined for the Plaintiff and Thomas
Hunt     Stone and Hugh Knox for Deft.  The Court gave in favor Plt.
         Judgment for 7s/8P.
```

```
Frederick Keel)
    vs        )  Judgment by Default
Jas. Phillips )
```

```
                    Richard Winn
                    Wm. Kirkland
                    M. Winn
                    James Craig
                    John Turner
                    Isaac Love
```

Thursday 11th May 1786.

The Court met according to adjournment.

Present

Minor Winn		William Kirkland
James Craig		John Turner
Richd Winn	and	Isaac Love Esquires.

Lewis   Nathaniel Durham and Edmund Morgan appeared in open Court and
to   being duly Sworn made Oath that they saw Warner Lewis Sign
Turner   Seal and deliver unto John Turner a Sett of Titles by way
         of Lease and Release for one hundred Acres Situate on the
North Fork of the Wateree Creek, for the uses and purposes within
mentioned.

Jno. Smith Sen.ʳ Edmund Strange came into Court and made Oath that he
to   was present and saw John Smith and Patence his Wife
Jno. Smith Jun.ʳ Sign Seal and deliver Titles by way of Lease and
              release to John Smith Jun.ʳ for Two Hundred and fifty
Acres of Land Situate on a Branch of Little River and the Wateree Creek
And did also see John Blake and William Nettles Sign their Names as
Evidences and the said John Blake having already proved the said Titles
by Oath before John Winn Esquire as appears on the release and he and
the other Evidence William Nettles being both dead the Court admitted
the proof made and Ordered the same to be recorded.

Lewis   In the Cause Lewis vs Hunt on the Record of yesterday. The
vs   Judges having deferred their final Judgment with respect to
Hunt   the Costs. Have now determined that the plaintiff do pay
      them.

Tho.ˢ Meredith)
vs   ) Was now called on. upon the Jurors being Sworn the
Hugh Minar) Plaintiff challenged John McKinney and Richard Gladney
           was appointed in his room when the following were
           impanned viz.

James McMullin	Joseph Cameron Foreman
Joseph Chapman	John Elliot
Sam.ᵗ Caldwell	Alexʳ McKaime
Robert Ewing	John Porter
And McDowl	Alexan.ʳ Robertson
James Russell	Richard Gladney

The Jury withdrew and brought in Ver.ᵈ for the plt and assign his
Damages at one pound Sterling. The Defendants Attorney moved for an
arrest of Judgment which was granted and ordered to be argued by both
the Council on both Sides on the Morrow.

Clerks fees in   The County Court Clerk informed the Court that his
Crim:Cases   Fees in Criminal Prosecutions was not Specified by
Same as Sup.ʳ   the County Court Act and wished to have the same
Court   fixed by the Court. Council having been heard upon
          the Case.

    Ordered that the Clerk Take the same fees as allowed in the Superior
Court, till a particular Law is passed for that purpose.

21

Robert Ellison On attachment. The Cause was called on and the
    vs   following Jurors were impannelled to try the same Viz
John Phillips

        Joseph Cameron F.   James Russell
        James McMullin   John Elliot
        Joseph Chapman   Alex.ͬ McKaime
        Sam.ͭ Caldwell   John Porter
        Robert Ewing   Alex.ͬ Robertson
        Andrew McDowl   Richard Gladney

    John Milling and John Ellison proved the Value of the Horse and
that Phillips never returned him & promised to pay Ellison the Value.
The Jury withdrew and brought in their Verdict for the Plaintiff and
assigned his Damages at Fifty pounds Sterling.

Will. Sibley
    vs   Case.
Jas. Owens   The Cause was now called and the Same Jury was appointed
                to try the same except John McKinney instead of
Richard Gladney. Judgment having been obtained by Default at last Court
upon the Writ of Inquiry.

    The Jury fixed for the Plaintiff one penny Damages and Costs of
Suit.

Thos. Miles   Thomas Miles appeared in open Court and acknowledged
    to   the Signing Sealing and delivering Titles to John
Jno. Woodward   Woodward for One Hundred Acres of Land Situate on the
                Branches of Cedar Creek for the Uses and purposes
therein mentioned.

Thos. Miles   Thomas Miles also at the same time acknowledged the
    to   Signing Sealing and delivering Titles to William
Wm. Summerall   Summerall for one Hundred Acres of Land Lying on the
                Branches of Cedar Creek for the Uses and purposes
                therein mentioned.

State   The State vs Edw.ᵈ Hancock on Indictment Racheul Hancock
    vs   prosecutor adknowledges herself bound in the sum of Ten
Hancock   pounds to prosecute at August Term.

                                    Rachel Hancock (L. S.)

    John Robinson acknowledges himself in the like manner in the Like
Sum

                                    John Robinson (L. S.)

State   The State vs Mary Kelly. on Indictment for Rescue bound in
    vs   Recognizance to appear at this Court in the Sum of
Mary Kelly   Fifty pounds was Solemnly called and failed to appear.
                This Court ordered the Recognizances to be forfeited
and that a Pure Facias Issue to show Cause for her non attendance at
next Court.

    John Kirkland and James Brown her Securities for her appearance
as aforesaid are also to be Cited to appear at the same time and place.

D.ᵒ Rottenbury State vs Henry Rottenbury for the same. bound as
                aforesaid. was called and failed to appear as afore-
                said is to be Cited as aforesaid.

    Andrew Spradling and Larkin Cardin his Securities for his appear-
ance as aforesaid are also to be Cited to appear at the same time and
place.

    Thos. McClurkin vs James Owens. Petition Defendant Confessed
Judgment for L 2.3.6 & Costs.

                              22

William Graves vs Richd Taylor. Petition.
    Judgment for L 4.13.4 and Costs

Elizabeth Graves vs Thomas Hill
    Case withdrawn and Costs paid.

                            Richard Winn
                            M. Winn
                            Isaac Love
                            John Turner
                            James Craig
                            William Kirkland

                    Friday 12th May 1786.

    The Court met according to adjournment.

                        Present

Richard Winn. Minor Winn. Jas. Craig. William Kirkland. John Turner.
and Isaac Love Esq^rs John Winn Esquire & John Buchanan Esqr

Richd Winn   Richard Winn Esquire appeared in open Court and
    to   acknowledged the Signing Sealing and delivering a Sett
John Winn   of Titles by Lease and Release to John Winn Esquire
                 for a Tract of Thirty three Acres of Land adjoining to
the Town of Winnsborough for the Uses and purposes therein mentioned.

Jno. Winn   John Winn Esquire appeared in open Court and acknow-
    to Jac. Brown ledged the Signing Sealing and Delivering a Sett of
                 Titles to Mr. Jacob Brown for Lot No. 103. Situate
in Zion Street within the said Town of Winnsborough for the Uses
and purposes therein mentioned.

Jno. Winn   John Winn Esquire at the same time acknowledged the
    to   Signing Sealing and Delivering to Samuel Littlejohn
Sam: Littlejohn a Sett of Titles for Five Hundred Acres of Land
                 Situate on Broad River for the Uses and purposes
                 therein mentioned

Henry Iceey   Edward Hancock and David Evans appeared in open Court
    to   and being duly Sworn made Oath that they Saw Henry
W. Willingham   Ivey Sign Seal and deliver unto William Willingham
                 Titles by way of Lease and Release for a Tract of
one Hundred and Fifty Acres of Land on Reedy Creek a branch of the
Wateree Creek.

Teyrie   William McTeyrie vs John Creg. Case Judgment confessed
  vs   by Deft for principal and Costs
J. Gregg

    The State vs William Bryant A. B.
      The Defend^r being called plead^d Guilty.
    Postponed.

    Christopher Huffman vs Willm. Dougharty Attachm^t
      Judg^t by Default

Meredith   The Judgment in this Cause deferred till this Day was fully
  vs   argued by the Council on both Sides, The Court ordered, for
Minar   reasons Shown, That Judgment be arrested and the Defendant
            recover his Costs

J. Appedaile   James Bowles appeared in open Court and being duly Sworn
    to   made Jane Appedaile Sign Seal and Deliver a certain
R. Gladney   paper purporting to be a Bill of Sale of a negroe Wench
                named Bess and one Small Brown mare to Richard Gladney
to him and his Heirs.

                            23

Ellison vs Phillips	In the Suit Robert Ellison vs John Phillips on Attachment. Ordered that the Sheriff expose the Lands to Sale.
State vs Bryant.	The State vs William Bryant A & B. The cause was now resumed and the following Jurors were impannelled to try the same Viz.

John McKinney F.	Andrew McDowl
Richd Gladney	James Russell
Jas. McMullin	Joseph Cameron
Joseph Chapman	John Elliot
Saml Caldwell	Alex^r McKaime
Robert Ewing	John Porter

Evidence Examined for the Prosectuion. Joseph Quarrel. James Austin. John Milling   Watson. For the Defendant.   Hunt.

The Jury without going out of Court brought in their Verdict.
                                                    Guilty.

Ordered that the said Defendant Wm. Bryant be taken into the Custody of the Sheriff, till further orders.

Thomas Johnston vs Jas. Wilson, Debt. The same Jury being impannelled. brought their Verdict for the Plaintiff and assigned his Damages at 1^d and costs.

Miller) vs) Owens)	Alex^r Miller vs Jas. Owens. Debt. discontinued at plts's Costs.
Rogers) vs) Goyen)	William Rogers vs Danl Goyen. Slander. Issue Joined. The same jury was Sworn and impannelled to try the same. Evidence heard and Case argued the Jury withdrew

and brought in their Verdict for the plaintiff and assigned his damages at forty Shillings and Costs.

Ellison vs Mattocks	Ellison vs Mattocks. Bryant & Aldridge writ of Enq^y The Same Jury being impannelled. It appeared that Mattocks had quitted the County. The Jury brought their Verdict for the plt against Mattocks for L 12. and Costs.
Graves vs Owens.	William Graves vs Joseph Owens. Case Referred to Arbitrators Viz. Ralp Jones. William Kirkland. William Cason, to make their Award and return to next Court and their Award to be a Rule of Court.
Randal vs Spradling	Hugh Randall vs Andrew Spradley Petition Discontinued at plts Costs.

Saml Nesbit vs Alexr. Miller. Case Discontinued at dfts. Costs	John Gray vs Saml. Beaty Discont^d at Defts. Costs
John Bell vs John Potts. All^t Default.	Richard Winn vs Fras. Edrington. Default

Isaac Love vs Thos. Meredith, Thos. Starke & McKenzie Mattocks. Refered as to Meredith and Starke to John King and Ralph Jones to return their Award to next Court which is to be a rule of Court ---

R^d Gladney vs J. Phillips	Richard Gladney vs John Phillips. Robert Martin Summoned as Garnishee who Says the goods were given in Securety for a debt.

Thos. Rousham vs John Smith All^t

24

Joseph Quarrell Summoned as Garnishee now appeared and Swore that there would due from him to Smith an note of Hand due in December next the Sum of L. 7. 1. 3

Adjourned to Eight O'Clock Tomorrow.

John Winn to Jos:Quarrell	John Winn Esquire acknowledged in open Court the Signing Sealing and delivering Titles to Joseph Quarrell for Lot No. 187 in the Town of Winnsborough
D. Gordon to H. Milling	David Gordon appeared in open Court and acknowledged the Signing Sealing and delivering Titles to Hugh Milling for 640. acres of Land Situate on the head Branches of the Wateree Creek and Little River and

that he Signed the receipt for the Consideration money thereon Indorsed.

Richard Winn
James Craig
John Turner
Isaac Love
M. Winn

Presententh
of Gd Jury We the Grand Jurors do present is a grievance that there is no Road Cut out from Winnsborough to Summers's Mill. with a Bridge over Little River where the said Road Crosseth it.

That the Road from Murfey's Mill on Little River to Fridays Ferry has not more than three miles a fit Cut and no one appointed to repair ot.

We present also the Road from Cockrells to Lees Mill as much out of repair.

We present it also as a great grievance the same that the Streets of Winnsborough are not kept Clean and well grubbed.

John Cooke Foreman	Moses Cockrell
Jacob Bethney	Robert Martin
Wm. Robertson	John King
Willm. Daniel	William Owens
William McMorris	John Lee
David McCreight	Wm. Durphey
Robt. Reed	

Saturday. May 13th. 1786.

The Court met according to Adjournment

Present

John Winn		Minor Winn
John Buchanan		Jas. Craig
John Turner	and	Isaac Love.

Gray vs Edrington	James Gray vs Francis Ederington. Case continued to next Court.
McMorris vs Yarborough	William McMorris Junr. vs Major Yarborough. Debt the Defendant being called and not appearing Ordered that Judgment be Entered according to Specialty.
Croslin vs Riley	Croslin vs Riley. Judgment by Default.

Spradling
vs   Andrew Spradling vs Henry Gregg. Case default.
Gregg

Norton
vs   James Norton vs. Charles Picket Trover. The Cause was now
Picket   called on and the following Jurors were impannelled &
              Sworn to try the Same. Viz.

          John McKinney Foreman
          Richard Gladney   Andrew McDowl
          James McMullin   James Russell
          Joseph Chapman   Joseph Cameron
          Saml. Caldwell   John Elliot
          Robert Ewing   John Porter

     The jury withdrew and brought in their Verdict for the Plaintiff
and assessed his Damages at nineteen pounds Sterling.

Lewis
vs   William Lewis vs James Hunt. Upon motion for a new Trial.
Hunt   Motion overruled.

Hutchison   John and Letitia Hutchison vs Richd. Walker an attachment
vs   The same Jury was Impannelled and Sworn to try the same.
Walker

     Proof having been made upon Oath of the Debt the Jury brought
their Verdict for the plaintiff in Twenty one pounds Two Shillings and
Eleven pence half penny.

     John Winn Esquire Summoned as Garnishee in the above Cause was now
Sworn acknowledged to have in hands about Three Hundred pounds South
the property of said Richard Walker.

Norton
vs   James Norton vs Charles Picket.
Picket

     The Defendant moved for an appeal which the Court Granted on the
Defendants giving Security for Judgment and Costs.

Rutland
vs   Rutland vs Gent. Debt. The Defendant came into Court and
Gent.   acknowledged Judgment. according to Specialty being Eight
              pounds 11/6.

     William McMorris Senr. vs James Neely. Debt. The Defendant
appeared in Court and confessed Judgment for Twenty four pounds Five
Shillings & 8.
                              John Winn
                              Jno. Buchanan
                              James Craig
                              John Turner
                              Isaac Love
                              M. Winn

Fairfield County   August Term. 14th. August 1786.

                         Present.

     Richard Winn. John Winn. Minor Winn. John Buchanan. James Craig.
Henry Hampton and Isaac Love Esquires

     The Court being opened the Revd. McCaule Preached an Excellent
Sermon on the Occasion.

Proceeded to ballot for Jurors for November. Term when the following persons were drawn to Serve on the Grand Jury. Viz.

James Gray	Micajah Picket
Lewis Pope	Andrew Gray
John Winn Junr.	John King
Willm. Dorch	Robert Reed.
Charnel Durham	John Gray
John Lee	Thos. Shannon
James Brown	John Alston
Wm. McMorris Senr.	Richd. Taylor
Robt. Reed	Burr Harrison
Benj. May	James Hart

Henry Crumpton.

The following Persons were drawn to Serve on the Petit Jury Viz.

John McComb	James Rogers
James Cameron	William Boyd
Christr. Huffman	MatW McClurkin
Morris Weaver.	Richd. Gladney
Andrew Cameron	Alexr Smith
John Stinson	John Elliot
Samuel Owens	John Roberson J. C.
John McKinney	James Russel Junr.
James Davis	Hugh Smith
Daniel Cockran.	John Porter
Alexr Robertson Junr.	Thos. Parrot Junr.
Saml Arnot	AndW McDole.
John Cameron	
Wm. Nelson	John McClurkin
Jesse Dunn	Daniel Wood
John Cork.	

Northward
vs
Jas. Harris

Attachment Frisell McTyri, Sworn as Garnishee Saith he hath in his hands on Hoghead of Tobacco prized and a parcel of damaged loose Tobacco Supposed to be 12. or 1400. Weight. Ordered that the Sheriff expose said Tobacco to Sale according to Law and that a Sure Facias, issue against James Igilvie to Show Cause why Judgment Shod not be entered against him as against the said James Harris.

Adjd till tomorrow at 9 o'Clock.

Richard Winn
Jno. Buchanan
James Craig
Isaac Love.

Fairfield County   Tuesday 15. August 1786.

The Court met according to adjournment.

Present.

John Winn, William Kirkland. John Buchanan. James Craig. Richard Winn and Isaac Love. Esquires and John Turner. Esquire Henry Hampton and John Pearson Esquires

Jas. Rogers
to
Ro:Rabb

John Buchanan and Henry Hunter Esqrs appeared in open Court and being duly Sworn Say that they Saw James Rogers Sign Seal and deliver to Robert Rabb a Conveyance by way of Lease and Release of 298 Acres of Land on Mill Creek a Branch of Little River and also Saw him Sign the Receipt for the Consideration Money thereon Indorsed.

Richd Walker
to   Joseph Cameron and John Rotten appeared in open Court
B. Harrison   and being duly Sworn Say They Saw Richard Walker and
                Major his Wife Sign Seal & deliver unto Burr Harrison
a Set of Titles for three Hundred Acres of Land Situate on Little River
and a Creek thereof called Little Creek.

Riley
to   Bryant Riley appeared in open Court and acknowledged
Turnipseed   the Signing Sealing and delivery to Bartholomew Turnipseed a Sett of Titles for Sixty Acres of Land Situate on Little River
being part of a Tract of Two Hundred and fifty acres originally granted
to Daniel Wootan.

J. Jenkins
to   John Jenkins appeared in open Court and acknowledged
Wm. Gladdin   the Signing Sealing and delivery of a Set of Titles to
                William Gladden for One Hundred Acres of Land
                Situate on Nixons Creek Waters of the Wateree.

J. Winn
to   John Winn Esqr appeared in open Court and acknowledged
J. Buchanan   the Signing Sealing and delivering to John Buchanan
                Esquire a Set of Titles for Two Hundred Acres of Land
                Situate on Miracks Creek Waters of Little River.

J. Campbell
to   John Winn and John Milling appeared in open Court and
J. Buchanan   being duly Sworn Say They Saw Jenny Campbell Sign
                Seal and deliver to John Buchanan a Set of Titles
by Lease and Release of Three Hundred and Fifty Acres of Land Situate
on the Branches of Reedy River.

Chapman
to   Charles D. Bradford and Thomas Parrot appeared in open
W. Rabb   Court and being duly Sworn Say They Saw William Chapman
                Sign Seal and deliver a Set of Titles to William Rabb
for Three Hundred Acres of Land Situate on Little River near the mouth
of Chapman Creek.

Cameron
to   Joseph Cameron appeared in open Court and acknowledged
Cameron   the Signing Sealing and delivering to James Cameron a
                Set of Titles by way of Lease and Release for Sixty Seven
Acres of Land on a small Branch of Jacksons Creek.

Marple
to   Thomas Marple appeared in open Court and acknowledged the
Craig   Signing Sealing and delivering to James Craig Esqr. a
                Set of Titles for one Hundred and Fifty Acres originally
                Granted to Jacob River and Situate on Mill Creek.

Winn
to   John Winn Esquire appeared in open Court and acknowledged
Boyd   the Signing Sealing and delivering to William Boyd Esquire
                a Sett of Titles for Lot No. 42 in the Town of
                Winnsborough.

Do.
to   Also acknowledged the Signing Sealing and delivering to
H. Hunter   Henry Hunter Esqr Titles for Lots No. 134. No. 70. &
                No. 75 in the said Town of Winnsborough.

Kirkland
to   William Roach and David Evans appeared in open Court and
H. Woodward   being duly Sworn Say They Saw Joseph Kirkland Esquire
                Sign Seal and deliver unto Henry Woodward a Sett of
Titles for Three Hundred Acres of Land and also to Henry Hunter Esqr

Two Titles or Two Hundred and Twenty two Acres of Land both Situate Lying and being on Little River and Mill Creek.

K. Strother
to
T. Baker
James Craig Esqr and David Evans appeared in open Court and being duly Sworn Say They Saw K. F. Strother Sign Seal and deliver to Thomas Baker Esqr Titles for Several Tracts of Land adjoining to the Town of Winnsborough.

Proceeded to call over the List of the Grand Jury when the following answered to their names Viz.

John Cooke Foreman
John Woodward
David McGraw
Moses Cockrell
Phillip Raiford
Aremanus Lisles
James Thomas

Moses Knighton
Robert Rabb
James Kincaid
Edward Martin
C. D. Bradford
William Rabb.

Having chosen their Foreman & received their Charge from the bench withdrew.

Called over the Petit Juror's List when the following appeared and answered to their names. Viz.

James Dodds
Joseph Cameron
William Ewing
Robert Ewing
Saml. Gladney
Lewis Owen

Adam Free
John Finley
Charles Montgomery
Simon Cameron
James Montie
Thos. Maple.

Samuel Lowrie Esquire produced his Certificate to the Court Signed by Richd. Hutson, Aedamus Burke and F. F. Grimke Esquires whereby it appears that he is admitted to practice as Sollicitor and Attorney in all the Courts within this State.

State
vs
Jas. Rabb
Indictment for assault and Battery. The deft appeared in Court and pleaded Guilty. Whereupon the Court Ordered that he be dismissed on paying a fine of 1^d and Costs.

Sam. Caldwell
vs
John Patton
Defendant appeared and confessed Judgment for L 8. 10. 5 and Costs

State
vs
Fred: Keel
Indictm^t for Bastardy. Pleaded not Guilty - whereupon the above named Jurors were Sowrn and Impannelled to try the Same. The Jury without going out of Court returned. We the Jurors find the Deft Guilty.

Hen: Hunter
vs
Richd. Taylor
Defendant appeared in Court and confessed Judgment for thirty six pounds Twelve Shillings with Interest from date of the note.

Fred. Keel
vs
Jas. Phillips
On Petition. Judgment for L 3.7.8. and Costs. Wm. Fowlers order to be paid.

Richd Winn
vs
Fra. Ederington
On Petition. Judgment confessed for L 3. 12. 6. & Costs.

C. D. Bradford and Thomas Parrot appeared in open Court and being duly Sworn Say they Saw John Davis Sign Seal and deliver Titles to

James Davis for Two Hundred and fifty Acres on Williams Creek a branch of Broad River.

John Milling and Daniel Cockran appeared in open Court and being duly Sworn Say they Saw John Buchanan Sign Seal and deliver to James Gray Titles for One Hundred acres Situate on Jacksons Creek.

Hugh Smith appeared in open Court and acknowledged delivering a Sett of Titles to John Sheins for Four Hundred and fifty Acres in Craven County.

John Lee appeared in open Court and acknowledged the delivering &c Titles to Armenos Liles for One Hundred and Fifty Acres on Broad River.

Northeward
vs
Jas. Harris

Attachm^t - Ordered Taht the Tobacco be Sold and the Amount of J. Harris's note & all Costs retained out of it.

The Court adj^d till tomorrow at 9. O'Clock.

> Richard Winn
> J. Pearson
> H. Hampton
> Wm. Kirkland

omitted to be Entered above.

Road.
Pet^n for

A Petition was presented Signed by Several of the Inhabitants on Little River requesting That a road might be ordered to be laid out from Mobley's Meeting House to Winnsborough leading by James Rogers. Which was granted - Ordered That Burr Harrison Esq. W. Thos. Shannon & Thos. Atterson be appointed Commissioners to mark out the same. And that ___ Butler be nominated Overseer from Mobleys Meeting House to Mr. Harrisons House on Little River, and Benj. Harrison from thence to the Winnsborough Road with power to appoint Warners &C.

Fairfield County

Wednesday August 16. 1786.

August Term

Present

Richard Winn. William Kirkland. John Pearson. Henry Hampton. John Buchanan. John Turner. James Craig. Minor Winn and Isaac Love Esquires. and John Winn Esquire.

Estes
to
M. Hill

Thomas Addison & Christ^r Addison appeared in open Court and being duly Sworn Say that they Saw Zachary Estes and Martha his wife Sign Seal and deliver Titles to Moses Hill for one hundred Acres of Land Situate on the Waters of Little River of Broad River.

Leggo
to
An:L Duggin

Maddern Leggo appeared in open Court and acknowledged Signing Sealing and delivering Titles to LeAndrew Duggin, of one Hundred Acres of Land on Dutchmans Creek.

E. Mucklervy
Pet^n for
Maintinance

Elizabeth Mucklervy Petitioned the Court for her Maintinance from James Davis and George Bell as Executors to her Husbands Effects, Ordered That the Executors provide the Petitioner with decent maintinance till next Court when all parties are to appear here to await the Final Judgment of the Court.

The Grand Jury brought in a true bill. State vs Joseph and John McDonald for Stealing Fifty Seven pounds of Bacon from Shadrack Jacobs.

Shaver
vs   Judgm^t for 40^s and Interest from March 1783.
Chapman

Jno. Bell
vs   Writ of Enquiry. on Attachm^t. The following Jurors were
Adm^r Potts   impannelled to try the same Viz.

James Dodds	Adam Free
Jos: Cameron	John Finley
Willm. Ewing	Chas. Montgomery
Saml. Gladney	Simon Cameron
Lewis Owens	James Moutie
Thos. Marple	

Jury found for Plaintiff for L 11.2.10.2 and Costs

Execution to Issue agn. Garnishee for what he may have in his hands according to what he Swore.

Hartin
vs   Crim. Con. The same Jury was Sworn and Impannelled to try the
Gibson   Same.

The Attorney for the plt moved that the following words in the Defts plea be Struck out as frivilous and Erased Viz. "And the s^d Jos: Gibson by his Atty Daniel Brown comes "And defends the force and Injury when &C. And Saith that "The Saith that "The said Rosey mentioned in the plts Declaration by the "Name of Rosey Hartin is not the Lawful Wife of of the said "Henry Hartin nor was the Wife of the said Henry at the "time of begetting of said Bastard Child mentioned in the "plts Declaration." which was agree to by the Court.

The Jury found for the plt Fifteen pounds Sterling.

J. Winn
to   John Winn Esqr. appeared in open Court and acknowledged
Wm. Moultrie   the Signing Sealing and delivering Titles to his
          Excellency Willm. Moultrie Esquire of Lotts No. 19.
          20. 53. & No. 54. in the Town of Winnsborough.

H. Hampton
to   Henry Hampton Esqr appeared in open Court and acknow-
Moultrie ledged the Signing Sealing and delivering Titles to
          William Moultrie Esqr of a Plantation on Tract of Land
Situate on the head of Jacksons Creek containing Two Hundred Acres of Land.

Minor
vs   Fra^s Coleman Sum^d as Garnishee swears he has no property in his
Liles   hands.

McCoy
vs   Att. John Greg, Garnishee Sworn Saith he owes the deft about
B Wilson L 15. Sterl. by notes of he and

Adj^d till tomorrow at 9 O'Clock.

                              John Winn
                              M. Winn
                              James Craig

31

Thursday August. 17. Aug. 1786

Fairfield
County   The Court met according to Adjournment

Present

    Henry Hampton. William Kirkland. Richd Winn. John Pearson. John Turner. Isaac Love. John Winn. and James Craig Esquires.

Rabb
to   William Rabb appeared in open Court and acknowledged the
J. Kincaid   Signing Sealing and delivering to James Kincaid Set of
              Titles for One Hundred Acres of Land on Little River a
              branch of Broad River

Picket
vs   Debt. The Suit withdrawn at Defendants Costs.
Sanders

Wells
vs   Sheriff having returned nearest Inventus. The Court ordered a
Beard   Judicial Attachment to Issue.

State
vs   Called, Forfeited her Recognizance. Sc: F. to Issue.
S. Harris

State
vs   Daniel Goyen as Principal & Alex. Goyen his Security
Danl Goyen forfeited their Recoginzance. Sc: Fa: to Issue.

McClintock
vs   Thomas Wright the Deft was Surrendered to the Custody
Thos. Wright of the Sheriff by his Bail James Austin.

State
vs   Appeared in Court agreeable to her Recognizance and
S. Bradley   Swore she has been delivered of a Female Child and that
              Daniel Goyen was the Father of it.

    Constables. William Nelson and John Anderson were appointed
Constables. When Wm. Nelson was Sworn

Winn
vs   In the Suit Minor Winn vs Jno. Liles an Attachm^t liveed on a
Liles   certain black Horse. Charles Coleman interpleads and Claims
              said Horse. Upon which it is ordered that a Jury come at
              next Court and try in whom the property of the said Horse is.

State
vs   Trespass. The Cause being called the following Jurors
Ed. Hancock   were Sworn and impannelled to try the Same Viz.

James Dods	Lewis Owens	Simon Cameron
Jos: Cameron	Thos. Marple	James Moutie
Wm. Ewing	Adam Free	
Wm. Beard	John Finley	
Saml. Gladney	Chas. Montgomery	

    The Jury brought their Verdict GUILTY
And Court Fined the Defendant 1^d

McCay
vs   Garnishee Sworn in Court to a Balance in his hands of L. 1.
Bargin   12. 11.
              Ordered that the Cause be dismissed as coming within
              Jurisdiction of a Single Magistrate.

State
vs   A & Battery. The defendant pleased Guilty. and the Court
Porter   fined him 1ᵈ

Isaac Love
vs   Referred to John King and Micajah Picket in case they
Thom: Stark disagree to chuse a third person and their Judgment or
            any Two of them to be returned and Entered as the
Judgment of the Court. Referres to meet at James Tollers on the Second
Monday in September next, and to Sit till the Business is finished and
the Witnesses Summoned to this Court are to attend at the same time &
place.

Tho. Saine
vs   Referred to the same Persons under the same Restrictions.
Meredith

Hollis
vs   On Petition. The Judges having heard the Evidence on both
Picket   sides. Being divided in opinion the action was continued
            for further hearing.

Greg
vs   The defendant confessed Judgment for one penny and Costs.
Ph: Riley

    George Lott was fined fourty Shillings for Contempt of Court and
ordered to give security for his behavior.

Gray
vs   Upon Plts. affidavit that he coᵈ not procure a very material
Ederington Evidence the trial was ordered to be put off.

    The Court adjᵈ till 9 O'Clock tomorrow.

N. B.   Lot appeared in Court the next day, and being sober, asked
        pardon for his rude behavior, and the court ordered him to be
        dismissed without Costs or Fine.

                            John Winn
                            Jno. Buchanan
                            James Craig
                            Richd. Winn
                            John Turner

Fairfield County   Friday 18. August 1786.

    The Court met according to Adjournment.

                        Present

    John Winn. Richard Winn. John Pearson. Minor Winn. John Buchanan
Esqʳˢ

M. Winn
to   Minor Winn Esquire appeared in open Court and acknowledged
Auston   the Signing Sealing and delivering to Robert Austen Titles
            to Lots No. 135. and Lot No. 69. in the Town of Winnsborough.

Miller
to   Alexander Miller appeared in open Court and acknowledged the
Arthur   Signing Sealing and delivering to James Arthur Two Hundred
            Acres of Land on Walkers Branch of the Wateree Creek.

Arthur
to   James Arthur appeared in open Court and acknowledged the
Watson   Signing Sealing and delivering Titles to John Watson for Six

33

Hundred and forty acres of Land on Walkers Branch of the Wateree Creek.

Petit Jurh.   The Petit Jury being called the following answered to their
viz.   names.

Jas. Dods	Lewis Owens	Simon Cameron
Jos. Cameron	Thos. Marple	James Montie
Wm. Ewing	Adam Free	Chas. Montgomery
Wm. Beard	John Finley	Wm. Watson

Road from
Little River   Ordered that a Road be cut from Winnsboro to Little
to   River and from thence to Shirers Ferry and that a
Shirers Ferry Bridge be built over Little River where the said
               Road crosses it.   And the Court appointed Wm. McMorris
from Winnsborough to Little River and Wm. Rabb from thence to the Ferry
overseers with power to appoint their own Warners.

State
  vs   Petit Larceny.   The above named Jury was Sworn to try
Jos. McDaniel the same.   when having heard the Evidence on both
               Sides, brought in their Verdict   GUILTY.

Hollis
  vs   Verdict for Defendant.
Picket   The Court Adjourned untill tomorrow at nine o'clock.

                          John Winn
                          Richard Winn
                          Jno. Buchanan

Fairfield County
                    Saturday. August 19th. 1786.

     The Court met according to Adjournment.

                          Present

     John Winn. Richard Winn. John Pearson. James Craig.

Rachel Hancock
  vs   Ordered to be continued.
Edw: Hancock

Henry Hunter
  vs   Ordered that an Interlocutory Judgment.
John Hicks

Jno. McCaw.
  vs
Wm. Graves   Judgment by Default.

Droslin
  vs   Ordered to be continued.
Riley

State
  vs   The Deft. was fined L 5. proclamation money. Ordered
Danl. Goyen   that he give bond in L 50. for Maintenance of the
               Child. payable to the Justices.

     Isaac Love vs Mark Fortune. Continued

State
  vs   Daniel Goyen having appeared this day and made such Excuse as
Goyen   was Satisfactory for not appearing when first called, the
               Fine or Forfeiture of his recognizance was remitted.

Wm. Boyd
    vs   Ordered that Judgment be Entered.
Jesse Gwin

J. Milling vs. Robinson & Mense. Default

      The Court adjourned for one Hour.

Overseers   William Lewis is appointed overseer on the road from
             Winnsborough to Camden from the Bridge on 25. mile Creek
             to Ross's Old Road. and Rowland Williamson from thence to
             the Wolf pit.

Road   Ordered that a road be opened from Moses Cockrells to or near
           James Turner's until it meets the Road ordered by Chester Court.
           John Lee to mark out the road from Cockrells to the County Line.

Overseer   John McCombs is appointed Overseer of the said Road.

State
   vs   Mr. O. Brown moved for an arrest of Judgment. and
Jos: McDaniel   filed his reasons which were argued by the Council for
                the State. as also by the Council for the Deft. and
the Court upon hearing the matter Ordered Judgment to be arrested.

Woodward
   to   William Woodward appeared in open Court and acknowledged
Strother   the Signing Sealing and delivering unto Kemp T. Strother
             Titles to Several Tracts of Land Situate on Mill Creek
             containing in the whole Five Hundred and one Acres of Land.

Sims
   vs   Judgment by Default.
Talbot

Rogers vs Thos. Hicks. Default. & SC: Fa. to go against the Garnishee.

Marg^t Larney
   vs   Judgm^t for 1^d and Costs.
John Richmond

Wm. Graves
   vs   Discontinued at Defts. Costs.
John Hunter.
                          John Winn
                          Richard Winn
                          James Craig
                          H. Hampton
                          Jn. Pearson

                    June Court 1791

      Monday the 13th day of June 1791
      The Court met according to adjournment.

      Judges Present: John Winn and James Craig Esq^rs

Ordered that John Winn Junior do continue to execute the office of
Sheriff of Fairfield County for the remaining term of four years as
prescribed by law.

Ordered that Burr Harrison Esqr be appointed Coroner for the County of
Fairfield.

Proceeded to call over the list of Grand Jurors summoned to appear at
this Court when the following persons answered to their names.

Gardinen Ford, Darling Jones, Jonathan Belton, Robert Rabb, William Hill.

Proceeded to call over the list of Petit Jurors Summoned to appear at this court when the following answered to their names.

Robert Smith, William Nelson, Samuel Caldwell.

Ordered that Letter of Administration be granted to Isaac Lansdale for the Estate of William Dent deceased with a copy of the nuncupative will annexed he proposing James Rabb as security of whom the court approved.

Ordered that Letters of Administration be granted to Elitia Owens (Widow of Lewis Owens) John Pearson. Joe Owens & John Mathews for the estate of Lewis Owens dec^d they proposing James Davis and William Nelson as Securities of whom the court approved.

Ordered that letters of Administration be granted to Elizabeth Miller for the estate of John Miller She proposing Thomas Hill and Michael Bird as securities of whom the court approved.

Court adjourned to tomorrow morning nine o'Clock.

John Winn
James Craig

June Term

Tuesday the 14th day of June 1791

The Court met according to adjournment.

Judges Present

John Winn. James Craig and Benjn Boyd. Esq^{rs}

Henry Fundenburg)
  vs   )   T. P. Judgment confessed according to specialty.
Jesse Wallis)

     Robert Martin petitioned the court that Elijah Ivey an orphan Boy might be bound to him to learn the planting trade which the court granted on condition that the said Robert Martin do at a proper time give the said orphan schooling to read write and cypher and when he attains the age of nineteen years to give him a decent suit of cloaths and during the time of his apprenticeship to find him in cloathing and wholesome food & lodging.

James Curry)
  vs   )   Debt Judgment - Confessed according to Specialty.
Hugh Smith   )
& Daniel Goyen)

Messrs McCleod)
& Belton   )   Debt Judgment - Confessed according to Specialty.
  vs   )
Joseph Cameron)

Jonathan Belton produced the will of Sarah Belton deceased in order to be proved but the evidences thereto living out of the county Ordered that a dismissal issue to one or more of the Justices of the county whereon the witness live.

Hezekiah Ford appeared in open court and upon Oath produced an instrument of writing purporting to be the last will and testament of James Graves deceased as nearly as he could recollect the original will appearing to be destroyed since the testators death. Ordered that the copy produced be established and that letters of administration be

36

granted to Hezekiah Ford and Milleyson Graves with the copy of the will annexed.

At the request of the administrators for the estate of Reuben Judd Woorston deceased Ordered that the estate be sold at the following credits - All sums of twenty shillings & under Cash - all sums not exceeding forty shillings payable on the 1st of January 1792 all sums above forty shillings payable on the 1st of January 1792 and 1st of January 1793.

Alexander Finley)
   vs   ) Debt Judgment confessed according to Specialty.
James Austin   )

Johnathan Belton produced the last will and testament of Sarah Bolton deceased which was accordingly proved Ordered that letters testamentary be granted to Jonathan Belton.

Ordered that the administrators of the estate of Colonel Joseph Kirkland deceased do sell all the personal Estate of the said Kirkland at the following credit that is to say all sums under forty shillings Cash all Sums above forty shillings to be paid the one half the first day of January 1792 the other half the first day of January 1793.

The Reverand Thomas Harris McCants petitioned the court that James McFadden an orphan Boy might be bound to him as an apprentice untill he attains the age of nineteen years. he giving him during the time sufficient food and cloathing and have him taught to read to write and cyphen and when his apprenticeship expires to give him a decent suit of cloathes.

Charles Darnel Bradford proved an Oath the signing and delivery of a bill of sale giving by William Dent to Isaac Lansdale.

Ordered that George Dougharty administrator of Daniel Dougharty deceased do sell the personal Estate of the said deceased on the following Credits Viz. all sums above twenty shillings one half payable January 1792 the other half January 1793 with legal interest from the date taking good security all sums under twenty shillings cash.

Jacob Gibson appears in open court and being duly sworn proved the last will and testament of Thomas Marple deceased which was ordered to be recorded.

John Means   )
   vs   ) Attch.ᵗ Dismissed by the Plaintiff
Heartwell Macon)

Proceeded to call over the list of Grand Jurors summoned to appear at this court when the following answered to their names.

Foreman	Johnathan Belton	Darling Jones	Joe Owens
	James Rabb	Robert Rabb	Henry Moore
	John Robinson	Alexander Gordon	Burrel Cooke
	Samuel Owen	Hugh Smith	William Hill
	James Ogilvie		

who accordingly were impannelled.

Thomas Means)
   vs   ) Debt. S. P. Dismissed by the Plaintiff.
Robert McTyre)

Ordered that the Sheriff of Fairfield County be allowed the sum of One pound twelve shillings and Eight pence for feeding the cattle taken under execution at the Suit of John Winn vs the Catawba Company.

McHale vs Will. Picket) Ind.ᵗ Riot. We grand jury returned a true
& al.   ) bill. Ordered that a Bench Warrant issue
                immediately.

```
The State  )
    vs     )  Riot
Will. Picket)  Same return and order
  & al.    )
```

```
The State    )
    vs       )  On the parties producing the body of Margaret Splawn
Shared Goyen )  in court the court ordered that their recognizances
Margaret Splawn)  be remitted and the Execution thereon returned unto
Robert Smith & )  the office and that Margaret Splawn be fined in the
James Marshall )  sum of five pounds proclamation Money.
```

```
The State    )
    vs       )  Bast^dy fined in the sum of ten pounds proclamation
William Daniel)  Money.
```

```
D. Evans Treasurer )
of Fairf^d County  )
    vs             )  Debt Judgment according to Specialty.
William Kirkland   )
& Alexander Finley )
```

John Winn
James Craig
Benj. Boyd.

June Term

Wednesday the 15th day of June 1791

The court met according to adjournment.

Judges Present: John Winn, James Craig and Benjn Boyd Esqr.

Susanna Arledge produced the last will and testament of Moses Arledge
deceased which was duly proved by John Yarborough a Subscribing witness
thereto. which was ordered to be recorded and letters testamentary to
be granted to Susanna Arledge she having taken the accustomed Oath.

Proceeded to Call over the Grand Jurors impannelled for this Court.

Foreman Jonathan Belton. Joe Owens. James Rabb. Robt. Rabb. Cooke.
Samuel Owen, Hugh Smith, William Hill James Ogilvie and Robert
Ellison who was sworn in the place of Darling Jones.

Jesse Havis appeared in open court and having taken the Oath of Office
and Allegiance prescribed by law was adjudged to be qualified to act
as constable in the County of Fairfield.

Proceeded to Call the Petit Jurors list when the following persons
answered to their names.

George Ashford. William Alsop. Richard Mansel. Thomas Sent. Thomas
Hendricks John Burns Lewis Boltner Thomas Hill. Thomas Parrot Junr.
William Nelson. John Goodrum. Robert Smith.

```
Stephen Brown)
    vs       )  On Motion of the Defendants attorney that the S. P.
John Compty  )  Judgment was obtained illegally.  Ordered that the
                cause be reinstated on the docket for a new trial and
that the Plaintiff have leave to prove his books before a magistrate and
the same to be allowed in Evidence.
```

```
John Compty   )
    vs        )  On Motion of the Defendants attorney that S. P. the
James Ogilvie)  Judgment was illegally obtained Ordered that the cause
                be reinstated on the Docket for a new trial.
```

Martyn Alken)
    vs   ) Case referred to be arbitrated by Thomas Harris McCaule
John Compty) and Minor Winn with leave to chose an umpire, their
               award to be returned during the sitting of the present
Court and the same to be a rule of Court.

State   )
   vs   ) Indt. Ordered that the said Sims be discharged from his
Lewis & Sims) recognizance and the execution thereon be returned into
               the office, and said Sims to pay Costs.

State   )
   vs   ) Indictment for stealing a Bell. The Grand Jury Returned
Samuel Burke) No Bill
               Jonathan Belton Foreman

State   )
   vs   ) Indictment for an assault & Battery. True Bill
William Willingham) Jonathan Belton foreman

State   )
   vs   ) Indictment for Stealing a Saddle. True Bill.
Robert Jennings) Jonathan Belton foreman

State   )
   vs   ) Indictment for marking and Disguising a Sow Pig.
Alexander Kincaid) No Bill Jonathan Belton Foreman

State   )
   vs   ) Indictment for an assault and Battery. a True Bill
Thomas Means) Jonathan Belton, foreman.

State   )
   vs   ) Recognizance for a Suspicion of Felony. Ordered
Burbidge Woodward) that the recognizance be discharged.

State   )
   vs   ) Ind. The cause was now called and the following Jury
Robert Jennings) Impannelled to try the same Viz.

     George Ashford, William Alsop, Thomas Sent, Thomas Hendricks,
John Burns, Lewis Beltnen, John Hill, John Goodrum, Robert Smith, John
Robertson, Benjamin Scot, Benjamin Harrison.

     The Jury returned the following Verdict. The Prisoner Jennings
found not Guilty of the charge, B. Harrison Foreman. Adjudged the
county pay Costs agreeable to the new acts.

State   )
   vs   ) Indictment for selling spiritous liquors without
Maddern Legge) license. No Bill Jonathan Belton Foreman.

Thomas Means)
    vs   ) Debt Judgment Confessed according to specialty by
David James) David James stay of Exon to next court in Course.
& Enoch James)

In the presentment of the grand Jury for Fairfield County Ordered that
letters issue to the magistrates to have the following Persons bound
over to next court for Bastardy That is to say. to John Cooke Esqr.
to Bind over Priscilla Seigler Mary Rhoda, and Elizabeth Dayley to
Hugh Milling Esqr. to bind over Mary Free. to Samuel Yongue Esqr. to
bind over Sarah Turner to John McKinney Esqr. to bind over Susannah
Bosier to John Gray Esqr. to bind over Elizabeth Die and Elizabeth
Poches Also that Sciere facias do issue to the overseers of the roads
mentioned in the presentment aforesaid. to show cause why they should
not be fined for not complying with the orders issued from the court.

Robert Duncan   )
Ad.ᵒʳ John Bowdre)   Case Referred to the award of four persons chosen
    vs   )   by the Parties and their umpire; whose names and
Phillip Sharer   )   award returned in writing to be made a rule of court.
                                                          J Y H.

John McClurken appeared in open court and proved his property in a certain brown bay horse called before J. Pearson Esqr. and sold as an
astray to Mr. John Winn for four pounds Ordered that the treasurer
refund said McClurken the Price of said horse deducting all charges.

James Nealy)
    vs   )   Debt Judgment according to specialty.
James Austen)

Samuel Caldwell)
    vs   )   Case Dismissed at the Plaintiffs costs
John Gray   )

James Hart)
    vs   )   Attcht. Dismissed at the plaintiffs Costs.
John Miles)

Samuel Johnston)
    vs   )   S. P. Dismissed by the Plaintiff
John Watson   )

Samuel Johnston)
    vs   )   S. P. Dismissed at the Defendants costs.
David Shelton)

William Watts   )
    vs   )   Att.ᵗ William McMorris in the name of the Deft. came
William Goldtrap)   into court and repleved the property and entered
                        himself Special Bail.

Lewis Boltner   )
    vs   )   Att. Continued.
Barrbary Rustick)

John Smith   )
    vs   )   Case the former Rule of Court to be cont.ᵈ
Phillip Raiford)

William Kirkland)
    vs   )   Att.ᵗ Judgment according to specialty.
James Rainey   )

John Means asse.)
of John Wauth   )   Debt Judgment Confessed according to Specialty.
    vs   )   Stay of Exon. till the 1st of September next.
Hugh Smith &   )
Robert Ewing   )

                                        John Winn
                                        James Craig

                              June Term

        Thursday 16th day June 1791

        The Court met according to adjournment.

Judges present: James Craig and Benjamin Boyd Esq.ʳˢ

John Winn Junr. having been duly elected Sheriff for Fairfield County
now produced his commission and took the oath of Office. proposing
Samuel Youngue and Robert Ellison and Charles Lewis of whom the Court

                                  40

approved. Securities Also Robert Craig was sworn in as Deputy at the Same Time.

Maddern Leggo)
     vs   ) S. P. Judgment by Default.
John Martin)

Taylors & Rea)
     vs   ) Debt. Judgment by Default.
Jacob Bethna)
& John Arrick)

Taylors & Rea)
     vs   ) Debt. Judgment by Default.
Nathan Dorch)

John Humphreys)
     vs   ) Debt. Award returned and made a rule of Court.
Richard Winn)

William Kirkland)
     vs   ) Attch^t Ordered that a venditious Exponas do issue
James Rainey   ) to sell the land.

Matthew Talbot)
     vs   ) Debt. Judgment by Default.
K. T. Strother)
& John Hunter)

Mathew Talbot)
     vs   ) Debt. Judgment by Default. Except William Strother.
William Dargan)
& Als.   )

Mathew Talbot)
     vs   )
Nathan Dorch) Debt. Judgment by Default.
& William Dorch)

Henry H. Tillinghast)
     vs   ) S. P. Dismissed by the Plaintiff
Rolland Williamson)

Alexander Johnson)
     vs   ) Case the award to be returned and made a rule of
John Ard   ) Court.

McCafferty)
     vs   ) S. P. Ordered that Ded-Po-issue to Meclenburgh County No.
Willingham) Carolina directed to three Magistrates to compared the
             Pltfs accounts with the books and return the same under
             their seals.

William Phillips   )
     vs   ) Debt. Dismissed at the Plaintiffs Costs
Henry Fundenburgh   )
Serv^d of Thomas Taylor)

Jacob Sumerland)
     vs   ) S. P. Dismissed at the Pltffs costs.
Maddern Leggo)

Daniel Brown)
     vs   ) Case Judgment by Default.
James Mumford)

Isaac Rix Pope   )
     vs   ) S. P. Judgment Confessed according to Specialty.
William Willingham)

41

John Turner   )
& James Johnston)   Att.ᵗ Ordered that the Defendant produce a true
  vs   ) Statement of his administration at next court and
John Burns   ) that his letters of administration be revoked.

Janet Downey)
  vs   ) Case. Dismissed at the Defendants Costs.
Robert Adams)

Richard Mansel)
  vs   ) Ags.ᵗ Bat.ʸ Dismissed at the Pltfs Costs.
Thomas Means)

Charles Lewis)
  vs   ) Diss.ᵈ Dismissed at Pltfs Costs.
Charles Picket)

Abraham Miller)
  vs   ) Debt. Dismissed at Defts Costs except two dollars to
James Mann   ) be paid by the Plaintiff.
& Robert Smith)

John King   )
  vs   ) Case. Opposed by force of arms.
Warner Lewis)

Martyn Alken)
  vs   ) Case. The cause was now called and the following Jury
John Compty) impannelled to try the same.

Thomas Sent, Lewis Boltnen, George Shed, Jos.ʰ Quarrell, John Workman, Robert Smith, Jacob Gibson, Saml. Arnot, William Hill, John McClurken, Joshua Durham, Jas. Barkley, who returned the following Verdict: We find for the Plaintiff fifteen pounds and the note that he gave for the home of the negro. Jacob Gibson foreman. The following persons were sworn to the attendance in the above cause. Christopher Brock fourteen days attendances out of the county and one day in 30 miles distance. James Rowe to Eleven days. Daniel Ward Eighteen days out of the county 30 miles.

James Craig
Benj. Boyd.

June Term

Friday the 17th day of June 1791.

The Court met according to adjournment.

Judges Present: John Winn and Benjamin Boyd Esq.ʳˢ

Ordered by the court that all actions dismissed from either of the Dockets of Court shall immediately after the rising of the court be transferred to the Exor docket. And on all Judgements either in favour of the plaintiff or Defendant for Debt or costs Exon shall issue immediately thereon and the tune of issuing be entered on the Exon Docket unless the same shall be expressely ordered to the contrary by the party obtaining the same or the Attorney. and that the Sheriff indorse on each Exon the day on which the same came into his hands. and the day and the property on which the same is levied and that the return of his proceedings be made and Entered at length on the Exon Docket four days before the sitting of each court for the inspection of the parties concerned.

Ordered that Benjamin Odear bound by this Court to Alexander Pedian in November Court 1787 be discharged from the service and delivered to the care of his mother at the request of said Pedian agreable to an agreement between the said Parties and filed in this Court.

Martyn Alken   )
     vs   ) Case Referred to Minor Winn & James Craig Esqr and
Nathaniel Majors) their award to be returned within three months.

Nathaniel Norwood)
     vs   ) Debt Ordered that the rule be dismissed this day
John Atcheson   ) unless the costs are discharged by three o'clock.

Same)
 vs) Debt.
Same)

Ad^{ors} of John Milling)
     vs   ) Case Continued under the rule of reference.
James Cooke   )

James Cooke   )
     vs   ) Case continued under the rule of reference.
Ad^{ors} of John Milling)

Thomas Bradford)
     vs   ) S. P. Dismissed at the Pltfs costs.
William Forch)

Martyn Alken   )
     vs   ) Case Refered to John Means & Hugh Milling with leave
Thomas Bradford) to chuse an umpire the award to be returned this day.

Benjamin Shurlds)
     vs   ) S. P. Nonsuit the pltf not appearing to prosecute
Drury Bishop   ) his suit.

Burrel Cooke)
     vs   ) Debt. The cause was now called and the following Jury
John Hawthorn) impannelled to try the same.

James Russel Senr., John McGlurken, William Nelson, Samuel Arnot,
John Workman, Samuel Moberly, William Hill, Alexander Gordon, Robert
Smith, Robert Coleman, Lewis Boltnen, Richard Hansel.

A Jur__ was withdrawn and the defendant withdrew his Plea whereon
Judgment was entered for the Debt & Int. agreable to the present
instalment law. Mr. John Pearson came into open Court and acknowledged
himself as a security for the Debt agreable to the aforesaid law.

Martyn Alken   )
     vs   ) S. P. Refered to Hugh Milling and John Means Esqr.
Thomas Bradford) with leave to chuse an umpire and the award to be
                  returned this day.

Nathaniel Norwood)
     vs   )
John Atcheson)   Deft. The Defendant having paid the cost. Ordered
    Same   )   that the order for new trial be made absolute.
     vs   )
    Same   )

Charles Derham)
     vs   ) Case The cause was now Called and the following
Alexander Gordon) Jury impannelled to try the same.

John McClurken	William Nelson	Samuel Arnot
John Workman	Samuel Moberly	William Hill
Robert Coleman	Lewis Boltnen	Richard Mansel
James Davis	William McMorris	Willm. Willingham

who returned the following verdict we Find for the Plaintiff two Pounds
one shilling.   James Davis Foreman

Joshua Derham swore to seven days attendance in the above suit. Robert Winfield Eckles one day sworn to William Graves swore to three days attendance on the above suit.

The State   )
    vs   )   Indictment for a Riot. The cause was now called and
William Picket)   the following Jury were Impannelled to try the same.
John Whitehead)
Wm. Whitehead)   Charles Lewis   Lewis Boltnen   Robert Coleman
                   Samuel Arnot   John Workman   James Davis
                   Benjamin Harrison   Joseph Quarrell   John McClurken
                   William Willingham   Samuel Moberly   Edwd. Martin

        who returned the following Verdict. Not Guilty. James Davis
Foreman.
                              John Winn
                              Benj. Boyd.

                              June Term

        Saturday the 10th day of June 1791.

        The Court met according to adjournment.

        Judges Present: John Winn and James Craig Esquires

William Evans appeared in open court and proved the Signing sealing and delivery of a Bill of sale from William Willingham to John Willingham for three negroes And also proved the signing sealing and delivery of a Deed from William Willingham to John Willingham and David Evans in trust for William Ashley an infant

David Evans being sworn proved the signing sealing and delivery of a conveyance of 3.250 Acres of Land from John & Minor Winn to Thomas Whitehouse.

Alex^r Pedian)
    vs   )   S. P. Judgment according to Specialty.
James Gamble)

James Crawford)
    vs   )   Debt. Judgment by Default according to Specialty.
James McCreight)

James Austin)
    vs   )   S. P. Judgement by confession.
Maddern Leggo)

Charles Picket)
& William Lewis)   Debt. Judgment confessed by Robert Starks the
    vs   )   Defendants Attorney.
James Rainey   )
& John Winn   )

Phillip Pool Exor)
of Georg Pool   )
    vs   )   S. P. Refered to Mr. McCaule and Captn. Farren
Lewis Boltner   )   and their umpire. the Deft. admits the pltfs demand
  Same   )   but pleads a set of
    vs   )
  Same   )

John Allen Thorpe)
    vs   )   Sc: fa. Dismissed
Mary Free   )

Thomas Bradford)
    vs   ) Attch.^{t} Nonsuit
William Dorch)

Minor Winn   )
    vs   ) Case Dismissed at the Defts Costs
David McCreight)

John Willson assg.)
    vs   ) S. P.   Judgement by Default according to Specialty.
William Taylor &)
Meredith Taylor)

William Burns)
    vs   ) Debt.   Nonsuit
Joshua Derham)

John & Thomas Means)
    vs   ) Debt.   Judgement according to specialty.
Charles D. Bradford)

Benjamin Boyd)
    vs   ) S. P. A. Decree for L 7"17"6 by Default
Robert Richardson)

Minor Winn   )
    vs   ) S. P. Judgement Confessed according to Specialty.   Stay
Francis Palmer) of Exon four Months.

Robert Ellison)
    vs   ) Attch.^{t} Judgement by Default
John Hutchinson) Ordered the defendant Pleads within twelve months.

Nathaniel Norwood)
    vs   ) Debt.   The cause was now called and the following
John Atcheson) Jury impannelled to try the same.

Robert Coleman	Thomas Bradford	John McClurken
George Kenedy	William Nelson	Lewis Boltnen
John Richmond	John Burns	Thomas Hendricks
William Hill	Samuel Owens	John Bell

who returned the following Verdict. We find for the Plaintiff L 2"6"0
with lawfull Interest on the two notes. Thomas Bradford Foreman.

Nicholas Ringer swore to five days attendance on the above suit. John
Bradford swore to four days. Philemon Halcomb. one day. Augustine
Smith to one days attendance.

Obediah Kirkland appeared in open court and being appointed deputy
sheriff of Fairfield County took the Oaths of office and allegeance
prescribed by law.

Samuel Neal   )
    vs   ) Att^{t} The Defendant appeared in court and repleved
Heartwell Macon) the property and Robert Coleman in open Court
                  acknowledge himself special Bail.   Ordered that the
property Attached he delivered up to the defendant.

Ordered that John Campell be remitted one half of his fees due the
county for licence.

Proceeded to ballot for Grand Jurors to serve at next Court. when the
following names were drawn.

Robert Martyn Junr., Nazareth Whitehead, Robert Martin, Jesse Simmons,
Rolland Williamson, Willm. Daniel, Jesse Ford, Thomas Lewers, Thomas
Starke, Wm. Kirkland, Alexr. Gordon, Zach.^{h} Nettles, Willm. Cason,

William Hoach, Alexr. Kenedy, John Pearson, Robert Hancock, Jas. McCreight, Daniel Mabry, Frirrle McTyre.

Petit Jurors drawn to serve at next Court.

Edwd. Day, Robt. Phillips Junr., David Campbell, Josh. Cammeron, Edmund Tidwell, Obeanh. Henson, James Phillips, Henry Page, Jacob Hoch, Willm. Calhoun, Willm. Cogan, James Arnot, Thomas Dukes, William Robinson, Jacob Turnepseed, Micajah Mobley, Edward Watts, Robert Shurley, Asaph Hill, Saml. McKee, Willm. Summerland, George Vandenear, Adam Blair, Jno. Tidwell, James Henning, Allen Goodrum, Thomas Mobley, Jas. Dodds, George Kenedy, Benjamin Helsey.

Ordered that the treasurer be impowered to contract with some person on the most reasonable terms to put Pillars under the Court House when necessary.

David Read Evans being appointed Deputy Clerk for the County Court of Fairfield took the Oaths of Office and Allegiance as prescribed by law.

William Strother appeared in court and proved the signing of a Bill of Sale from K. T. Strother to Benjamin Harris on for a negroe.

John Turner)
   vs   )   Case   Refered to Micajah Picket and Charles Lewis and
John Burns) their umpire their award to be returned to the clerk
             within two months and be made a rule of Court.

Nathaniel Norwood)
   vs   )
John Atcheson)   Debt Ordered that the actions be consolidated and
  Same   )   the cost of one only taxed.
   vs   )
  Same   )

Adjourned to January
Court next in course.
                        John Winn
                        James Craig

January Term 1792.

Thursday the 12th Day of January 1792.

The Court met according to adjournment

Judges Present. John Winn and James Craig Esquires.

Adjourned to tomorrow morning ten 0'Clock.

                        John Winn
                        James Craig

January Term 1792

Friday the 13th January 1792.

The court met according to adjourment.

Judges Present: John Winn and James Craig Esquires.

Proceeded the call over the list of grand Jurors appointed to serve at this court when the following answered to names, Nazareth Whitehead, Jesse Simmons. Proceeded to call the Petit Juror List. The following answered to their names, Allen Goodram, John Winn Esqr. appeared in open court and acknowledged the signing, sealing and Delivery of a Conveyance of a tract of Land containing two hundred and twenty five acres situate on Lick creek conveyed by the said John Winn to James Akin, Ordered that letters of administration be granted to James Brown and Samuel Alston for the estate of William Boyd deceased they giving securityas the laws requires.

Stafford Curry was Qualified as an Executor with John Turner and Abraham Miller for the estate of Samuel Neal deceased.

William Watts   )
    vs   )   Attachment dismissed at the plaintiffs costs.
William Goldtrap)

Nicholas Peay appeared in open court and proved the Last will and testament of George Peay deceased duly executed. Ordered the same be recorded. Elizabeth Peay Executrix appointed in will of George Peay deceased was duly qualified to Act. having taken the accustomed oath. Ordered Letters testamentary be granted to the said Elizabeth Peay.

James Davis)
    vs   )   On Scire facias. Judgment on the Installment and
James Dillard)   Execution to issue.
William Hogan)
John Wilking)

Same)
  vs) On Sci. fa Judgment for Instalment & Execution.
Same)

Same)
  vs) On Sci. fa Judgment for Installment of Execution.
Same)

William Nelson)   [case stricken]
    vs   )   Appeal from Mr. Justice pearson's judgement Ordered
William McMoris)   the judgement be Confirmed

Phileman Halcomb)
    vs   )   Appeal from Mr. Justice Grays Judgement Ordered the
William Holly)   Judgt be reversed. & Decreed that William Holly pay
                    Phileman Halcomb L 1. and costs of suit.

                              John Winn
                              James Craig

                           January Term

Saturday the 14th day of January 1792

The Court met according to adjournment.

Judges Present. John Winn and James Craig Esquires

Several of the Inhabitants of Fairfield County petitioned for a road to be cut out from Morris branch to Dennis Burns on the Winnsborough road to Camden. Ordered the same be granted and John Turner Esquire. Charles Lewis and Thomas Starks appointed commissioners to Lay off the same, also Charles Lewis appinted overseer for the said road.

Daniel Huffman)
    vs   )   Case. Dismissed by the Plaintiff.
James Swann   )

Drury Bishop)
     vs   ) S. P. Dismissed by the Plaintiff
Henry Robinson)

William Roach   )
     vs   ) Case. Dismissed by the Plaintiff
Zachariah Kirkland)

Hugh Boyd   )
     vs   ) Case Dismissed at the Defts. costs.
Thomas McClurken)

Mathew McCreight)
     vs   ) Case refered to be arbitrated by John Pearson and
John Martin   ) William McMorris.

Clator Smith)
     vs   ) Appeal Magistrates Judg^t confirmed no attorneys fee
John McCullock) to be tax'd.

James Gordon   )
     vs   ) S. P. Judgment confessed according to specialty by
Thomas McClurken) Thomas McClurkin.
Arthur McCrackin)

James Camble)
     vs   ) Attachment. Dismissed by the plaintiff.
Joseph Rogers)

Anderson Pannel, Peter Holsey and Benjamin Pannel appeared in open
court and being duly sworn made oath that they saw Benjamin Holsey,
Sarah Holsey and Margaret Holsey sign seal and as their act and deed
deliver to John Stip a certain paper writing (then shown to them)
purporting to be conveyance to the said John Stip of three hundred
ninety five acres of Land situate in Berkly County Virginia and that they
also saw the said parties sign the receipt for the consideration money
thereon indorsed and that they signed their names as witnesses thereto
and that Anderson Thomas signed his name as a witness thereto at the
same time, which is ordered to be certified.

Samuel Proctor   )
     vs   ) S. P. Continued to June court next by consent.
Thomas Parrot Junr.)

Areemans Liles and Albert Bean appointed commissioners and Richard Hill
overseer on a road to be opened from Mean's Store to Liles's ford on
Broad River.

James Dodds appeared in court and proved the due Execution of the last
will and testament of John Dodds deceased Ordered that the same be
recorded.

David Hamilton Simon Cameron the executors and Elizabeth Dodds executrix
appointed in the will of John Dodds deceased were duly qualified in
open court. Ordered that Letter's of Ad testamentary be granted to
the same.

John Wilson appeared in open court and acknowledged the signing sealing
and delivery of conveyance of a tract Land containing One hundred acres
situate on the west side of the Wateree river, conveyed by the said
John Wilson to Aron Wooten.

Phillip Martin)
     vs   ) Debt. Abraham Smith proved the signing of the note in
John Sims   ) suit given by said Sims to Martin and also swore to
                 2 days Attendance living in York County fifty five
                 miles.

48

Ordered that a store licence be granted to William Gibson to retail
spiritous liquors to commence from the date of the permit.

Ordered also that a tavern licence be granted John Haris in like manner.

Ordered that the new road from Winnsborough to the new meeting house on
Jacksons Creek be a public road and that the same be kept open. and
William Beard overseer for the same.

Phillip Martin)
 vs   ) Debt. Judgment confessed according to specialty with
John Sims) stay of execution three months.

Proceeded to call the Grand Jury the following answered Nazareth White-
head, Jesse Simmons, Rolland Williamson, William Daniel, Alexander
Kenedy, James McCreight, Frirrle McTyre, John Wilson, Francis Kirkland,
Henry Moore, Benjamin May, John Means, who were accordingly impannelled.

The last will and testament of Robert Phillips deceased was produced
in court duly proved ordered that the same be recorded, and Agnes
Phillips Exeuctrix and Robert Reid & David Hamilton Executors appointed
in said were duly qualified in open court.

Henry Funderburgh)
 vs   ) S. P. Judgment confessed according to specialty.
James Phillips)

Samuel Neal)
 vs   ) Att^t abated by the death of the plaintiff. Robert
Heartwell Macon) Coleman swore to six days attendance on the said
       suit.

The grand jury returned on the following indictments.

State   )
 vs   ) Indt. for Larceny. a true bill.
William Adams)

State   )
 vs   ) Indt. for assault & Battery. a true bill.
William Willingham)

State   )
 vs   ) Indt. for admisdemeanon a true Bill
Henry McBride) Continued to June court on affidavit.

Adors of Bowdre)
 vs   ) Case trial continued to June court and a commission
Phillip Shaver) to take the Deposition of Robert Duncan debeneese.

Adjourned to Monday 10 o'clock
          John Winn
          James Craig

         January Term 1792

Monday the 16th day of January 1792
The Court met according to adjournment.

Judges Present: Benjamin Boyd & John Winn Esq^{rs}

Martyn Alken)
 vs   ) Case dismissed at the plaintiff's costs.
John Pair)

Abraham Gibson)
    vs   )   S. P.   award returned the Defendants to pay costs of
John Briant)   suit.

Zachariah Kirkland appeared in open court and took the oath of office
and allegiance as one of the magistrates appointed to keep the peace in
the county of Fairfield.

Thomas Hill appeared in open court and took the oath of office and
allegiance as one of the constables appointed for the county of Fairfield.

James Hoy appeared in open court and took the oath of office and
allegiance as one of the constables & appointed for the county of
Fairfield.

David Shelton appeared in open Court and acknowledged the signing sealing and delivery of a Deed conveying a tract of one hundred and fifty
acres of Land conveyed from the said David Shelton & Lucy Shelton to
Daniel Mabry.

Anderson Thomas appeared in open court and proved the signing, sealing
and delivery of a deed conveying a tract of Land containing one hundred
and fifty acres on the North side of Broad River conveyed by Abel
Gassaway to David Shelton.

Anderson Thomas also proved the signing sealing and Delivery of a Deed
conveying a tract of one hundred and fifty acres of Land situate on
McClures branch & Beaver creek conveyed from David Hopkins to David
Shelton.

Exor of George Pool)
          S. P.)
    vs   )
Lewis Boltner.   )
) Award returned by consent of parties Six pence
Exor. of George Pool) for the defendant in each Cause and Costs
         S. P.) of Suit found
    vs   )
Lewis Boltner   )

Allowed Robert Lathan seven shillings and Eight pence on account of
keeping a Stray mare.

William Strother)
    vs   )   S. P. Decree for L S.14"S with interest from the
Maddern Leggo)   14th of July 1787. and costs of suit.

Ordered that a rule of court be issued to John Bradford to show cause
why he should not be fined for neglect of duty in not executing certain
warrants directed by John Cooke Esquire.

Ordered that a rule of Court be issued to James Bawles late Deputy
Sheriff to show cause why he has not returned the papers of the Late
Sheriff of Fairfield County to the Clerks office.

                        John Winn
                        Benjm. Boyd

                    January Term 1792

Tuesday the 17th day of January 1792.
The Court met according to adjournment.

Judges present: John Winn and Benjamin Boyd Esq.rs

Ordered that a tavern License be granted to Francis McCall to retail
spiritous liquors and keep a house of entertainment for travellers.

State   )
    vs   )   Bastardy. Fined L 5 proclamation money & costs of suit.
Keziah Frost)   Ordered to give security.

State   )
    vs   )   Bastardy. Fined L 5 proclamation money & costs of suit.
Peter Larrows)   Ordered security be given.

John Winn   )
    vs   )   Debt. Judgment confessed according to specialty.
Richard Featherstone)   stay of execution to the first day of March next.

State   )
    vs   )   Bastardy. Ordered that the recognizance be continued.
William Lathan)

Ordered that a rule of court issue to John Turner Esqr to show cause why
he did not bind over the woman who has charged the above said William
Lathan with being the father of her bastard Child.

State   )
    vs   )   Mis.vs Recognizances discharged.
John Richmond)

State   )
    vs   )   Ind^t Riot. Continued.
William Picket)
and alias.   )

State   )
    vs   )   Assault & Battery. Continued.
William Willingham)

State   )
    vs   )   Asst. & Battery. Continued. Ordered that Samue Yongue
Maddern Leggo)   Esqr. to issue a warrant to bind over Samuel Burke to
                 prosecute the Indictment at next Court.

State   )
    vs   )   Indict^t Ordered that bench warrant do issue against the
William Adams)   defendant.

Fairfield County)
    vs   )   Scire facias for not working on the roads as
Victor Nealy   )   directed, on making a sufficient excuse they
David McCreight   )   were dismissed without costs. Ordered that
Charles Montgomery)   Letters do issue again to the said overseers
Robert Phillips   )   for their respective roads and that the same be
                          served personally or left at their dwellings by
                          the sheriff.

State   )
    vs   )   Bast^{dy} Ordered that a scire facias do issue against
Mary Hatcher)   Mary Hatcher and Elisha Haigood to show cause why their
                 recognizances should not be forfeited.

State   )
    vs   )   Sci. fa. Dismissed on the Defendants paying costs.
Samuel Caldwell)

State   )
    vs   )   Sci. fa. Dismissed on the defendants paying Costs,
Alexander Gordon)   and the county for one years Licence for retailing
                    of spiritous Liquors.

```
State      )
   vs      )   Indictment for an assault and Battery.  The cause was
Thomas Means)  now called and the following Jury impannelled to try the
               same
```

Thomas Malone	William Allsap	Daniel Mabry
William Hill	William Nelson	John Martin
Edward McGraw	Adam Pool	Boling Wright
Allen Goodrum	Edward Watts	Anderson Thomas

Foreman being impannelled & sworn

They returned the following verdict. The Jury finds him Guilty. Anderson Thomas foreman. On a Motion made by James Davis, Ordered that a
rule of court do issue to Denis Crosby Executor of Thomas Crosby
deceased to show cause why the Execution Obtained by Thomas Brannan vs
the said James Davis and sold by the said Thomas Bradford to Thomas
Crosby should not be returned by the sheriff satisfied.

```
Exors of Alexander Miller)
        vs               )   S. P.
Thomas Baker Franklin    )   Continued on the Defendants paying the
                             plaintiffs attorney his fee
```

Ordered that Zachariah Kirkland be appointed overseer on the main road
Leading to McCords ferry in the place of Jacob Bethna.

```
John Todd )
    vs    )   S. P. Decree for L 4"6"2. a rehearing granted by consent
John Means)   of the attorney the Deft making no objection to the
              legality of the pltfs Testimony.
```

```
James Cooke  )
     vs      )   Appeal from Mr. Justices Yongues Judgt. the Magistrates
James Cameron)   Judgement confirmed.
```

```
State              )
   vs              )   Indictment for an assault and Battery.  The same
William Willingham)    Jury were impannelled to try the cause except
                      David James in the place of Edward McGraw who
returned the following verdict we agree and find the Defendant GUILTY.
Anderson Thomas foreman.  whereupon the court fined the Defendant the
sum of four pounds Sterling money.
```

```
State       )
   vs       )   Asst. & Bat.ʸ  The Jury having found the defendant GUILTY.
Thomas Means)   The Court thereupon fined the defendant in the sum of
                six pence.
```

```
Samuel Nesbit)
    vs       )   S. P.  Ordered for trial on tomorrow.
Walter Akins )
                           John Winn
                           Benjn. Boyd.
```

January Term 1792.

Wednesday the 18th day of January 1792.
Court met according to adjournment

Judges Present. John Winn, Benjamin Boyd & James Craig, Esquires.

Ordered that Wm. Willingham be taken into Custody untill he shall give
security for his appearance to answer to an Indictment the State vs
William Willingham and that he also give security for his good behavior
in the mean time.

John Todd)
   vs   )   S. P. Decree for two pounds Eighteen shillings and two
John Means)   pence.

John McCants   )
   vs   )   Debt on Attachment. The Defendants Attorney Daniel
John Hobrendorf) Brown confessed Judgment on the bond which is only to
                be charged on the Land under Attachment and not against
any other Attachment property of the said Hobrendorf. Ordered that
a writ of venditioni expenas do issue.

Martyn Alken   )
   vs   )   Case refered to Benjamin Boyd and John Wilson
Thomas Bradford) Esquires.

Martyn Alken   )
   vs   )   S. P. referred as above.
Thomas Bradford)

Samuel Nesbit)
   vs   )   S. P. Decree for six pounds with Interest & costs
Walter Akin   )   Thomas Nesbitt swore to four days attendance.

State   )
   vs   )   Sci. fi. James Dodds swore to six days attendance
Samuel Caldwell) as an evidence on the above suit.

Minor Winn   )
   vs   )   Case Judgment confessed for L6"13.
John Woodward)

William Daniel)
   vs   )   S. P. Decree for L4"4"6 with Interest.
Maddern Leggo)

Robert Haswell)
   vs   )   Att^t Abated by Pltfs. death.
Richard H. Homan)

David James   )
   vs   )   Att^t Dismissed by Pltf.
Heartwell Macon)

William Hill)
   vs   )   Att^t Diss^d by pltf.
Eleasar Mobley)

John Means   )
   vs   )   Case Dismissed at the Defts. costs.
Anderson Thomas)

Samuel Johnston)
   vs   )   Attachment. Heartwell Macon Junior was Sworn
Spencer Brunnett) as garnishee. Ordered to lye over till Friday.

                          John Winn
                          James Craig

                  January Term 1792

Thursday the 19th day of January 1792.
Court met according to adjournment.

Judges present. John Winn, James Craig and Benjn Boyd Esquires

Elisha Haigood proved the signing sealing and delivery of a deed
conveying a tract of One Hundred and fifty acres of Land situate in

Fairfield county conveyed from John Busby and Obedience Busby to Hardy Miles.

Ordered that Isaac Lansdale administrator of William Dent deceased do sell the property belonging to the said Estate at a credit to twelve months taking good security and that the said Ad^{or} do make his return of sales at the next court of Ordinary.

On a motion made against the administrators of William Durphey late sheriff of Fairfield County, that the said sheriff had received certain monies on sundry executions in his hands the property of Messrs Graaff Scibels, Beaselman & Co. Ordered that the said Ad^{ors} have thirty days to adjust the said Exons for the monies then appearing to have been received or not received by the default of the said sheriff on the aforesaid Exons and the same not paid on accounted for to the said Company.

Margaret Godfrey)
   vs   )   Case the cause was now called and the following
Thomas Malone)   Jury was impannelled to try the same

John Woodward, Phillip Raiford, Robert Rabb, Wm. Nelson, Thomas Bradford, Joseph McDaniel, Wm. Hill, Wm. Alsop, John Watson, George Karson, Nathaniel Major, Edwd Watts who returned for the following verdict. We find for the plaintiff L15"3"2   John Woodard foreman

Daniel Mabry swore to six days attendance. Thomas Stone swore to five days Attendance.

James Atkins)
   vs   )   On Attachment dismissed
John Clayton)

Martyn Alken)
   vs   )   Case
Thomas Bradford)

Martyn Alken)
   vs   )   S. P. Referred. award to be returned on the 12th
Thomas Bradford)   day of June next and the same to be final.

William Hill Exor   )
of William Hill   )
   vs   )
John Buchanan   )   S. P. Continued at the plaintiffs Costs
& Robert Read   )   Ruled for trial at next term.
Exors. of Robt. Campbell)

Francis Coleman)
   vs   )
David Shelton)   Debt. Judgment case Stay of Execution two months.
Henson Day &   )
James McCemont)

William McCafferty)
   vs   )   S. P. Nonsuit.
Willm. Willingham)

Isaac Love)
   vs   )   Case. Dismissed at Plaintiffs costs.
John Mickle)

Benjamin Boyd)
   vs   )   S. P. Withdrawn each paying an equal part of the costs.
James Winn)

John Means vs George Karson & John Buchanan) S. P. Judgment according
                                            to specialty.

John Means   )
    vs   ) Debt. Judgement. Stay of Exon six months.
John Buchanan)

John Smith   )
    vs   )   Case Refered to James Craig & Minor Winn Esq[rs]
Phillip Raiford)   who awarded that the suit be dismissed at the
                   plaintiffs costs.

Minor Winn)
    vs   ) Case Writ of enquiry.
Samuel Baity)
           Same the Jury were impannelled except Boling Weight
Thom John Dunlap. Andrew Gibson, David James Willm. Scot Jesse Sibley,
Lee Dugan.

John Winn   )
asse of John Smith) Debt. Judgement confessed stay of Exon to 1st
    vs   ) April next.
James McCreight   )
                              John Winn
                              Benjn. Boyd

                        January Term 1792

Friday the 20th day of January 1792.
Court met according to adjournment

Judges present, John Winn, Benjn. Boyd and James Craig Esquires.

William Alsup)
    vs   ) S. P. Decree for six pounds
Thomas Nelson)

William Alsup)
    vs   ) Case Dismissed error
James Phillips)

Francis Coleman)
    vs   ) Debt. Plea withdrawn. Judgement according to
William Rabb   ) Specialty.

James Auten)
    vs   ) S. P. Decree for L 5"6"1
James Harris)

Robert Ellison)
    vs   ) Debt. Judgement according to specialty.
Madern Leggo)

John L. Bradford)
    vs   ) Debt. Judgment according to specialty.
William Alsup   )

Martyn Alken)   Referred to Minor Winn & James Craig Esquires
    vs   ) Case   who award that Nathaniel Majors do pay the
Nathaniel Majors)   said Alken the sum of Thirty shillings and
                          costs of suit.

James McCreight appeared in open court and proved the due Execution of
the last Will and testament of William McCreight deceased. Ordered
that the same be recorded and Letters testamentary be granted to the
said Executors named in the said will.

Samuel Caldwell)
    vs   )   Debt. On Motion Ordered that a scire facias do issue
John McCown   )   to the defendants to show cause why Execution should
& Widow Campbell) not issue.

William Willingham)
    vs   )   Case the cause was now called and the following
Jesse Havis   )   Jury impannelled to try the same.

William Burns, Robert Smith, John Martin, William Alsup, Richard Gladney,
Joseph McDaniel, William Hill, David James, Joseph Quarrel, James
Johnstone, John Woodard, William Owens, who returned the following
verdict. We find for the plaintiff the sum of L 12" 13" 8. John
Woodard Foreman.

Ordered that John McCray a poor boy be bound to the Rev.d Thomas Harris
McCaule untill he attains the age of twenty one years, the said McCaule
to find him in board Lodging and decent cloathing and to give him one
years schooling within that time and at the expiration of the term to
give him a good suit of Cloaths agreable to the custom of the Country.

Wm. Willingham)
    vs   )   Case Jacob Gibson swore to one days attendance.
Jesse Haris   )

Exors of Alex.^{r} Miller)
    vs   )   S. P. Judgment according to specialty. Stay
John Jenkins   )   of Exon to the first day of March next.

William Alsup)
    vs   )   Case. Dismissed by the pltf.
James Phillips)

Christian Graddick)
    vs   )   Debt. Judgement according to note confessed.
William Strother)
& Minor Winn   )

Jesse Haris came into court and took the oaths as one of the Deputy
Sheriffs for the County of Fairfield.

Maddern Leggo   )
Ind.^{ore} Stokes)
Ind.^{ore} Womack)   Debt The same Jury were impannelled to try the
Ind.^{ore} of Dargan) same except Jacob Gibson, James Austen and John
    vs   )   Haris. The Jury found a special Verdict which
Enoch James   )   was ordered to be recorded.

Thomas H. McCaule   )
    vs   )   Debt Judgement Confessed.
The Administrators)
of John Milling dec.^{d})

Miley Beard)
    vs   )   Case. Dismissed
William Scot)   John Bell swore to 5 days Attendance Horp Parrot one
                 day Attendance.

Samuel Johnstone)
    vs   )   On Att.^{t} A Collateral issue between Samuel Johnstone
Spencer Brumete) and Heartwell Macon Junior was Ordered to be tried
Hartwell Macon) and following Jury impannelled to try the same John
                 Martin, Wm. Alsup, Robert Swann, Thomas Shannon,
Richard Gladney, Jos.h McDaniel, William Hill, Joseph Quarrell, Wm.
Owens, John Haris, James Austen, John.^{n} Harrison who returned the
following verdict We find that Heartwell Macon Junr is Indebted to
Spencer Brumett in the Amount of L 23" 6" 8.

                                Thomas. Shannon Fore.^{m}

Robert Cooke   )
        vs   )   Att.^t Dismissed.
Heartwell Macon)

Ad.^{ors} of Briant Riley)
        vs   )   Continued
John Morrison   )
& William Canle   )

David James   )
        vs   )   S. P. Dismissed at Plt.fs Costs.
Heartwell Macon)

John Woodard   )
        vs   )   S. P. Decree for five pounds.
Thomas Bradford)

Warring Winn & Co.   )
        vs   )   Sci fa. Rule discharged.
Adors of Joseph Kirkland)

Joel Smith   )
        vs   )   Debt Judgement by Default according to specialty.
Charles Williamson)

Richard Bolan   )
        vs   )   Att.^t Dismissed.
Richard H. Homan)

Robert Cooke   )
        vs   )   Att.^t Ordered that the property attached be returned
Heartwell Macon)   to the Defendant.

Samuel Johnston)
        vs   )   Att.^t Ordered that the property Attached be
Spencer Brumette)   returned to the Defendant on the collaterall
                     Juse Heartwell Macon.

Benjn May Ad.^{or})
of Briant Riley) S. P. Judgement by Default according to specialty.
        vs   )
John Jenkins   )

Benjn May Ad.^{or})
of Briant Riley) S. P. Judgement according to Specialty.
        vs   )
Elijah Gibson   )

                          John Winn
                          James Craig

                    Grand Jurors

Hugh Milling, Richd. Winn Esqr., James Winn, James Gray, Alex.^r
Robinson Senr., William Rabb, Wm. McMorris Junr., John Watson, John
Woodard, Phillip Raiford, Captn. Jno. Robertson, John Gray, John King,
John Means, Robert Adams, Daniel Cockran, James Ogilvie, John Bell,
Samuel Owens, James Rabb.

                    Petit Jurors

Frek. Arrick, John Cork, John Shane, David James, Danl. McCoy, Thomas
Seal, James Bishop, Nathl Majors, James Smith, Willm. Morgan, James
Mann, Robt. McCreight, Nath.^k Saunders, Peter Cooper, John Bishop,
Thomas Meek, David Doughty, John Cameron, Wm. Mobley, James Hall,
Robert Williams, Jas. Cameron, James Turner, James Kincaid, John
Mathews, Aron Duke, William Aikin, William Paul, James Nealy, Aron
Jones.

June Court 1792.

Tuesday the 12th Day of June 1792

Judges Present. John Winn, James Craig and Benjn Boyd Esqrs.

Proceeded to ballot for Grand Jurors to serve at next Cour when the following were drawn. Edwd. Maynard, Turner Starks, Gardner Ford, Captn. Wm. Robertson, Jona^n Belton, Captn. Henry Moore, Minor Winn, And^W Grey, Burrel Cooke, Saml. McKinney, Saml. Yongue, John Woodard, John Robertson, John Cooke Esqr , Henry Rugeby, Nazareth Whitehead, John Buchanan, Micajah Picket, John McKinney, Jacob Lewis.

Proceeded to Ballot for Petit Jurors.

John Yarborough, Daniel Malone, Wm. Harbin, Robt. Kilpatrick, Robert Gray, Robert Hood, Henry Haigood, John Richardson, John Gregg, John Johnston, John Coying, Saml. Nesbitt, Jacob Neats, John Broom, Daniel Collings, Davis Thomphson, Richard Gladney, Robert Tidwell, George Leighnen, Jas. Russel, James Rogers, Henry Haston, Saml. Mayfield, Benjn. Dove, Harris Freeman, Wm. Randal, Joseph Helms, Thos. Malone, Josiah Knighton, William Casten.

On a petition of several of the inhabitants of Fairfield County praying an examination of the clerks and treasurers books and a suspension of Sheriff Sales of property under execution for the county tax.

Whereupon the court granted the said petition so far as to allow a Delegation of five or seven of the people to inspect the clerks and treasurers books and also every matter relating to recognizance of fines, forfeitures, Licences and sales of estrays in which committee of the people the Judges and to be present. Also the court upon the said petition granted a Stay of Execution upon all property Levied on by the sheriff for the county tax untill the next intermediate court at which time the said committee shall make their report.

Whereupon the following Committee was appointed to meet at the Court house of Fairfield County on the second Monday in July next. Hezekiah Ford, Willm. Watson, Anderson Thomas, John Pearson, Phillip Pearson, William Roach, Thomas Means, Thomas Lewis, Jonathan Belton & Areamanus Liles. The latter five persons being nominated by the court and that the said persons be notified thereof.

John Winn
James Craig
Benjn Boyd

June Term 1792

Wednesday the 13th day of June 1792
The Court met according to adjournment

Judges Present. John Winn, James Craig and Benjn. Boyd Esquires.

Ordered that a commission do issue directed to William Farr Esqr. one of the Judges of the county court of Union to take Ann Gasaways renunciation of dower. Also that a commission do issue directed to Joseph Brown Esqr. one of the Judges of Chester County impowering him to take Mary Hopkins's renunication of dower.

John Brown and Cullen Mobley appeared in court and proved the last will and testament of Henry Fundenburgh dec^d Daniel Mabry and Thomas Mobley Exors appointed in the said will were duly Qualified and letters testamentary granted.

John Cameron appeared in open court and proved the last will and testament of John Calhoun deceased, and William Calhoun sole executor

58

appointed in the said will was duly qualified and Letters testamentary ordered to be granted to the said William Calhoung.

On a petition of Heziah Frost, Ordered. That Peter Lareaux do pay two Shillings per week to Heziah Frost for the support of her bastard child, the payment to be made monthly, and in case of Failure his bond to be put in suit, and that he be served with a copy of this order.

Proceeded to Call the grand Jurors appointed to serve at this court when the following persons were impannelled and sworn.

Jona[n] Belton, James Winn, Jacob Gibson, Robt. Ellison, Wm. McMorris Junr., Samuel Owens, Jas. Rabb, Phillip Raiford, James Ogilvie, John Robinson, John Bell, Wm. Rabb.

State)
vs) Asst. & Batry. Continued
Barnaby McKinney Pope)

Court adjourned untill three o'clock.

William Owens and James Marshall were appointed constables in the place of James Austen who resigned his office and were accordingly qualified as constables for the county of Fairfield.

Thomas Johnston)
vs) Debt. Thomas McDaniel swore to six days attendance
David Shelton) on the said suit living out of this county 33 miles
and crossing a Ferry on Board river. six times and
six pence each time.

David Hamilton appeared in open Court and proved the last will and testament of Samuel Gamble. deceased.

State)
vs) Indict[a]. A nole prosequi entered by the county Attorney.
Daniel Mabry)

State)
vs) Ind[a]. Ordered that the recognizances be continued. and
Randal Gibson) that one of the Justices of Chester County be directed
to bind over Robert Bullard in behalf of the State as
an evidence in the said case.

State)
vs) Indict[t] for assault and Battery.
William Jackson) A True Bill Jonathan Belton Foreman.

State)
vs) Indict[t] for an assault and Battery.
Randal Gibson) A true bill. Jona[n] Belton Foreman

A Set of Tittles from John Isaac and Margaret his Wife to William Lowry dated the 17th of April 1774 conveying a tract of 100 Acres of Land situate in Craven County on the wateree creek was now produced to the court which was very much torn and injured by the war. John Turner Esquire one of the witnesses thereto now appeared and having presented the said deed and being duly sworn says that his name signed as a witness thereto as well as to the receipt thereof is his hand writing and that his brothers name Alexander Turner he truly believe to be his hand writing and that his brother and Robert Harper signed their names as Evidences thereto together with him and that he verily believes John Isaac & Margaret his Wife signed sealed and delivered the same for the uses therein mentioned.

Jonas Beard)
vs) Debt. Judgement confessed for forty two pounds, nine-
John Buchanan) teen Shill[s] & 9& 1/4 by John Buchanan.

William Nelson)
    vs   ) App^l Referred to Benjn Boyd & James Craig Esquires
William McMorris) with power to chuse an umpire and their award to be
             final.

                        John Winn
                        James Craig
                        Benj. Boyd.

June Term 1792

Thursday the 14th day of June 1792.
The Court met according to adjournment.

Judges Present. John Winn, James Craig and Benjn Boyd Esq^{rs}

George Owens being appointed by the court to the office of constable for
Fairfield County, was accordingly duly qualified.

John Compty)
    vs   ) Continued.
James Ogilvie)

State   )
    vs   ) Ind^t A none presequi. entered by the county attorney.
Jesse Shutts) Ordered that recognizances be discharged.

State   )
    vs   ) On Indictment for Misdemeanor.
Henry McBride) The cause was now called and the following Jury
              impannelled to try the same.

James Winn, John Martin, Willm. Paul, William Aikin, Adam Pool Senr.,
Adam Pool Junr., John Winn, Daniel Mabry, William Hill, Adam Effert,
Fred^t Arrick, Nathl. Majors, who returned the following verdict. Not
Guilty Danl. Mabry. Foreman.

James Dodds   )
    vs   ) Debt. Judgement confessed by Thomas McClurken
Thomas McClurken) according to specialty stay of execution untill
& George Purvis) January court next.

John Carson   )
by Phillip Walker)   Carson vs Richmond att^t
    vs   )   On an attachment refered by consent of Parties
John Richmond   )   to Daniel Brown and Samuel W. Yongue Esquire who
                    returned the following award, We. Samuel Yongue
& Daniel Brown have liquidated the debts & Demands of the parties and
find two pounds 10/. due the plaintiff which we award to be paid with
Interest from the 20th of April 1785 & costs of Suit.
Winnsboro 14th June 1792
                        Daniel Brown
                        W. W. Yongue

also that the execution be lodged in the sheriffs office but not levied
untill the 14th of September next.

Citations for the estates of John Miles and Thomas Franklin late of
Fairfield County dec^d were returned having been published but not
certified as the law directs, and no consent having been entered.

Ordered that Letters of Administration be granted to Frederick Ansminger
for the said Estates of John Miles and Thomas Franklin dec^d upon the
said Frederick Ansininger returning the citations duly certified and
taking the usual oaths and giving securities as the law requires.

State   )
  vs   )   Ordered that the Bench warrant be continued.
William Adams)

State   )
  vs   )
William Picket   )
William Whitehead)   On Indictment. Ordered that the county attorney do
John Whitehead   )   enter a nole prosequi the defendants having agreed
James Johnston   )   to pay the costs of the prosecution.
Robert Adams   )
Samuel Starks   )

John Winn Esquire Ador. of the estate of Joseph Kirkland dec.d having
made return and statement of the debts and credits of the said estate,
Ordered that the same be recorded.

Elijah Jones having Petitioned the court for a Licence to retail
spiritous Liquors as a store keeper. Ordered that the same be granted.
Also a Licence for six months granted Moses Cockrill.

Ordered that all Defaulters of the grand and petit Jurors be advertised
to appear at next court to show cause why they should not be fined for
non attendance.

State   )
  vs   )   Indictment for an assault and Battery. Patience
William Willingham)   McGraw prosecutrix. The cause was called and
                      the same Jury impannelled to try it the same
except William Robertson in the place of Frederick Arrick. Who without
returned the following verdict GUILTY. Daniel Mabry. Foreman. whereupon
the court fined the defendant in the sum of three pounds.

Joseph McDaniel)
  vs   )   On appeal. Ordered for trial on tomorrow evening.
Shad.k Jacobs)

Martyn Alken   )
  vs   )   Case
Thomas Bradford)

Martyn Alken   )
  vs   )   On Summons and Petition.
Thomas Bradford)   Refered to John Wilson and Benjn. Boyd Esquires.
                      The arbitrators to whom was refered to (by nomina-
tion of the parties) the account of Martyn Alken and Thomas Bradford
after having examined the witnesses and minutely examined the accounts
find them to ballance, therefore award that the parties pay each half
the costs. Daniel Hewitt swore to 8 days attendance as Evidence Jesse
Haris 10 days do-as-do.

State   )
  vs   )   Bast.dy The deft. having appeared in court and swore
Margaret Stewert)   her child to George Kanimous & Joseph McDanil security
                     for her appearance was discharged from his recog-
nizance. fined L 5 proc payable in 2 years & to give security for the
maintenance of the said bastard child.

Samuel Proctor   )
  vs   )   S. P. Continued by consent of parties. John
Thomas Parrot Junr.)   Norwoods deposition to be taken before a magis-
                       trate and the same to be allowed in evidence on
                       trial.

State   )
  vs   )   Pricilla McGraw swore seven days attendance on
William Willingham)   the said suit as an evidence living out of the
                      county 25 miles.

State   )
vs   ) Ind^t for an Assault & Battery. Continued.
William Jackson)

State   )
vs   ) Indict^t for an assault and Battery.
Maddern Leggo)   Dismissed the defendant to pay the costs.

State   )
vs   ) Basd^y Ordered that Burrell Cooke security for the
Mary Rhoda)   defendants appearance be discharged from his recognizance.

Exors. of Alex^r Miller)
vs   ) S. P. John Bell Esquire swore to four days
Thomas B. Franklin   ) attendances as an evidence on the said cause.

State   )
vs   ) Scire Facias to wait another calling of the docket.
Mary Hatcher   )
& Elisha Haigood)

State   )
vs   ) Rule. discharged.
John Bradford)

Evans Winn & Co.   )
vs   ) Rule. Continued
Thomas Parrot Senr.)
Thomas Parrot Junr.)

Fairfield County)
vs   ) Information filed before the county attorney of the
Andrew McDowell) defendants retailing spiritous liquors without a
                   licence. and to be continued.

State   )
vs   ) Ind^t Diss^d on the defts. paying Costs.
Henry Gowen)

State   )
vs   ) Ind.^{t} Diss^d on the Defts. paying costs.
Barby McKinney Pope)
                                    John Winn
                                    James Craig

                              June Term 1792

Friday the 15th day of June 1792.
The Court met according adjournment.

Judges Present. John Winn, James Craig and Benjn Boyd Esquires.

                              Tavern Rates

Jamaica Rum when carried away per quart ----------------- " 3 "
West India ----- do ------------------------------------- " 2 " 6
Northward --- do -- and Taffia -------------------------- " 2 "
Good West India do --------- per 1/2 pint --------------- " 1 "
Northward ----- do ----- or Taffia ----- per -- do ------ "   " 7
Good Peach Brandy ------- per quart ----------)
      when carried away ----------------------)   " 2 " 6
Good Peach Brandy - drank in grog at the tavern
      per 1/2 pint -------------------------------------- " 1 "
Good Proof whiskey per Quart ---------------------------- " 2 " 4
do ---- do ----- do ----drank in grog per 1/2 pint ----- "   " 9
Gin ----------- per glass ------------------------------- "   " 3

                                  62

do ------ do ------ do ----- per 1/2 pint drank in grog - " 1 "
Madeira Wine ---- per Bottle -------------------------- " 4 " 8
Nidonia Wine per ----- do -------------------------- " 4 " 8
Port ------ Wine per ---- do -------------------------- " 4 " 8
Madeira Wine per ---- do Qt. or port Wine --------------- " 3 " 6
All other inferior Wines per do ----------------------- " 2 " 6
Bottled porter --------- per Bottle --------------------- " 2 " 4
Draught do ------- per quart -------------------------- " 1 " 6
Bottled Cyder ---- per bottle -------------------------." 2 ."
Draught do ------ per quart -------------------------- "   " 7

Meals of Good Healthy Provisions

Breakfast 8^d --- dinner 1^{8S}/2^d --- Supper 8^d --- all bespoke dinners
where a Bill of fare is given to the parties to agree on the price.

Lodging

In a feather bed with clean sheets 6^d each night.
In a mattress --- with do --- do --- 4^d each -- do ---
For Stabling a horse one night on corn blades or good Hay --- 8^d ---
     for 2 quarts of Indian corn or 3 qts. of oats 4^d
For one night in a good pasture ----------- 3^d

Ordered that there Rates be strictly adhered to by all concerned and
that the same be affixed and constantly kept up by the persons Licenced
in the most publick room in their respective houses. Otherwise in
failure thereof be fined for contempt of the Court.

John Turner &)
James Johnston)   On Att^t a writ of Enquiry to be executed.
    vs   )
John Burns   )

John Woodard)
    vs   )   Case. Refered to Jacob Bethany, Zachariah Kirkland and
Alex^r Kennedy) John Wilson, who returned the following Award. We the
                arbitrators for the cause between John Woodard and
Alexander Kennedy have determined that Mr. John Woodward shall pay all
cost and draw the suit out of court.

                         Jacob Bethny
                         Zach^h Kirkland
                         John Wilson

Jas. Hoy swore to 6 days attendance, James Kennedy 6 days attendance
Zachariah Kirkland 4 days John Wilson 6 days 20 miles out of the county
Jacob Bethany 7 days 30 miles out of the county on the above suit.

John Bell)
    vs   )   Case. Diss^d at the defendants costs.
John Arrick)

John Wilson swore to 5 days 20 miles out of the county & James Hoy
5 days attendance on the above suit.

James Bowles keeper of the court house produced his bill for the same.
Ordered that he be paid the sum of one L 1 in full and dismissed untill
the court house is finished.

Ado.^{rs} of John Milling)
    vs   )   Case Refered to General Winn and David Read
James Cooke   )   Evans with leave to chuse an umpire.

James Cooke   )
    vs   ) Case
Ad.^{ors} of John Milling)

63

Robert Duncan   )
Ad.^{or} of John Bowdre dec^d)   Case. The cause was now called and the
     vs   )   following Jury impannelled to try the same.
Phillip Shaver   )

Joseph McDaniel, John McCown, Burr Harrison, Jno. Martin, Jno. Richmond,
Edward Andrews, Willm. Hill, John Parr, David Campbell, Andrew McDowel,
James Gamble, Shad.^k Jacob, who returned the following verdict. We find
for the pltf plaintiff L 7"15"o. Burr Harrison, foreman.

Exors of Alex^r Miller dec.d)
     vs   )   Sum^{ry} Pros^s Decreed to the plaintiff six
Thomas Baker Franklin   )   shilling and eleven pence.

Willm. Hill   )
Exor of Willm. Hill)
     vs   )   S. P. Judg.t according to specialty with Interest.
John Buchanan   )   William McMorris swore to 4 days and Charles
& Robert Read Exors)   D. Bradford 4 days attendance on the above suit
of Robert Campbell)   as evidence.
& James Phillips   )
   deceased   )

Robert Duncan   )
Ador. of Bowdre)   Case. Hugh Norrell swore to 9 days attendance
     vs   )   living out of the county 20 miles four different
Phillip Shaver)   courts. James Duncan 9 days out of the county 20
                          miles. five different courts. Harris Freeman 6 days
                          John Robertson Eight days as evidence on the above
                          said suit. George Ashford swore to 8 days attendance
                          as an evidence on the said suit.

James Austen   )
     vs   )   Case   Judgment by default
Thomas Meredith)

Robert Ellison)
     vs   )   On attachment final Judgement according to specialty
John Hutchinson)   the note to be depreciated and order for sale granted.

Daniel Brown)
     vs   )   Case. Discontinued at the pltfs costs.
James Mumford)

Samuel Owens   )
     vs   )   On Att^t refered to arbitration by consent of parties.
Johnathan Owens)

Charles D. Bradford)
     vs   )   Case settled by arbitration. the defendant to
Henry McCoy   )   pay costs.

James Dillard   )
     vs   )   Case Abated by Defendants death.
Henry Fundenburgh)

Quinten Craig   )
     vs   )   On Attachment Judgement by default.
Richard H. Homan)

State   )
     vs   )   Bast.^{dy} It appearing that the offence was committed in
Mary Hatcher)   Richland County and the defendant now residing there.
                      Ordered that the recognizance giving by the defendant
                      and Elisha Haigood for the defendants appearance be
                      discharged.

Daniel Brown)
   vs   )   Sci. fa. Dismissed.
John Winn)

James Green Hunt)
   vs   ) On app[l] The Judgement Confirmed for the plaintiff
Shaddrick Jacobs) payable in specia with costs - and according to
               amo[t] of the Specialty - Henry McCoy swore to 4 days
and John Bradford 2 days attendance as evidence on the above suit.

John Winn
James Craig
Benj[n] Boyd

June Term 1792

Saturday the 16th day of June 1792.
The Court met according to adjournment.

Judges Present. John Winn, James Craig and Benj[n] Boyd Esquires.

Ordered that James Cooke and Richard Hightower be cited to show cause
why they should not be fined for removing the court house benches
without lease, and that Henry Hall and William Reece be summoned as
Evidences ----- discharged -----

James McCreight)
   vs   ) Case. Dismissed by the plaintiff.
James Gamble)

Richard Billops)
Ass. of Cole   )   Debt. Discontinued.
   vs   )
Frirrle McTyre)

Jesse Havis   )
   vs   ) Special action on the case
William Willingham)
John Willingham   ) The cause was now called and the following Jury
Edward Willingham) Impannelled to try the same.

Burr Harrison, James Winn, James Cameron, Josh. Cameron, Jas. Johnston,
Samuel Youngue, Jno. Woodard, Hugh Carson, Heartwell Macon Junr., Jas.
Barkely, Wm. Aikin, Jas. McCreight, who returned the following verdict.
We find for the plaintiff five pounds S. W. Yongue foreman.

Benjn. Boyd)
   vs   ) On appeal. Magistrates Judgement confirmed for the
Robert McTyre) plaintiff for L 2"18"4[d] and costs.

Jesse Haris   )
   vs   ) Case Elizabeth Austen swore to 7 days Nancy
William Willingham) Haris 5 days & John Haris 5 days attendance as
& Others   ) evidences on the said suit.

Bar[by] McKinney Pope)
   vs   ) On appeal. Magistrates Judgement reversed and the
Benjn. Boyd   ) defendant pay costs.

John Winn
James Craig
Benjn. Boyd

Adjourn[d] till Monday morn[g] 10 o'clock.

65

June Term 1792

Monday the 18th day of June 1792
The Court met according to adjournt.

Judges Present. John Winn, James Craig and Benjn Boyd, Esquires

Frederick Ansminger returned the citations for the estates of John
Miles and Thomas Frankling decd duly certified agreeable to an order
of court passed the 14th day of June 1792 and proposed George Smith
and Samuel Crosslin as securities for the said administrations of whom
the court approved.

Adors of Briant Riley)
   vs   )   S. P. Judgement by default according to
Elijah Gibson   )   specialty L 4" with interest & costs.

John Sweat)
   vs   ) Case Arbitrated each party to pay an equal part of the
Willm. Randal) costs.

Benjn May ador)
of Briant Riley) S. P. decree for L 8"12" 8d according to specialty
   vs   ) with interest & costs to be paid by installments.
Willm. Boyd)
& Robert Boyd)

William Daniel)
& Charles McDonald) Debt. Judgement according to specialty.
   vs   )
James Hart   )

Hugh Gamble and James Gamble exors. appointed in the last will and
testament of Samuel Gamble deceased appeared in open court and were
duly qualified.

Samuel Caldwell)
   vs   ) Ordered that Scire Facias. The Judgement against
John McCown &   ) John McCown be revised and that Elizabeth Campbell
Elizabeth Campbell) be allowed untill the next ensuing term to put in
                 her plea.

Thomas Bradford)
   vs   ) On Attachment. dismissed.
James Dougharty)

Jacob Bethna)
   vs   ) On Attachment. Dismissed.
William Dorch)

Joseph Brevard)
   vs   ) Case Continued at the plaintiffs costs.
Samuel Crosslin)

William Daniel)
& Chas. McDonald) Debt. Judgement According to specialty.
   vs   )
Willm. Nelson)

John Turner &   )
James Johnston   )
   vs   ) On Citation dissd. at the defts. costs. Ordered
John Burns ador   ) that the cause. John Turner and James Johnston vs
of Amos Goyen decd) John Burns on attachment be dismissed from the
                 docket as an error.

John Turner) Case. Arbitrated each party to pay an equal part of the
   vs   ) costs.
John Burns) Evidence 17/6.

66

Benj.ⁿ May Ad^{or})
of Briant Riley)   Debt. Judgement according to the specialties.
    vs   )
John Morrison)
& Willm. Caule)

William Willingham)
    vs   )   Case. The cause was now called and the following
James Andrews)   Jury impannelled to try the same.

Hugh Gamble, Robert Coleman, John Richmond, Wm. Burns, Frizzle McTyre,
John McCown, Jas. Cameron, Josh. Cameron, John Bell, Robert Gamble,
Heartwell Macon, Jno. Workman who returned the following verdict we
find for the plaintiff thirty five pounds exclusive of the notes.
Heartwell Macon Senr. Foreman.

Joseph McDaniel)
    vs   )   Debt. Judgement according to specialty.
David Shelton)

William Willingham)
    vs   )   Case. Diss.d at the plaintiffs costs.
Jesse Haris   )

Hugh Norrell)
    vs   )   Debt   Judgement according to specialty.
John Gray   )

Willingham)
    vs   )   Case Joshua Durham swore to five days attendance on the
Andrews   )   above suit.

Samuel Johnston)
    vs   )   On Attachment. the cause was now called and the
Spencer Brumett)   following Jury impannelled to execute a writ of
                     enquiry.

John Turner, Samuel Yongue, Richd. F. Winn, Samuel Proctor, David McGraw,
Charles D. Bradford, Phillip Raiford, William Robertson, Thos. Means,
William Roach, James Winn, Elijah Jones, We find for the plaintiff
L 10"19"2^d with interest from the 1st January 1791 Wm. Roach Foreman.
Judgement Ordered to be entered against Heartwell Macon Junior as
garnishee with costs of suit.

                         John Winn
                         James Craig

                      June Term 1792

Tuesday the 19th day of June 1792
The Court met according to adjournment.

Judges Present. John Winn and James Craig Esquires.

Enoch James)
    vs   )   Case. dismissed at the Defendants costs.
Robert Gamble)

On the presentment of the grand Jury for this term. Ordered that a
Bench Warrant do issue to take the bodies of Issac Young and Mary Frost
to answer to the complaint contained in the said presentment.

Minor Winn   )
    vs   )   Rule. Judgement Revised.
Thomas Nelson)

Evans Winn & Co.)
    vs   )   Rule. The Judgement revised. and the defendant
Saml. Proctor)   to be allowed three months to produce his offset.

Minor Winn Ass^e^)
    vs   ) Rule. Judgement revised.
John Robertson)
& Lewis Pope)

Minor Winn   )
    vs   ) Rule. Judgement revised.
Thomas Muse)
& John McKinney)

Robert Craig)
    vs   ) S. P. Dismissed at the defendants Costs.
David McCreight)

Samuel Johnston)
    vs   ) On Att.^t^ Constables Costs 7/2 Justice 5/ taxed.
Spencer Brumett) Joseph McDaniel swore to 4 days attendance as an
                  evidence on the said suit.

William Burns)
    vs   ) Case. Refered to James Craig, Jacob Gibson Junr.
Joshu Derham) Minor Winn, Benjn. Boyd and Phillip Pearson and their
                  award to be returned at next court and be final.

Heartwell Macon Junr.)
    vs   )   On Appeal. Magistrates Judgement for the
Robert Cooke   )   defendant confirmed, with costs.

Nicholas Ringer)
    vs   ) On appeal Ordered that the proceedings be remanded
John Atcheson) to the magistrate, and that the Judg.^t^ be revised
                  and that in case of appeal. the Magistrate do certify
                  the proceedings up fully, with the depositions of all
                  the evidences, and the cause stated in an ample
                  manner.

John Jenkins)
    vs   ) On Att.^t^ Dismissed
Richard Dorkins)

Hugh Gourly)
    vs   ) Case. Dismissed
Willm. Evans)
& Richd Winn)

Robert Craig)
    vs   ) On Attatch.^t^ John Winn Junior and David Evans summoned
James Dougharty) as Garnishee. Judgement for four pounds 9/3 to be
                  paid by the garnishee should they appear and settle-
                  ment of their accounts to have any money of the
                  defendants in their hands.

William Willingham)
    vs   ) Case. On motion of the Defendants att.^t^ for a new
James Andrews) trial. The court granted the same on proper
                  grounds being shown. John Haris swore to 7 days
                  attendance as an evidence on the above suit.

Richd. Winn Esquire)
    vs   ) S. P. Judgement according to specialty.
Hugh Milling   )
& Saml. Caldwell   )
Exors. of Alex. Miller)

Minor Winn)
   vs   )   S. P. Judgement according to specialty stay of Exon.
Thomas Bell)   to the 1st of September next.

Richard Winn   )
Ador. of Baker)   Debt. Judgement according to specialty.
   vs   )
John Richmond   )
& David Campbell)

Lewis Boltner)
   vs   )   S. P. Diss.d at the defendants Costs.
Henry McCoy)

Mary Young   )
   vs   )
Hugh Milling   )   S. P. Judgement according to specialty.
& Saml. Caldwell   )
Exors of Alex. Miller)
& Thomas McClurken)

Jonathan Belton)
   vs   )   On Attatch.t Withdrawn by the plaintiff at his own
John Dozier   )   Costs.

Ordered that the county attorney do issue a process against John Badgers
in behalf of the county for abusing a stray horse in his possession.
and that Jacob Gibson John Cooke. McKinney Pope & Peter Curry. as
evidences to prove the same.

Robert Hawthorn)
   vs   )   Debt. Ordered that a commission do issue directed
Victor Nealy   )   to three Justices of Kershaw county. to take the
                 deposition of Charles C. Pinckney Esquire in behalf
                 of the defendant.

Ordered that the Sheriff of Fairfield county do pay all the monies
hitherto collected and received by him (on account of the county tax
assessed for the building of the court house &c) towards discharging
the bond entered into by the Justices of the said county for the purposes aforesaid. And that he do return a due statement thereof to the
Judges of the said county court on the second Monday in September -
next.

Ordered that the accounts of all persons who have any demands against
the county of Fairfield (for monies paid towards the satisfaction of
the bond given for the erecting of the court house) be allowed the
same as a credit or set off against the amount of fines assumed by them
& the amount of estrays purchased at the county sales, they producing
to the treasurer of the said county sufficient vouchers of the payments
on the said Bond.

Ordered that William Kirkland and James Craig Esquires be appointed
commissioners (to the county lines between the counties of Richland,
Kershaw & Fairfield) on the part of Fairfield County. And that notices
be sent to the Judges of the said county courts to appoint the time and
the com.ms for running the said lines on their respective parts.

Court adjourned untill 12th Jan.y next.

                        John Winn
                        James Craig.

                  January Term 1793

Saturday the 12th day of January 1793.
The court was opened accordg to adjournt
Judges Present. James Craig Esquire

The last will and testament of John McClurken was produced in open court proved and approved of Ordered that Letters Testamentary be granted.

James Craig

Court adjourned untill Monday Morng 9 O'Clock.

January Term 1793

Monday the 14th Day of January 1793.

The Court met according to adjournment.

Judges Present. James Craig. John Winn and Benjn. Boyd Esquires.

D. Evans petitioned the court for a Licence to retail spiritous liquors &c. Ordered that the same be granted. To commence from the date of the permit and continue untill 12th of January 1794.

On a petition of several of the Inhabitants of Fairfield County for a road to be opened from the upper Wateree Creek to the Camden road at Boilstones place. beginning at John Goodrums on the new road that leads from rocky mount to Winnsboro from thence the nearest and best way to the lower Wateree Creek to cross at the Widow Halls from thence the nearest and best way to the Dutchmans creek to cross a McDanields ford from thence the nearest and best to Boilstones place on the Camden Road from Winnsboro. Ordered that the same be granted and that John Hollis and William Hollis be appointed overseers to open and clear out the same in a proper manner.

James Craig

Court adjourned untill 3 O'Clock
The court met according to adjournment
Court adjourned untill Tomorrow at 9 O'Clock.

John Winn
Benjn. Boyd
James Craig

January Term 1793

Tuesday the 15th day of January 1793.

The Court met according to adjournment.

Judges present. John Winn, James Craig & Benjn. Boyd Esquires.

James Butler appeared in open Court and having taken the oaths of office and allegiance as prescribed by law was admitted to act in the office of Constable in the County of Fairfield.

Ordered that John Owens be allowed the sum of ten shillings for the keeping of an Estray horse tolled by him and sold for the use of the County.

On application of the admors. of James Thomas deceased that an equitable division of the negroes be now made in order to fix the widows share on thirds as she is lately married. which the court ordered accordingly and by the consent & approbation of the parties nominated Major Liles, Thomas Means and Andrew Feister to make such division and that Robert Moorman do enter into a Bond with good security that if any Claim or demand should be hereafter made against the said Estate he shall Contribute his share to discharge the same.

Ordered that James Long be appointed overseer to lay out and open a
road from Badgers Ford on Little River to Summers Mill on Broad River.
Also that John Cooke Esquire be appointed Com^r to assist in laying out
the same.

The Grand Jury was now called and the following persons sworn.

Minor Winn, Robert Rabb, Jno. Robertson, Wm. Robertson, Saml. W. Yongue,
Thos. Means, Henry Moore, Jno. Cooke, Burt Cooke, Thos. Muse, Rolld.
Williamson, Phillip Raiford, Jacob Lewis.

Ordered that Sheriff do imediately proceed to collect the county tax
agreable to his former instructions and according to the assessment for
that purpose made and that he do without fail proceed to advertise the
people of the same.

Basil Wheat)
   vs   )   On Attat^t Thomas Stokes being sworn as Garnishee acknow-
John Miller)   ledged have in his hands 14 Barrels of Corn and 500 lbs.
               of Tobacco the property of the Defendant.

The Citation for the estate of Benjn. McKinney deceased being returned
duly certified. Ordered that letters of Administration for the said
Estate be granted. to Jane McKinney. Reuben Harrison and John Boykin
they taking the oaths and giving security as the law directs.

Mary Stewart and George Beazely returned the Citation for the estate of
John Stewart deceased duly certified. Ordered that Letters of Administration be granted to the said Mary Stewart and George Bearely for the
said Estate they taking the oaths and giving security as the law
directs.

Ordered that Mrs. Elizabeth Austen do make a proper distribution of the
Estate of Drury Austen deceased agreable to the will of the said
deceased among the heirs and Legatees, and that Hugh Milling & John
Gray Esquires.

with Mr. John Robertson be appointed to make the same in order to do
Justice to the said Elizabeth Austen and the orphans and that they do
report their proceedings to the Court on the second Monday in April
next.

Ordered that Alexander Smith be allowed the sum of 5/ for the keeping
of an Estray Steer Tolled by him and sold for the use of the County.

The Grand Jury by their Foreman John Cooke Esquire returned the following bills.

The State   )
   vs   )   Indict^t for Petit Larceny. A True Bill.
John Crosslin)

The State   )
   vs   )   Ind^t for Stealing. A True Bill.
Thomas Hines)

The State   )
   vs   )   Ind^t for Petit Larceny. A True Bill.
Daniel Goyen)

Daniel Mabry appeared in court and having taken the Oaths of office and
Allegiance, as the law directs, was appointed to act as constable in
the County of Fairfield.

Areomanus Liles Esquire appeared in Court and took the Oaths of office
and allegiance being appointed One of the Justices assigned to keep the
peace in the County of Fairfield.

Ordered that the Court house be finished out of the Sum that County is now assessed for and that the Clerk do advertise for any person or persons willing to undertake the finishing the same.

State)
vs) Ind.ᵗ for Ass.ᵗ & Bat.ʸ. True Bill
Frizzle McTyre)

State)
vs) Ind.ᵗ for Ass.ᵗ & Bt.ʸ. True Bill
Frizzle McTyre)

                              John Winn
                              Benjn. Boyd.

                    January Term 1793

Wednesday 16th January 1793.
The Court met according to adjournment.

Judges Present. John Winn, James Craig.

Alex.ʳ Boughter)
vs) Case Dismissed at the Defts. Costs.
Benj.ⁿ Halsey)

Nicholas Ringer)
vs) On App.ˡ Ordered for a new trial before the magistrate
John Atcheson)
Elizabeth Lockridge and James Picket returned the Citation for the estate of Pamuel Lockridge deceased duly certified Ordered that Letters of Administration be granted to the said Elizabeth Lockridge and James Picket for the said estate, they taking the accustomed Oaths and giving security as the Law requires.

The State)
vs) Indict.ᵗ for Stealing
Willm. Adams)

The Cause was now Called and the following Jury sworn to try the same.

John Turner, John Richardson, Thomas Parrot Sen.ʳ, Abraham Miller, John Bell, Henry Haigood, John Broom, Jacob Neats, Henry Hearten, Thomas Malone, Jos.ʰ Helms, Issac Hussey.

The Jury returned the following verdict. Guilty. John Turner Foreman.

Whereupon the court Ordered the deft into Confinement.

The State)
vs) Indict.ᵗ for Petit Larceny. The Indictment traversed.
Thomas Hines) Ordered that the recognizances be continued to next
                Court.

James Bowles)
vs) On appeal. Ordered that the magistrates judgement be
John Havis) confirmed.

Ordered that a road be opened from Badge-s Ford on Little River to Hunts Ford on Borad River, and that Mr. Burrel Cooke be permitted to place a gate on the river bank to prevent creatures tresspassing on his fields.

The Grand Jury by their foreman John Cooke Esquire returned.

The State)
vs) Indict.ᵗ for Murder. A True Bill
Samuel Clampet)

72

James Cooke   )
vs   )
Admors. of Jno. Milling)
)   Case. Refered to Arbitration. Award affirmed
Admors. of Jno. Milling) for L 1.7"9 with costs in favour of the
vs   )   admors of Jno. Milling.
James Cooke   )

Quintin Craig   )
vs   )   On attachment the Cause was now called and the
Richd Hattfield Homan) following Jury impannelled to try the same.

William Kirland,Jno. Richardson, Thos. Malone, Henry Hartin, Henry
Haigood, John Broom, Joseph Helms, John Bell, Jacob Neats, Edwd.
McGraw, David Long. Hanspot Turnepseed, who being sworn to Execute a
writ of Enquiry returned the following verdict. We find for the
plaintiff Fifteen pounds with Interest. Willm. Kirkland Foreman.

The State   )
vs   )   Ind.^t for Stealing. the Defent. being found Guilty. The
William Adams)   Court Ordered that he do receive 15 Stripes on his
                 bare back at the public whipping post.

The State   )
vs   )   Ind.^t for Felony. Ordered that Deft. be Liberated on
Samuel Clampet) giving good & sufficient Bail for his appearance at
                 Camden Court next April Sessions.

Charles Johnston)
vs   )   On Att.^t Sebara Splawn and Rosa Splawn being summoned
Jesse Goyen   )   as Garnishees and duly sworn say upon Oath that
                     they have no property of the defendants in their
                     hands.

State   )
vs   )   Ordered that Saml. Young Esquire be directed bind over
Saml. Clampet)   the prosecutor and Evidences in this Case to appear
                 a Camden Court next April Sessions.

                         John Winn
                         James Craig

                    January Term 1793

Thursday the 17th Day of January 1793.
The Court met according to adjournment.

Judges present. James Craig & John Winn, Esquires.

Maddern Leggo)
vs   )   Case Dissd at Defts. Costs.
Jesse Shuts)

Exors of Jos. Kershaw)
vs   )   Debt. Abated by Defts. death.
Wm. Lashley   )

James McCreight)
vs   )   Case. Arbitrated the pltf to pay costs.
Jane Appedale)

Alex.^r Bookter)
vs   )   Case. Discont.^d at Defts. Costs.
Benjn. Halsey)

Graaff & Co.   )
    vs   ) S. P. Abated by Alex.[r] Johnstons death
Alexr. Johnston   )
& Thos. B. Franklin)

Robert Rabb)
    vs   ) S. P. Ref.[d] Arromanus Liles. Levi Daniel William
Thomas May) Hadridges with leave to chuse an umpire.

Hugh Carson   )
    vs   ) Debt. Diss.[d] at Defts. Costs.
Robert Ewing   )
& Willm. Gibson)

Wadsworth & Turpin)
    vs   ) Debt. Withdrawn at Defts. Costs.
Anderson Thomas   )

James Craig   )
    vs   ) Debt Judgt. Confessed. Stay of Exon, Six months.
William Huston)

James Craig   )
    vs   ) P & S. Diss.[d] at the Defts. Costs.
Levi Goyen   )
& James Scott)

Lewis Boltner   )
    vs   ) Att.[t] Diss.[d] at the pltfs. Costs.
Barbara Ruistick)

Samuel Owens   )
    vs   ) Att.[t] Refered to Arbitration award affirmed for the
Jonathan Owens) pltf for L 2"2"4.

John Wilson   )
    vs   ) Debt. Discontinued.
George Watts   )
& Daniel Williams)

Saml. Proctor   )
    vs   ) S. P. Refered to Mr. Benjn. Boyd and Major Liles.
Thomas Parrot Jun.) their award to be a rule of Court.

William Nelson)
    vs   ) On appl. S. P. Refered Award returned & affirmed in
Willm. McMorris) favr. of Wm. McMorris against William Nelson for the
                  sum of six pounds Sterling with the Costs of suit.

Evans Winn & Co.   )
    vs   ) Rule. Judgement revised.
Thomas Parrot Senr.)
& Thos. Parrot Junr.)

Isaac Love   )
    vs   ) Case. Diss.[d] at the Defendants Costs.
Reuben Harrison)

John Compty)
    vs   ) S. P. Nonsuit.
James Ogilvie)

The Grand Jury being requested to inspect the Goal and report to the
Court upon the same. Reported as follows It is the opinion of the
Grand Jury that the Goal as far as it is gone is executed to the plan
delivered Mr. Strother and also that when finished will be equal to the
purposes intended. Jany term. 1793. John Cooke Foreman.

The following persons have been Legally warned to work on the road from Winnsborough to Little River but neglected to attend, The Court have fined each Defaulter agreable to Law.

Defaulters Names

Thomas Owens, James Barkley, Randal Gibson, Hugh Carson & Wm. Durphey, Robert McCreight, Joseph Quarell, James Workman, David McCreight, John Hussey.

Hanspot Turnepseed)
    vs   ) On Attachment. Decree according to Specialty.
Willm. McTyre   ) Ordered that the property Attached be Condemned.

On a petition of several of the inhabitants of Fairfield County for a road to be opened from Archibald Palls on Jacksons Creek. the nearest and best way by Hutchinsons old Field to Chester County Line near Doughtys Plantation. Ordered that the same be Granted. and that Mr. Burr Harrison, Thomas Shannon and Ephraim Butler be appointed Commissors to lay out the said road. Also t hat Henson Keath be appointed overseer from Gladneys Old place to Little River and Thomas Shannon from Little river to the County Line.

Ordered that Gardner Ford be appointed Guardian to Mary Love an orphan on his giving security as the law requires.

Robert Hawthorn)
    vs   ) Case. The cause was now called and the following
Victor Nealy   ) Jury sworn to try the same.

John Richardson, David Thompson, Jacob Neats, Henry Hartin, Thomas Malone, Elisha Haigood, Henry Haigood, Issac Hussey, James Austen, James Hunt, Crispin Morgan, Henry McCoy.

who returned the following verdict. It is the opinion this Jury that the plaintiff is non suited. James Hunt Foreman. Whereupon the plaintiffs attorney gave notice to the defendants attorney that on tomorrow he should move for a new trial.

Minor Winn)
    vs   ) Case. Judg^t Confessed for L 10"16"10.
David James)

It appearing to the court that the County Attorney is by sickness rendered incapable of attending to the Business of the County. Ordered that all State matters and recognizances do lie over untill June term next.

William Langley of Rockey Mount pettioned the Court for a Licence to retail Spirritous Liquors for one year Ordered that the same be granted he giving security as the law requires.

Exors. of Saml. Neal)
    vs   ) Ordered that the Deft. be ruled to Special Bail.
Hartwell Macon Senr.) whereupon the Heart^l Macon Junr. Ent^d himself as
                    special bail with the said defendant.

The State   )
    vs   ) Ind^t for Ass^t & Batt^y Phillip Mathews prosecutor.
Frizzle McTyre) Diss^d on the defendants paying costs.

John Henington)
    vs   ) Case. Judgt. by default.
Robert Walker)

John Hampton   )
    vs   ) Debt. Judg^t Confessed Stay of Exon four months.
John Owen Wallace)

James Davis)
    vs   )   Rule. Judgement Revised.
James Dillard)
& others   )

Jesse Havis Indor.^e)
    vs   )   S. P. Abated by Deft.^s death.
Samuel Dodds   )

Jon.^a Belton)
    vs   ) S. P. Diss.^d at Defts Costs.
Jas. Arnet)

Field Farrer)
    vs   ) Case The Plaintiff residing out of the State, Minor
John Buchanan) Winn Esquire entered himself as security for the
                  Costs.

Richard Winn)
    vs   )   Debt. Judgement by default.
William Hughes)

James Craig   )
    vs   )   Debt. Diss.^d at the plaintiffs Costs
John Owen Wallace)

James Green Hunt   )
    vs   )   Debt. Judg.^t according to Specialty by Default
James Johnstone et als)

                        John Winn
                        James Craig

January Term 1793

Friday the 18th Day of January 1793.
The Court met according to adjourn.^t

Judges Present. John Winn, Benj.ⁿ Boyd & James Craig Esq^{rs}

Ordered that the following Orphans be bound out as underwritten, and to
be cloathed, fed and schooled agreable to the custom adopted by this
court. viz.

Absolam Lord to be bound to Patrick Gladney
Thomas Goodrum to ----Robert Phillips
Ross Straisner to ----Wm. McDill.
Shadrack Cameron to---Moses Cockerill
Jacob Richards to ----James Alcorn or James Rabb

Willm. Sibley)
    vs   ) On appeal. Ordered the appeal be dismissed.
Andrew Bay)

Robert Hawthorn)
    vs   ) Debt. Joseph McDaniel swore to 15 days and William
Victor Nealy) Hill to 21 days attendance as evidences on the above
                  suit. The Pltfs attorney in this case having given
                  notice that this day he should move for a new trial
                  the matter was now argued before the Court whereupon
                  it was Ordered that a new trial should be Granted.

Samuel Johnston and John Means Petitioned the Court for Licences to
retail spiritous liquors &c. Ordered that the same be granted they
giving security as the law requires.

Austen Smith)
    vs   )   Case. Diss.^d at the plaintiffs Costs.
James Rabb)

Burbage Woodard)
    vs   )   Case the cause was now Called the following Jury
John L. Bradford) impannelled to try the same

John Winn, Minor Winn, David Thompson, James Barkley, Henry Hartin,
John Broom, And^w McDoule, Jacob Neats, William Dansby, Thomas Malone,
John Hutchinson, Henry Haigood, John Richardson, who returned the
following Verdict We find for the plaintiff five shillings
John Winn Foreman

John Means   )
    vs   )   On Attachment. Levied on two negroe girls in the
Spencer Brumett) possession of Heartwell Macon Senr. whereupon
                 Heartwell Macon Senr. and Heartwell Macon Junr. came
in open Court and Entered special Bail Ordered that the property be
delivered up when Called for agreable to the order of Court.

> We Heartwell Macon Senior and
> Heartwell Macon Junio do hereby
> enter ourselves special bail in the
> above action.
> > Heartwell Macon
> > Macon Junr.

The State   )
    vs   )   On Indict. the Indictment Traversed but on motion of
John Crosslin) the County Atty, that the same could not be legally
              traversed Ordered that the deft. do produce his
              witnesses for trial on Monday next.

James Webber)
    vs   )   Debt. Judgement by Default.
the Admors. of)
Willm. Durphey)
deceased   )

Burbage Woodward)
    vs   )   Case. On Motion of the defendants atty. that the
John L. Bradford) verdict in this case being less than 40/ and that
              the plaintiffs should not recover Cost. Ordered
              that the same be post-poned for discussion untill
              tomorrow.

> John Winn
> James Craig
> Benjn. Boyd

January Term 1793

Saturday the 19th Day of January 1793
The Court met according to adjournment.

Judges Present. John Winn, Benjn. Boyd.

Jonathan Belton)
    vs   )   Debt. Judgement Confessed for L 16" " 9d with
William Johnston) Costs of Suit Exon. to be lodged in the sheriff's
              office but not Levied untill ordered.

Archibald Jamieson   )
& Co. Indor.^e of Jno. Dorch) S. P. Decree by default according to
    vs   ) specialty.
Phillip Ryley   )
& Richard Thompson   )

John Means   )
    vs   )   On Att.^t Ordered that Dedimus potestatem do issue
Spencer Brumett)   directed, to John Macon, Jenkins Devaney, John
                     Hawkins and Henry Hill or any two of them to take
                     the deposition of James Glen of Warren County in
                     the State of No. Carolina.

Robert Cooke   )
    vs   )   Case. The cause was called and the following
Heartwell Macon Senr.) Jury sworn to try the same

Robert Coleman, John Richardson, William Nelson, Charles Johnston,
Jacob Neats, James Austen, Thomas Malone, Henry Hartin, Henry Haigood,
John Workman, Jas. Workman, Abraham Gibson. who returned the
following verdict. We find for the Defendant. Robert Coleman Foreman.

Robert Rabb   )
    vs   )   Rule, Judgement Reversed.
Frizzle McTyre)

Burbage Woodard)
    vs   )   Case. The defts. atty. brought on the motion for
John L. Bradford)   the plaintiff should pay Costs the verdict being
                     under 40/. after hearing the arguments the Court
                     adjudged the Deft. was to pay the Costs.

Basel Wheat)
    vs   )   On Attat.^t Decree for L 6"6. Ordered that the property
John Miller)   Attached be condemned to Satisfy the decree.

Ordered that the Sheriff do pay the County tax into the hands of the
treasurer as he receives same taking his receipts for the amount and
that the treasurer do pay Mr. William Strother the sum of L 40 as
soon as so much shall come into his hands taking Mr. Strothers receipt
for so much on account of his Contract with the court for Building the
County Goal and that the Clerk do imediately proceed to have all the
fines and forfeitures and moneys arising from the sales of Estrays
collected and render an account of the same at the next intermediate
court together with the remainder of the Collection of the County tax
to be applied to discharge the Creditors of the County &c.

William Kirkland   )
      vs   )   On App.^1 Dismissed at the defendants Costs
Fred.^k Ansminger)
Admor of Jno. Miles)

Christian Graddick   )
assee Jacob Boughter)   S. P.
      vs   )   This Cause moved by Consent to the Superior
Henry Hunter &   )   Court and the Costs to the suit in this Court
Minor Winn   )   to depend upon the determination of the
                         district Court.

On application of Fred.^k Ansminger admors. on John Miles Estate.
Ordered that the said admor. do sell the personal Estate of the said
John Miles on a Credit of 12 months.

Obed Kirkland appeared in open court and chose Capt. William Kirkland
as his guardian of whom the Court approved on his giving security as
the Law directs.

The Exors. of Neal)
    vs _1   )   Debt. Refered by Consent to Saml. W. Yongue and
Heart.^l Macon Senr.)   William Roach, Esqr. with leave to chuse an
                        umpire, Award to be returned on Tuesday next and
                        to be a rule of Court.

78

Joseph Brevard)
    vs   )   Case. Cont^d untill Monday.
Samuel Crosslin)
John Buchanan &   )
Thomas Harris McCaule   )
assignees   )   Cont^d untill Monday.
    vs   )
the admors. of Jno. Milling)

                    John Winn
                    James Craig

              January Term 1793

Monday the 25th Day of January 1793.
The Court met according to adjournment.

Judges present. John Winn, James Craig

Burbage Woodard)
    vs   )   Case. Thomas Nelson swore to 13 days John Lewelling
John Bradford)   to 8 days and Nancy Lewelling to 8 days attendance
               as Evidences on the above suit.

Edward Maynard appear in open Court and acknowledged the signing
sealing and delivery of a certain Deed conveying a tract of Land
Containing 100 Acres situate on both sides of Dutchman's Creek to
Robert Eckles the word winfield being erased before proving. Ferabee
Maynard wife of the above Edward Maynard appeared in Court and
renounced all Claim in right of Dower to the above conveyed tract
of Land.

The State   )
    vs   )   On Indictment for petit Larceny.
John Crosslin)   The Cause was called and the following Jury sworn
               to try the same.

John Richardson, John Stone, James Workman, Thomas Malone, John Porter,
Hugh Gamble, Hugh Smith, John McKewn, Henry Haigood, John Tidwell,
William Caldwell, Jas Gamble who returned the following verdict.
NOT GUILTY HUGH GAMBLE FOREMAN.

Ordered that Jacob Gibson be appointed overseer on the road from
Badgers ford on Little River to Hunts ford on Broad River.

Ansminger Adm^r.)
of John Miles)   S. P. Agreed the Deff^s. to pay Costs
    vs   )
Phillip Goats)

State   )
    vs   )   On Indt. Diss^d on Deft^s paying Costs.
Daniel Gowen)

On petition of several inhabitants of the Wateree Creek Ordered that
a road be opened from William Ewings place to the Rocky Mount Road
into Starkes road at Charles Pickets place the nearest and best way
and that William Coggins be appointed overseer to open & clear out
the same.

                    John Winn
                    James Craig

Tuesday the 22nd Day of January 1793
The Court met according to adjournt.

Judges Present.   John Winn, James Craig and Benjn Boyd Esq^{rs}

Admors. of Reuben Judd)
Worster   ) Case The cause was called and the following
    vs   ) Jury sworn to try the same
Field Farren   )

John Richardson, John Stone, Jas. Workman, Thos Malone, John Porter,
Hugh Gamble, Saml. W. Yongue, Thos. Harris, McCall, James Barklie,
Robert Barklie, James Winn, Elijah Jones, James McCreight, Hugh Carson,
Henry Haigood, on a writ of inquirey returned the following verdict.
We find for the plaintiff L 14"10"9½ Thos. H. McCants Foreman

Admors. of Reuben)
Judd Worster   ) Case Diss^d at the Defendants Costs
    vs   )
Willm. Roach   )

Joseph Brevard)
    vs   ) Case The cause was called and the same Jury sworn to
Samuel Crosslin)   try the same except Minor Robert Rabb, John Broom
                    in place of Hugh Carson, Saml. W. Yongue, and James
                    Winn who returned the following verdict We find for
                    the plaintiff five pounds Sterling F. H. McCall
                    foreman.

William Burns)
    vs   ) Case The court adjudged that there appears to be due
Joshua Durham)   the plaintiff the sum of L 7"4"11 with Interest from
                    the 12th day of December 1788.

Hawthorn)
    vs   ) Case. Joshua Durham appeared in Court and swore to 9 days
Nealy   ) attendance as an Evidence on the above suit.

Willingham)
    vs   ) Case Joshua Derham swore to attendance of 8 days in
Andrews   ) Evidence this Court on the above suit and Jacob Gibson to
             5 days attend.

John Cameron   )
    vs   ) Debt. Judgement by Default according to the
John Craig   ) Specialty.
& Creighton Buchanan)

Brevard)
    vs   ) Case. Samuel Smith sowre to 17 days attendance as an
Crosslin) Evidence on the above suit.

Samuel Johnston)
    vs   ) On Att.t attached a mare in the hands of Heartwell
Spencer Brumett) Macon Junr. 'On a collateral issue tried in January
                 term 1791 the property attached being found by the
                 Jury to be the property of Heartwell Macon Junior
                 adjudged that the Plaintiff to pay the Constable the
                 sum of 40/ for keeping the said Mare and the sum of
                 7/6 for levying on the said property.

Robert Cooke   )
    vs   ) On motion of the pltfs attorney that exception
Heartwell Macon Senr.) was taken to the jury and praying for a new
                        trial. Ordered that the same be granted and
that the rule for new trial be dismissed unless the plaintiff pays all
Costs hitherto accused on above case on the second day of next term.

The Exors of Samuel Neal)
    vs   )   Debt. Refered to the arbitration of Samuel
Heartwell Macon Senr.   )   W. Yongue and William Roach Esquire who
                             agreeable to the rule of Court returned the
following aware We Award and decree that the plaintiff recover of the
Defendant Heartwell Macon Senr. L 14"16"6 and Costs. Willm. Roach
S. W. Yongue.

The State   )
    vs   )   Indt. for Asst. & Battery. The cause was now called
William Jackson)   and the same Jury impannelled to try the Indictment
                  who returned the following verdict. Guilty
H. M. McCaule Foreman. whereupon the Court fined the defendant in the
sum of five shillings.

The State   )
    vs   )   Indictment for assault and battery. The Cause was
Randal Gibson)   now called and the same Jury sworn to try the same,
                  who returned the following verdict, Guilty. Thomas H.
McCall Foreman. Whereupon the court fined the defendant 20/. and
Ordered to be Confined untill paid Ordered that the real estate of
the case John Milling Esquire deceased mortgaged to several persons
and foreclosed by John Buchanan and Thomas Harris McCall be now sold
at 6 months Credit subject to the widows dower in order to Satisfy
the said Mortgages and other Creditors and that the admors. of the said
Estate do proceed imediately to advertise the same for the term of two
months.

Thomas Malone)
    vs   )   Case. The cause was now called and the following
The Admors. of)   Jury sworn to try the same. except Samuel W. Yongue
James Thomas)   in the place of Thomas Malone who returned the
                verdict. We find for the Plaintiff L 20"19d Costs
                H McCall Foreman

James Austen   )
    vs   )   Case. The Admors. appeared and pleaded they
Admors. of Jno Milling)   had no assets in their hands at this time.
dec.d   )

Cooke)
  vs)   Robert Coleman appeared in Court and swore to 14 days attend-
Macon)   ance as Evidence in the above suit.

John Smith   )
    vs   )   On Att^t. Judg^t. by Default.
Mathew Talbot)

Phillip Raiford)
    vs   )   S. P. Ordered that the Deposition of Captn. Jno.
Abraham Gibson)   Robertson be taken De Bone esse and that the same be
                allowed in evidence on trial.

John Cameron)
    vs   )   Debt. Judg^t Confessed according to Specialty
William Gibson)   subject to such set offs as may be allowed by David
& Robert Ewing)   Evans Esq.r to be produced in three months otherwise
               Exon. to issue.

                           John Winn
                           James Craig
                           Benjn Boyd

January Term 1793

Wednesday the 23rd Day of January 1793
The Court met according to adjournment
Judges Present. John Winn, James Craig and Benjn Boyd Esq^{rs}

Proceeded to ballot for Grand Jurors when the following Persons were Drawn.

Jno. Buchanan, Edwd. Martin, Benjn Harrison, And^W Thomas, Thos. Hill, Junr., John Watson, David McGraw, Willm. Cloud, Wm. McMorris Senr., James Davis, Thomas Muse, Thos. Parrot Senr., David Shelton, Reuben Harrison, John Hickle, John Derham, Robert Adams, David Andrews, Hezekiah Ford, Moses Cockrill.

Petit Jury

James Barkley, Lemuel Perry, James Austen, Clement Arledge, Adam Free, John Hill Senr., Alexr. McCane, Ballard Day, Jno. Dodds, Alexr. Roseborough, Willm. Smithwick, Pottey Turnepseed, Saml. Gladney, Jeremiah Pearson, William Johnston, Robert Read, Peter Curry, Jno. Willingham, Creighton Buchanan, Jacob Gibson Junior, Adam Byerly, Joseph Arledge, Moses Hornsby, Thos. Robinson, Richard Mansel, Aron Gossy, John Briant, Thos. Meredith, George Levi, Thomas Parrot Junior.

Robert McTyre)
   vs   )   Debt. Judg^t by Default according to the Specialty.
Thomas Nelson)

Robert Cooke)
   vs$_1$)   On Att^t Levied on two little negroes. the plaintiff
Heart^t Macon)   being nonsuit. Adjudged that the constable be
                  allowed the sum of 40/ for keeping the above attch^d
                  negroes 40 days.

Ordered the defaulters on the grand and petit jurors lists be fined unless they make sufficient excuse at the next term and that Scire Vacias do issue for that purpose.

Ordered that Clerk do have the demessions of the upper floor of the court house together with the partitions for Jury rooms taken and a bill of the same made out. the flooring plant to be inch thick. for the partitions inch and quarter also inch plank for Jury Tables, Benches and doors for Jury Rooms & Window Shutters and that the Clk do purchase the same at the most convenient mill and on the cheapest terms also plank for the staircase.

Ordered that process do issue against the overseers of the different roads presented by the grnad Jury. Also against the persons presented for Bastardy and the parties prosecuted for incess.

Minor Winn   )
   vs   )   On App^l Judg^y affirmed.
Richd Shother)

Ordered that as soon as the goal is completed that the Sheriff do take charge of the same.

Adjourned to the 12th June next.
                        John Winn
                        James Craig
                        Benjn Boyd

June Term 1793

Wednesday the 12th Day of June 1793
The Court met according to adjournment

Judges Present. James Craig and Benjamin Boyd Esquires.

Proceeded to Ballot for Jurors to serve at Jany Term.

82

Grand Jurors

John Arrick, James Hart, Arees Liles, Jesse Simmons, Thos. Means, Saml. Simmons, Geo. Peay, Thos. Shannon, Job Owens, Wm. Cato, Charnel Durham, Dav^d Hamilton, John Turner, Chas. Lewis, Benjn May, Jas. Nelson, Jas. Russel, Moses Knighton, Robt. Rabb, Saml. Johnstone.

Petit Jurors

Saml. Caldwell, And^W Martin, Benjn Lindsey, Jas. Brice, Elijah Jones, James Hendricks, John Lewelling, John Gwinn, Joseph Howthorn, Edwd Watts, Joseph Dodds, Joseph Barker, William Dunn, James Gamble, Robt. Marshall, Jas. McDowell, Nicholas Ringer, George Lott, Robt. Phillips, Richd. Nealy, John Goodrum, John Flowers, Drury Bishop, Joseph Quarrel.

Daniel Frazer appeared in Court and proved the Last will and testament of William Frazer deceased. William Frazer Junior the executor appointed in the said being duly sworn. Ordered that Letters testamentary be granted.

James Craig
Benjn Boyd

June Term 1793

Thursday the 13th Day of June 1793
The Court met according to adjournment.

Judges Present. John Winn and Benjamin Boyd Esquires.

The grand jurors appointed to serve at this court were called and the following answered to their names.

Robert Adams, Thos. Parrot Senr., Thomas Hill, Wm. Cloud, Edward Martin, Wm. McMorris Senior, David Andrews, Jas. Davis, David Shelton, Anderson Thomas, Thos. Muse, Moses Cockrill, John Buchanan Foreman.

Archibald Douglas appeared in Court and was duly qualified to act in the office of Constable for the County of Fairfield.

John Winn
Benjn Boyd

June Term 1793

Friday the 14th Day of June 1793
The Court met according to adjournment.

Judges Present. John Winn & Benjamin Boyd Esquires.

Ordered that John Turner and Micajah Picket and William Watson be commissioners to view the road leading through the mountain gap and to Judge wether the said road can conveniently be turned by the plant^n of John Tidwell or wether the old may be more practicable and make a report thereof st Septr court next.

John Wilson)
  vs) Debt. Judg^t Considered by George Watts according
Geo^e Watts) to Specialty.
& Danl. Williams)

David Milling)
& Hugh Milling) Debt. Judg.t according to specialty confessed by
  vs) John Winn. Stay of Exon. untill 1st February next.
John Winn)
& Randolph Wright)

Joseph McAdams)
    vs   )   Case Judg^t. Confessed according to specialty
Thomas Lewers)   tobacco rated as 11/ & Cost. stay of Exon. untill
                 1st January next.

Ordered that letters testamentary of Administration be granted to Minor Winn for the estate of James Winn deceased. He talking the accustomed oaths and giving security as the law directs.

Robert Barkley)
    vs   )   S. P. decree for L 8"14".
Francis McCall)
& Elijah Jones)

John Harrison appeared in Court and was duly qualified to act as constable in the county of Fairfield.

State   )
  vs   )   Ind^t. for assault and battery.
John Havis)   No Bill. John Buchanan foreman.

State   )
  vs   )   Ind^t for hog stealing.
William Hollis)   A true bill. John Buchanan foreman
et alios   )

Ordered that Willis Dent an orphan boy be bound to Marcellus Littlejohn untill he attains the age of 21 years and that the said Littlejohn do give him one years schooling previous to his attaining that age. and one suit of good cloathing at the expiration of his time.

State   )
  vs   )   Indic^t for hog stealing.
William Hollis)   the cause was now called and the following jury sworn
& als.   )   to try the same.

James Barkley, Creighton Buchanan, Alexr. Roseboro, Saml. Gladney, Jere^h. Pearson, Thomas Meredith, Thomas Parrot Junr., Ballard Day, Jno. Willingham, Saml. Perry, Clement Arledge, Peter Curry. who returned the following verdict. We find William Hollis Guilty and the others not guilty. Thomas Parrot Junr. foreman.

State   )
  vs   )   Ind^t. for Larciney. a true bill John Buchanan foreman.
John McBride)

State   )
  vs   )   Indict^t for assault. True bill John Buchanan foreman
Jno. Willingham)

State   )
  vs   )   Indict^t malicious killing a horse not a true bill.
Shadrack Jacobs)   Jno. Buchanan foreman.
& Wm. Alexander)

                          John Winn
                          Benjn Boyd

                    June Term 1793

Saturday June 15th 1793. Court met according to adjournment.

Judges Present. John Winn and Benjamin Boyd Esquires.

John Means)
  vs   )   Ordered that Samuel W. Yongue and Zachariah Kirkland
Spencer Brumet)   be authorized to take the deposition of James Glenn
                in this Case.

State   )
    vs   )   Indict^t for Larciney.
John McBride)   The following Jury were sworn to try the same

Creighton Buchanan, Alexr. Roseborough, Jacob Gibson, Thomas Meredith,
Thomas Parrot Junior, Samuel Gladney, Alexander McCane, Clement Arledge,
Ballard Day, Jeremiah Pearson, John Willingham, Peter Curry, who
returned the following verdict. Guilty. Thomas Parrot foreman.

Ordered that the defendant be imprisoned untill the 8th day of July
next and then publickly to receive ten lashes on his bare back and
stand committed till the costs be fully discharged.

State   )   t
    vs   )   Ind. for an assault & false imprisonment. True bill
Thomas Hanley)   John Buchanan foreman.
Jane Hanley)

State   )
    vs   )   Ind^t for Larciny.
Owen Andrews)   No bill. John Buchanan foreman

State   )
    vs   )   Ind^t for Assult & false imprison^t True bill. John
Samuel Crosslin)   Buchanan fore^m

State   )
    vs   )   Ind^t for Assault & false imprisonment true bill John
Joshua Derham)   Buchanan foreman.

State   )
    vs   )   In^t for hog stealing. William Hollis one of the
William Hollis)   defendants being found guilty Ordered that he said
et alias   )   defendant do give good security for his appearance
                  at January term next to receive his sentence of the
                  Court.

State   )
    vs   )   Information for retailing spiritous liquors without
Andrew McDoule)   Licence. The cause was called and the same Jury sworn
                  to try the same. Who returned the following verdict
                  NOT GUILTY Thomas Parrot Junr. foreman.

State   )
    vs   )   Taken and committed as a vagrant Ordered that the deft.
William Adams)   be discharged on giving good security for twelve months
                  & a day.

State   )
    vs   )   Ind^t for assault &c. James Handley. Elizt. Hill.
Thomas Handley)   John Hill and Mary Owens. a true Bill. Thomas Handley
et alias   )   & James Handley no bill John Buchanan foreman.

                        James Craig
                        Benjn. Boyd

                        June Term 1793

Monday the 17th Day of June 1793.
Court met according to adjournment.

Judges Present. John Winn and James Craig Esquires

The grand Jury by their foreman John Buchanan returned the following
bills.

State)
  vs) Ind^t for assault &c. no Bill, Jno Buchanan foreman.
Lee Duggins)

State)
  vs   ) Ind^t for assault &c. Wm. Hendricks prosr.
Saml. Crosslin) True Bill. John Buchanan foreman.

State)
  vs   ) Indt. for assault &c. Wm. Hendricks prosr.
William Hill) True Bill Jno. Buchanan foren.

State)
  vs   ) Ind^t for assault &c Wm. Hendricks pros^r
Frederick Arrick) True Bill Jno. Buchanan fore^n

State)
  vs) Ind.^{t} for assault &c. Wm. Hendricks pros^r
Jesse Sibley) True bill Jno. Buchanan fore^n

State)
  vs) Ind^t for assault &c Wm. Hendricks Pros^r true Bill
Rolly Hughes) Jno. Buchanan fore^n

State)
  vs) Ind^t for assault &c Wm. Hendricks pros^r true Bill John
John Sibley) Buchanan fore.n

State)
  vs) Indt for assault &c no Bill John Buchanan foreman.
Benjn Owens)
Junr)

Court adjourned untill 3 O'Clock   John Winn
               James Craig

Court met according to adjournment
Adjourned untill tomorrow 9 o'Clock

Samuel Proctor)
  vs   ) S. P. dismissed at the plaintiffs costs William
Thomas Parrot) Cato swore to days attendance as an evidence on the
Junr) above suit.

        John Winn
        James Craig

June Term 1793

Tuesday the 18th Day of June 1793
Court met according to adjournment.

Judges Present. John Winn, James Craig and Benjamin Boyd Esquires.

Joseph McDaniel)
  vs   ) On Att^t Diss^d at Defendants costs.
Lewis Boltner)

James Douglass)
  vs   ) S. P. Abated by defts. death.
James Winn)

Henry Page)
  vs   ) Case Diss^d at the pltfs costs.
Jona^n Belton)

Lewis Boltner) vs) Willm. Gordon &) James Nealy)	Rule Judgement revised.

James Milligan) vs) James McCreight) & John Ellison)	Diss^d at Defts costs.

Burbage Woodard) vs) William Nelson)	Case diss^d at the pltfs. costs.

Jonathan Belton) vs) Charles Johnstone)	Debt. Judg^t confess^d according to specialty say L38.3:4 Exon. to issue but not be levied for six months.

Samuel Dodds appeared in Court and proved the last will and testament of Joseph Dodds deceased. Ordered that letters testamentary be granted to the Exors. therein nominated.

The Citation for the estate of James Scott being returned Duly certified. Ordered that letters of administration be granted Nancy Scott and Edward Goyen they taking the accustomed Oaths and giving security as the law requires.

James Kincade having petitioned for a Licence to retail spiritous liquors for the term of one year. Ordered that the same granted he giving security as the law requires.

Ordered that John Gray esquire be appointed guardian to an orphan boy named John Smith. on complying with the requisitions of the law in that case made.

State) vs) William Lathan)	To be discharged on giving security to indemnify the County and on paying costs.

State) vs) Randal Gibson)	Ind^t for felony abated by the death of the Defendant.

State) vs) Frederick Arrick)	Int^t for assault &c. traversed and recognizances continued. Wm. Hendricks pros^r

State) vs) Mary Tidwell)	Recognizance continued.

State) vs) Isaac Young) & James Rabb)	Recognizances forfeited scire facias to issue.

State) vs) Millia Nelson)	Continued

State) vs) Elizt^h Watts) Geo^e Watts) Jesse Perry)	Recognizances forfeited scire facias to issue.

State   )
  vs   ) Ind.^t for ass.^t &c. William Hendricks pros.^r
Samuel Crosslin) recog.^a continued. traversed.

Proceeding to call over the list of petit jurors when the following
answered to their names.

John Willingham, Alexander McCane, Robert Read, Alexr. Roseborough,
Jacob Gibson, Peter Curry, James Barkley, Thomas Meredith.

Ordered that all summoned on the grand Jury who did not appear to sit
on the same be fined agreable to Law unelss they make sufficient
excuse on Oath on the first or second day of next term.

Also that all persons summoned to appear on the petit jury and failed
therein on this day be fined unless they appear and make excuse in
like manner and that the names of the defaulters on the grand and
petit jury be published at the court house door.

Ordered that Tavern Licence be granted William Gibson for the term of
one year he giving security as the law requires.

William Irvin   )
  vs   ) Judgement confessed by Maddern Leggo according
Maddern Leggo   ) to specialty.
& Willm. Morrison)

State   )
  vs   ) Int. felony. Alexr. Gordon pros.^d
Hugh Yongue) prosecution withdrawn at Pros.^{rs} Costs.

State   )
  vs   ) Ind. for felony Hugh Yongue Pros.^r
Francis Lee) prosecution withdrawn at prosrs. costs.

John Winn   )
  vs   ) Dismissed at defendants costs.
Wm. Morris   )
& John Lucas)

State   )
  vs   ) The defendant having charged Benjamin Carter
Catherine McClurken)

State vs Rachel Tidwell & John Goodrum. Rocognizances. Continued.

State vs John Smith. Ordered that Rule issue to show Cause why
information should not be filed.

State vs Thomas Hines & Thomas Muse. Recognizances forfeited. scire
facias to issue.

Robert Barkley vs William Gibson & William Ewing. Judgement confessed
according to specialty Stay of execution three months.

Admors of Lewis Owens vs John McCamey. S. P. Decree for L 4:12:6.
with Interest from the 1st June 1790.

William Nelson vs Robert Derham. On appeal. the Magistrate's Judgment.
vs William Nelson affirmed for 36/. with Costs.

Richard F. Winn vs James Wilson. S. P. decree by Default according to
specialty.

James Brown vs Thomos Whitehouse & William Roach. S. P. Decree for
L 5:13:6 with interest from 21st July 1788.

Mathew Talbot vs Maddern Leggo. Debt. Judgement by default according to specialty.

John Adair vs James Craig & Alexr. Kennedy. Nonsuit the Plantff. not appearing to prosecute.

Nathan King vs John Bell. Judgement Confessed. Stay of Exon one month.

David Evans treasr vs David Shelton. Judget by default according to specialty.

John Tidwell vs John Whitehed. Nonsuit the Pltf not appearing to prosecute.

John Cooke Exor. of Gindart vs Frizzle McTyre. Rule made absolute.

Thomas Nelson vs John Drennan. Case. Judgt by default a writ of inquiry to be executed.

Richard Mansel vs Frizzle McTyre. Dismissed.

David McGraw vs Reuben McGraw. On appeal. Ordered that the Judgement be reversed and the Deft. on appeal to pay the costs.

William Hollis vs Dennis Burns. On a Replevin. Ordered that the property under exon. be delivered up to the pltf and that the Defendant be charted with the costs of the replevin.

Ester Nuttewill vs Thomas May. On appeal. Judgement affirmed.

> John Winn
> James Craig
> Benjn Boyd

June Term 1793

Wednesday the 19th Day of June 1793.
Court met according to adjournment.

Judges Present. John Winn, Benjamin Boyd & James Craig Esqr.

Ester Nuttevill)
   vs   ) Edward Willingham appeared in Court and swore to 2
Thomas May   ) days attendance as an evidence on the above suit.

William Martin vs Heartwell Macon Junior. Judgt by Default a writ of enquiry to be executed.

Ordered that Willm. Willingham be committed to Goal untill he pays his fine and all the costs accrued thereon.

Ordered that a tavern licence be granted to John Stinson for the term of one year he giving security as the law requires.

Ordered that the Clerk do tax the County attorneys fees in all State causes and return the same in order to be passed at September term next. for payment in January term next.

Ordered that a rule issue vs the sheriff to show cause why he has not complied with an order made in June term 1791 respecting the returning of Writs of Scire facias &c.

Ordered that a Bench warrant issue against John Hendricks to appear in the behalf of the state & prosecute certain bills of indictment prefered against sundry persons for a breach of the peace &c.

David Huston vs John Goyen. Dismissed.

Benjamin Boyd vs Hugh Carson, John Winn admors & Prudence Durphey adm.t of Wm. Durphey decd. Case. Judgement confessed on an open account for L 30:16. princi.l with interest L 14:11:1. with lawful Interest on the principal untill paid from this day. Stay of Exon 12 months.

Lewis Boltner vs Joseph McDaniel. Appl. Dismissed at appellants costs.

Several propositions for undertaking the finishing of the Court house having been laid before the court. it appearing to the court that the proposals of Francis Palmer were the lowest whereupon it was agreed that he should be employed for the above work agreable to the proposals by him rendered in on his giving bond and security for the completing the same on or before the 12th day of January next in a workmanlike manner Also that the Clerk be empowered to procure the necessary Iron Mongory and have the plank brought to the Court house.

Adjourned untill the 12th day of January next.

> John Winn
> Benj.n Boyd
> James Craig

January Term 1794

Monday the 13th day of January 1794.
The Court met according to adjourn.t

Judges Present. James Craig esquire.

Appeared in open Court John Goodrum and James Alexander Watson and proved the last will and testament of Peter Cassity deceased. Ordered that the same be recorded. and Letters testamentary granted Also appeared William Watson one of executors appointed in the above said will was duly qualified.

Ordered that the administrators for the estate of William Gladden deceased do sell all the personal estate of the said deceased within twenty days from this date. (giving fourteen days public notice thereof) on a credit untill the first day of January next taking bond and good security for the property sold.

Charles Picket being appointed to the office of a Justice of the peace for the county of Fairfield now appeared in open Court and took the oaths of office and allegiance as by law required.

> James Craig

January Term 1794

Tuesday the 14th day of January 1794
Court met according to adjournment.

Judge Present. James Craig, Esquire.

The Citation for the estate of John Robinson deceased was returned duly certified Ordered that Letters of Administration be granted to Hannah Robinson and John Thomas Robinson. they taking the accustomed Oaths and giving security as the law requires.

Ordered that the perishable property of the said estate be sold within twenty days from this date giving due notice thereof on a credit of nine months. taking bond and good security.

The last will and testament of Nathan Saunders was proved in open Court. Ordered that Letters testamentary be granted to the executors therein named.

The Last Will and Testament of William Phillips was proved in open Court. Ordered that Letters testamentary be granted to the executors therein named.

The Last Will and testament of Mathew Hays was proved in open Court. Ordered that letters testamentary be granted to the executors therein nominated.

The Citation for the estate of Hugh Morrison deceased was returned duly certified Ordered that Letters of administration be granted to John Turner esquire. Henry Moore and Abraham Miller for the said estate. they taking the accusomed Oaths and giving security as the law requires Ordered that the personal property of the said Estate be sold on a Credit untill the first day of January next. taking bond and good security giving twenty days notice thereof from this date.

James Craig

January Term 1794

Wednesday the 15th Day of January 1794
Court met according to adjournment.

Judges Present. James Craig and John Gray Esq^{rs}

John Gray Esqr. being appointed one of the Judges for the County of Fairfield now appeared in open court and took the oaths of office and allegiance and office as by Law required.

The Last will and testament of Epraim Pettypool deceased was proved in open court by John Yarbrough. Ordered that the same be recorded and Ursula Pettypool Executrix appointed in the said will was duly Qualified.

William McMorris vs William Austin. S. P. Judgement Confessed according to specialty.

Ordered that a rule issue against William Owens constable to show cause why he permitted Thomas Handley then in his custody to escape.

Ordered that the administrators of the estate of James Thomas deceased do divide the personal property of the said estate among the heirs intitled by law to receive the same. the said heirs giving bond and security to the said administrators to discharge their proportianate part of any unsettled demands that may hereafter come against the said estate.

Thomas Parrot Junior being appointed constable for the County of Fairfield took the oaths of office and allegiance as by law required.

State   )
   vs   ) Scire facias. to show cause why their recognizances
Thomas Hines) should not be forfeited. Ordered that Scire facias be
Thomas Muse) made absolute.

Ordered that the above cause and order be postponed for a rehearing on Monday next.

State vs James Phillips. Ind^t for ass^t & Bat^y George Knowland pros^r Ordered a nole prosequi be entered.

Ordered that a dedimus issue directed to the Judges on John Irons Esqr one of the magistrates of the County of Richland to examine Elizabeth McLemore late Elizabeth Kennerly respecting the execution of the last will and testament of Jacob Gibson deceased.

The grand Jurors drawn to serve at this term were now called when the following persons answered to their names Charles Lewis. John Arrick.

Moses Knighton, Saml. Simmons. James Nelson Are§ Liles. Benj. May.
Robert Rabb. Charnel Durham. Wm. Cato. Saml. Johnstone. Joe Owens.
Thomas Means foreman.

The Citation for the Estate of Samuel Hollis deceased was returned
duly certified Ordered that letters of administration be granted to
Elizabeth Hollis and Berry Hollis they taking the accustomed oaths
and giving security as the law requires.

The citation for the estate of James Burke deceased was returned duly
certified. Ordered that letters of administration be granted to
Thomas Harden he giving security and taking the accustomed Oath as by
law required.

James Craig

January Term 1794

Thursday the 16th day of January 1794.
Court met according to adjournment.

Judges Present.   James Craig and John Gray esqʳˢ

Ordered that a road be opened from Strothers ferry to the Presbyterian
meeting house on Hancocks road. and that Colonel John Pearson do
superintent the laying out of the same and Charles Montgomery be
appointed overseer Also that Colonel John Pearson John Cook esquire
and Mr. Joshua Derham do meet and divide the inhabitants liable to
work on the road in their quarter in such a manner as to have their
work as nearly equal as possible. from the negroe burning and Strothers
ferry to the county line between Little and broad rivers.

Ordered that the personal estate of Phillip Shaver deceased be sold
on a credit of nine months credit taking good security and giving 14
days notice thereof.

Ordered that the following persons who were summoned to appear on the
grand Jury at last term and failed in their attendance be fined in the
sum of three pounds each. John Watson. David McGraw. Reuben Harrison.
John Mickle. Hezekiah Ford.

Also that the Petit Jurors who failed to attend on the same on the
18th day of June last. be fined in the sum of 30/ each Lemuel Perry.
Clement Arledge. John Hill senᵗ John Dodds Potley Turnepseed. Samuel
Gladney Jeremiah Pearson. William Johnstone. Creighton Buchanan. Adam
Byerly. Joseph Arledge, Moses Hornsby, Thomas Robinson, Richard Mansel,
Aron Gossy, John Briant, George Lewry ordered that execution issue
again the above defaulters for their respective fines.

Ordered that Robert Neil be paid the sum of nine shillings and four
pence for feeding an estray heifer and steer also the sum of six
shillings for fees paid by him for telling the same.

Ordered that all persons applying for Licences to retail spiritous
liquors do give their notes with security payable to the County
treasurer in six months from the time of Obtaining the same for the
monies the county may be intitled to receive for such Licence.

Ordered that Samuel Gladneys fine for non attendance as a petit Juror
at last term be remitted.

James Craig
J. Gray

January Term 1794

Friday the 17th day of January 1794. Court met according to adjournmt.

92

Judges Present. James Craig and John Gray esquires.

Ordered that a rule issue against the sheriff Clerk and County attorney to show cause why they should not be fined for neglect of their respective duties.

State)
vs) Ind^t The defendant appeared in Court to receive his
William Hollis) sentence. Sentence the defendant to pay fifteen
pounds and be committed untill Tuesday next at one O'Clock at which time if the said sum is not paid. the said defendant is then to receive 25 lashes on his bare back at the publick whipping post.

State vs James Hardridge & others. Recognizances discharged.

State vs William Briant. Recognizance discharged.

John Johnstone vs Heartwell Macon Junr. Judgement confessed by the defendant according to specialty. stay of execution untill the 12th day of June next.

James Knox vs Andrew McDowel. S. P. Dismissed at plaintiffs Costs.

Edward Lacey vs James Davis. S. P. Case agreed each to pay an equal share of the cost.

Levi Moberly appeared in court and took the Oaths of Allegiance and office as a constable for the County of Fairfield.

Ordered that Nancy Taylor. Tabitha Hughes and William Morrison be bound unto William Hughes untill they attain the age of 18 years or Marry. he complying with the usual requisites in such cases. as education cloathing &c.

John Winn vs Isaac Gibson. Refered. awarded to the plaintiff twelve pounds & costs of suit.

Ordered that a road be opened from Chester county line to Robert Ewings. Robert Wilson overseer. from there to Dutchman's Creek. James Gamble overseer from thence to the head of twenty-five mile creek Charnel Durham overseer from thence to the Charleston road below Doughartys Lewuel Perry overseer. and that John Turner esquire Jesse Haris Charnel Durham James Hoy. and Zachariah Kirkland esquire be appointed comissioners to lay out the same.

Ordered that the bill of Francis Palmer for work done to the court house amounting to L 23:7: be paid.

State vs Benjn Cassels alias Benjn Wooley. Ind^t for Larciny. true bill. Thomas Means foreman.

State vs John Allen Thorpe. Ind^t for assault & Batery. No bill Thos. Means foreman.

Ordered that a rule issue against all the grand Jurors who have failed to attend at this term. also against Robert Rabb who has failed to attend this day. Also against the following persons who have failed to attend on the petit Jury. to show cause why they should not be fined Benjamin Lindsay. James Brice. John Lewelling. John Gwinn. George Lott. Richard Nealy. John Flowers. Drury Bishop.

State)
vs) Bast^y The defendant fined in five pounds proclama-
Emilia Nelson) tion money each. Ordered that the said William
& William Dansby) Dansby do give security to indemnify the County.
also that he do pay the said Emilia Nelson the sum of 40/ per annum towards the support of the child for the term of ten years.

John Means vs Spencer Brumett. On att. Ordered that the deposition of Francis Coleman be taken before Samuel W. Yongue Esquire.

James Butter vs Willm. Malone. Att. Ordered that the property attached be condemned and sold nend expo. to issue.

James Craig
J. Gray.

January Term 1794

Saturday 18th day of January 1794.
The Court met according to adjournment.

Judges Present. James Craig and John Gray esquires.

Ordered that Amy Wooleys recognizances be continued.

Peter Conway vs Mosely Collins. S. P. Judgement Confessed according to specialty.

Hugh Donnelly vs Joseph Cameron. Case. abated by plaintiffs death.

John Gray vs Jane Phillips. Case dismissed at the defendants cost.

William Coggin vs William Johnstone. Case Judgement by default. writ of enquiry to be executed.

Alexander Purvis vs Robert McTyre. Attat.^{t} Robert Craig Garnishee.

Thomas Parrot Junior vs John Surgoner. On appeal. Ordered the magistrates Judgement be affirmed for L5.

Thomas Parrot Junior vs John Surjoiner. On appeal. Ordered the magistrates Judgement be affirmed for L5.

Thomas Parrot Junr vs John Surjoiner. On appeal. Ordered the magistrates Judgement be affirmed for L5.

James Austen vs Thomas Meredith. Case dismissed at equal Costs.

Christian Graddick vs Henry Hunter & Minor Winn. S. P. decree according to specialty.

Mathew McCreight vs John Martin. Case abated by Defendants death.

James Hollis vs Isaac Arledge. Case dismissed at plaintiffs cost.

Daniel McBride vs Moses Duke Exor. of Robert Dukes. Debt. Judgement by default.

Micajah Pickett vs Ephiarm Pettypool. Ordered the Clerk do receive the award out of Court.

John Winn vs Elisha Dye. S. P. Judgement by default.

James Burke vs John Burns. S. P. Abated by plaintiffs death.

Proceeded to ballot for grand Jurors to serve at next term when the following persons were drawn.

Nazareth Whitehead. David Andrews. Alexr. Gordon. Wm. McMorris Senior. James Rabb. Burwell Cooke. William Cloud. Hugh Milling. Henry Moore. Thomas Parrot senior. Alexr. Robinson senior. John Cook. James Brown. Jesse Fort. John Bonner. James Daniel. Samuel McKinney. John Woodard. Captain John Robertson. James Gray.

Petit Jury

Hugh Gamble Junior. Quintin Craig. James Aikin. Hugh Montgomery. James Lockridge Samuel Craig. David Dunn. Alexr. Kincaid. Wm. Holley. Peter Curry. Wm. Coggin. Wm. Bonner. Obediah Henson. John Cubit. Jesse Beam. Saml. Alston. Andrew McDoule. James Hoy. Wm. Lathan. Benjn. Halsey. John Hollis. Andrew Fester. Wm. Calhoun. Dudley Curry.

Thomas Johnston vs Samuel Lowry. On appeal. Judgement reversed. decree for Deft. 6d.

Ordered that John Smith be appointed overseer on the Columbia Charleston road from Cedar creek to Daniels fight.

Robert Rabb vs Frizzle McTyre. Rule. continued.

Ordered that the road leading from Enoch Grubs to Means's Stone be altered and Cleared out the best and straightest way. Robert Coleman and Levi Moberly. Commissioners to lay out the same.

Stephen Gibson being committed to Goal on an escape from the officer of Justice in Orangeburgh district for a charge of horse stealing Ordered that he be continued in prison in order to be delivered over to the said officers if applied for in one month otherwise to be discharged.

State vs Benjn Cassels alias Benjn Wooley. Ordered that the defendant be admitted to bail in the sum of L 20.

Ordered that Robert Manning be admitted to bail Ordered that David Doute be committed to Camden Goal and that the sheriff do press a guard for that purpose.

                    James Craig
                    J. Gray

                    July Term 1794

Wednesday the 16th day of July 1794. Court met according to adjournmt.

Judge Present. John Winn Esquire.

The Citations for the estates of the persons underwritten were returned duly certified Ordered that Letters of administration be granted to the following persons for the respective estates hereunder mentioned (that is to say)

To Edward McGraw for the estate of Aurther McGraw.
To Peter Grim Quel. for the estate of William Crim.
To Catherine McCabe for the estate of Patrick McCabe.
To Elizabeth Dunlap for the estate of Robert Dunlap.
To James Gordon for the estate of Nathl. Gordon.
To Mary Obrian for the estate of Daniel Obrian.
To William Scott for the estate of George Scott
all of the District of Camden deceased.

The Last will and testament of Jacob Gibson deceased being duly proved ordered that the same be recorded and Jacob Gibson Junior the executor therein appointed being duly qualified ordered that Letters testamentary be granted.

William Robinson appeared in open Court and Chose William McMorris Senior for his guardian of whom the Court approved and ordered that Letters of Guardianship be granted. The said McMorris giving security as the law requires.

Ordered that the administrators of John Robertson deceased be empowered to sell the personal estate of the said deceased any time after the

95

first day of November next giving fifteen days public notice of such
sale and making the sale to take place in time to return an account
thereof to the Judges of this court at January term next.

John Winn
James Craig
John Turner

July Term 1794

Friday 18th day of July 1794.

Judges Present. James Craig and John Turner Esq^{rs}

John Turner Esquire acknowledged the signing and sealing of a Coneyance
of a tract of fifty acres of Land in Fairfield County to Robert Hood.

Reuben Harrison and John Mickle having been fined for non attendance
as grand Jurors in June term 1793 and having now made sufficient
excuse. Ordered that their respective fines be remitted.

John Crosby vs Henson Day. Acc^t L 40:0:10 3/4

Mathew Day appeared in court and acknowledges himself Special Bail
in this action. and undertaker in case the defendant be cast in the
action to pay the Condemnation money or render the body of the defendant in execution.

Mathew Day

Field Farren vs James Cooke. Case Abated by defendants death

James Cooke vs Field Farren. Case Abated by plaintiffs death

Kirkland & Co. vs John Robertson Exor of Littlejohn. Case Dismissed.

Christina Ringer vs Jacob Ringer & Grispin Morgan. Debt.

Thomas McClurken vs John McCombs. Case. The following Jury were
sworn to execute a writ of Inquiry.

James Aiken. Hugh Gamble Junior. Alexander Kincaide. Peter Curry.
William Coggins William Bonner. Obediah Henson. John Cubit. Samuel
Alston. Andrew McDoule. Benj. Halsey. Dudley Curry Verdict. We find
for the plaintiff with Interest according to the note and fix the
value of the whisky at 2/ per Gallon.

Hugh Gamble foreman

Ordered that the petit Jury be allowed the sum of five shillings on
every verdict to be taxed against the parties cost in any action to be
paid by the plaintiff in the first instance.

Thomas Nelson sen^r vs William McTyre & Frizzle McTyre. S. P. on note.
Decree according to the specialty.

William Martin vs Heartwell Macon Junr Case. Writ inquiry before the
same Jury Verdict we find for the pltf. L 10:16:-7 Int. from 20th
March 1790.

Hugh Gambel foreman

John Means vs Joseph Stanton. Debt. Judgement according to the
specialty by nihil dicit.

Wm. Martin vs Hl. Macon Junr. Case. John Martin swore to four days
attendance as an evidence on the above suit.

Thomas Nelson vs John Drennan. Case settled at defendants Cost.

John Crosslin vs William Broome. Case Dismissed at equal Costs each party paying his own attorney.

Phillip Pearson vs Mathew Raiford. Att^t Dismissed at plaintiffs Costs.

Josiah Knighton swore in as a Constable for the County of Fairfield.

Francis Papp vs Henry Goyen et als. Case. Dismissed at Defendants Costs.

William Coggin vs William Johnstone. Case. Dismissed at defendants costs.

McCleod & Belton vs Robert Shirley & Robert Henson. Debt. Dismissed.

William Gray vs Thomas Phillips. Attachment. Judgement of default.

Richard Gladney vs William Bradley. Att^t abated by plaintiffs death.

David R. Evans vs Mary Wedon. Att^t Dismissed

Licence to Retail spiritous liquors granted to Thomas Lesley for six months. Also to Moses Cockerill for the same time. Also to James McCreight for one year.

James Hoy vs William Bradley. Att^t Dismissed.

Thomas Johnstone vs David Shelton & Elijah Major. Debt. remanded from the circuit Court. The cause was now called and the same Jury sworn. Verdict. We find for the pltf the sum which appears due on Mr. Sheltons bond.   Hugh Gamble foreman.

State vs James Stevenson. Bast^{dy} fined L 5 proclamation money and costs.

Ordered that the adm^{ors} of the estate of Samuel Hollis be empowered to sell the personal estate on a Credit of nine months taking bond and good security.

State vs Benjamin Carter. Basd^y fined L 5 proclamation money and costs.

State vs John Sims. Bastd^y recognizance discharged.

Minor Winn vs William Hughes. Diss^d at Defendants Costs.

                    James Craig
                    John Turner

July Term 1794

Saturday the 19th Day of July 1794.
Court met according to adjournment.

Judges Present. James Craig. John Gray and John Turner Esquires.

Henry Myers vs Henry Rugeby. Case. Abraham Myers swore to 3 days attendance as an evidence in this case living 40 miles from the co^t House.

State vs Frederick Arrick. Ind^t Wm. Hendricks pros^r Ordered that John Smith. Zack^l Kirkland Esqr Simon Shaver. James Nelson & Samuel Nelson witnesses in behalf of the state do attend the Court on Monday next otherwise that attachment do issue against them and they be served with a notice of this order.

```
State        )
  vs         )  Ordered that the recognizance be forfeited and Scire
William Lathan )  facias to issue. unless William Lathan shall within
James Johnstone)  one month Comply with the former order of Court. and
                  that the Clerk do give the said William Lathan
                  notice thereof.

Christina Ringer)
  vs           )  Debt.  The cause was now called and the Jury sworn
Jacob Ringer   )  except Samuel Craig and Joshua Durham in the place
Crispin Morgan )  of Peter Curry and William Bonner.
```

Verdict. We find verdict in favour of the plaintiff L 57:3: Ster^g with interest from Decr 25th, 1777.

Hugh Gamble foreman

```
State        )
  vs         )  Ind$^t$ Mary Ingleman prost.  Ordered that James Davis and
Joshua Derham)  John Allen Thorpe Witnesses in behalf of the state do
                attend on Monday next otherwise that attachment do
                issue against for contempt of Court.
```

State vs Rachael Tidwell. Ordered that the defendant do attend on Monday next. or that her recognizance be forfeited and Scire facias to issue.

State vs Mary Tidwell. Ordered that the defendant do attend on Monday next or that her recognizances be forfeited and scire facias to issue.

State vs Benjamin Cassells alias Benjamin Wooley. Ind^t for Larciny. Wm. Lockwood pros^t The following Jury impannelled

John Cubit. Samuel Craig. Benjamin Halsey. William Bonner. Hugh Gamble. James Aikins. Alexr. Kincaide. William Dudley Curry. Obediah Henson. Andrew McCoule. Saml. Alston. Guilty and recommended to mercy.

Hugh Gamble foreman.

Sentenced to receive fifteen lashes on his bare back at the public whipping post on the second Monday in August next.

```
Thomas Johnstone)
  vs            )  Thomas Johnston swore to 10 days attendance as an
David Shelton   )  evidence. living 40 miles from the Court house.
& Elijah Majors )  4 ferriagers. the attendance of Robert Johnston
                   not allowed to be taxed.
```

```
Robert Hawthorn)
  vs           )  Debt.  Agreed that this cause be settled as follows:
Victor Nealy   )  That each party pays his own Costs. that one third
                  (to wit) the cash part is considered as already paid
```
and that the defendant do on Monday next pay and deliver to Mr. John Means at Winnsboro a good like Horse or horses or other usefull and serviceable property such as shall be approved of and valued by David R. Evans, and Arsomanus Liles or such other Arbitrators as the said Means and Nealy may mutually agree on the amount of the remaining two thirds of the note on which the action is brought.

James Craig
John Gray
John Turner

July Term 1794

Monday the 21st day of July 1794. Court met according to adjournment.

Judges Present. John Gray and John Turner Esq^{rs}

Jonathan Belton vs William Sibley. Debt. Judg^t confessed for L 21:2/ Sterling and interest from the 20th April 1794.

State vs Mary Ginn. Recognizance forfeited and scire facias to issue against the defendant and securities unless the body be produced on the last day of the term.

State vs James Adams Junior. Recognizances forfeited and Ordered that scire facias do issue against the defendant and his securities unless the body of Deft be produced on the last day of the term.

State vs William Adams. Recognizances forfeited and Ordered that scire facias do issue against the deft and sureties unless the body of the defendant be produced in Court by the last day of the term.

State vs Frederick Arrick. Ind^t for ass^t & Bat^y & false Impst Wm. Hendricks pros^r. Jury were as follows sworn.

Hugh Gamble. Quintin Craig. James Aiken, Saml. Craig, Peter Curry, Wm. Coggin, Wm. Benner, Obed^h Henson. John Cubit. Samuel Alston. And^w McDoule, Dudley Curry. Verdict. Guilty
                                   Hugh Gamble foreman.

Christopher Ederington)
     vs   )   On att^t James Talent garnishee swore he was
Thomas Ederington   )   indebted to Thomas Ederington in the amount of
)   three thousand lbs weight of Tobacco payable
as follows. 1000 Weight on the 1st Jany 1795. 1000 W. do on 1st Jany. 1796 & 1000 W do on 1st Jany. 1797.

David R. Evans vs James Rogers. On appeal Judgement affirmed.

Henry Rugety vs Henry Maskall. On att^t writ of inquiry executed. Verdict we do find for the plaintiff L 400 with the interest due.
                                   Hugh Gamble foreman

State vs George Ederington. Ass^t & Bat^y. Thomas Ederington Pros^r. The defendant in the case claimed his trial.

State vs Elijah Gibson. Ordered that the recognizance be forfeited and Scire facias to issue vs Defft. and his sureties.

State vs Mary Tidwell. Rule absolute.

State vs Rachael Tidwell. Rule made absolute.

State vs Thomas Handley, Jane Handley. Ind^t for ass^t & Bat^y & false imprisonment Mary Ingleman pros^r. Ordered that a bench warrant do issue against the defendants.

State
   vs
John Willingham. Ind^t for assault and Battery. John Haris p^r. Same Jury sworn. Verdict Guilty. Hugh Gamble foreman.

State vs William Bradley, Temperance Ivey. Gastardy fined L 5 proclamation money and Ordered to give security to indemnify the County.

State   )
   vs   )   Upon the defendants request and application
Benjn. Wooley)   Ordered that the former sentence be rendered. and that
alias   )   the defendant do receive fifteen stripes instanter
Benjn. Cassels)   and be liberated.

Samuel Oats sworn in as a Constable for the County of Fairfield.

                              John Gray
                              John Turner

                                  99

Tuesday the 22nd July 1794. Court met according to adjournment.

Judges Present. James Craig. John Gray and John Turner Esquires.

Ordered upon the petition of John Richmond. That John Burns admor. of the estate of Amos Gowen deceased be cited to appear at next term and renew his bond and security for the due administration of said estate.

Peter Patterson vs Charles Picket	)	
Peter Paterson vs Hugh Menar	)	Actions of ass^t & Bat^y
Peter Patterson vs Isaac Arledge	)	Dismissed at plaintiffs costs.
Peter Patterson vs Christopher Boler	)	

Ordered that a tavern licence be granted to Jesse Havis for the space of one year.

John Smith vs Mathew Talbot. Att^t Dismissed.

William Martin vs David Shelton. Debt. John Martin appeared in open court and acknowledged himself security for Costs.

Ordered that personal estate of George Lewy deceased be sold as directed by the will giving twelve months Credit and taking good security.

State vs Jesse Sibley. Ind^t for ass^t & Bat^y. Elizth Hendricks pros^r. The following Jury sworn

Hugh Gamble. Peter Curry. William Coggin. John Cubit. Andrew McDowell. Saml. Craig. Benjn. Halsey. James Aikin. Thomas Hill. John Hollis. Willm. Bonner. John Smith. Verdict. Guilty. Hugh Gamble foreman.

State vs Samuel Crosslin. Ind^t for ass^t & Battery &c. Mary Ingleman pros^r. Same Jury sworn except Dudley Curry in the place of John Smith. Verdict. Guilty. Hugh Gamble fore^n.

State   )
   vs   ) On suspicion of Murder. the defendant claimed
Christopher Ederington) his trial. Ordered that the defendant do
              give security for his appearance to stand his trial at the district court of Camden. and that said security be given in open court before the last day of the term and upon which all former recognizances to be discharged.

David Hamilton appeared in open court and proved the last will and testament of David McCreight deceased. Ordered that the same be recorded and letters testamentary granted.

State vs Joshua Derham. Indictment for ass^t &c Mary Ingleman pros^r. same Jury sworn Verdict. not Guilty
                    Hugh Gamble foreman

Elizabeth Gibson vs John Jenkins. On a replevin of property Executed as that of Jacob Gibson. Ordered that the property executed be condemned.
                         James Craig
                         John Gray
                         John Turner

Wednesday the 23rd Day of July 1794.
Court met according to adjournment.

Judges present. James Craig, John Gray & John Turner, esq^{rs}

Jonathan Belton)
  vs   )   Debt. Judg^t confessed according to specialty with
Nusse Bowler)   stay of Exon. untill 1st January 1795. Exon nonethe-
                  less to be issued but not levied.

Robert Duncan vs Harris Freeman. Debt. Diss^d at Defendants Costs.

Christopher Ederington vs Thomas Ederington. On attachment. Dismissed
Joseph McDaniel swore to six days attendance as an evidence.

State vs John Sibley. Ind^t for ass^t & Bat^y &c. Elizth Hendricks pros^x.
The defendant pleads Guilty.

State vs Rolly Hughes. Ind^t for A & B &c. Eliz^h Hendrix pros^x.
Recognizance forfeited.

State vs William Hill. Ind^t for A & B &c. Wm. Hendricks pros^x. abated
by defendants death.

State vs Samuel Crosslin. Ind^t for A & B &c Eliz^h Hendricks pros^x.
The defendants pleads guilty.

State   )
  vs   )   Ind^t ass^t & Bat^y &c. Elizabeth Hendricks pros^x.
Jane Handley) John Hill and Mary Owens pleads guilty
Elizth Hill) Ordered that Bench warrants do issue against Jane
John Hill   ) Handley and Elizabeth Hill.
Mary Owens)

State vs John Arrick. Indt. asst. & Baty. &c. Anne Smith prosx.
Compromised at Defendants costs.

State vs Samuel Crosslin. Indt. asst. & Baty. & c John Hendricks
prosr. The defendant discharged.

State vs Elisha Owens. Indt. asst. & Baty. &c. John Hendricks prosr.
The defendant discharged.

State vs Catherine McClurken. Bastdy. Recognizance forfeited and
scire facias to issue.

State vs Rachael McGraw. Basdy. fined 5L proclamation money.

Fairfield County vs Joshua Badgers. Case The cause was now called
the following Jury sworn.

Hugh Gamble, Obediah Henson, Peter Curry, Dudley Curry, Willm. Coggin,
Benjamin Halsey, John Cubit, Saml. Craig, Andw. McDowell, John Hollis,
Samuel Alston, James Aikin. Verdict in favr. of the County L8:10
& Costs. H. Gamble foren.

James Hunt vs James Phillips. On appeal. Judgt. affirmed for 28/ &
Costs.

State vs John Goodrum. Bastdy. Deft. discharged for want of prosecutor.

State vs James Andrew. A & B^{ty} James Turner pros^r. Discharged
each party paying their own costs.

State vs James Andrew. A & Bt^y Alexander Robinson pros^r. Discharged
each party paying their own costs.

State vs Willm. Nelson. Archibald Douglass pros^r. recognizance
Continued.

State vs Mary Ginn. Ordered that the rule for the forfeiture of her
recognizance be reversed and that her present recognizances be
continued.

State vs Samuel Simmons. Recognizance continued.

State vs Robert Mannion. A Bench warrant to issue.

State vs Annie Wooley. Ordered a noli prosequi be entered.

State   )
vs   ) On Scire Facias Ordered that the recognizance so far
Thomas Hines) as relates to Thomas Muse be discharged on his paying
& Thomas Muse) the Costs of the prosecution of Hines and the scire
              facias &c.

State vs John Smith. Rule. Dissmissed.

State vs Isaac Young & James Rabb. Scire Facias. Dissmissed.

State vs William Alexander. Fraud. Michael Hoke. Ordered that a
bench warrant be issued against the defendant to renew and give better
security.

Ordered that all recognizances not discharged be continued over unto
next term.

State   )
vs   ) Ordered that the defendant be committed untill he
Joseph Strange) shall give security for his appearance at the district
              court of Pinkney on the first day of November next
which security is to be taken by Samuel W. Yongue and Zachariah
Kirkland esquires who are directed to bind over the evidence against
the defendant to appear at the same Time and place.

William Sibley   )
vs   ) S. P. Wrightman Bagley swore to five days
Martha Dansby   ) attendance as an evidence in this case.
Adm^X of Dl. Dansby)

William Willingham)
vs   ) Case the cause was now called and the same Jury
James Andrews) sworn Verdict. we do find Damage in favour of
              the plaintiff L 41:8:6. Hugh Gamble foren

Minor Winn   )
vs   ) S. P. Dissmissed at Defts. Costs.
Jonan Lewelling)
Samuel Caldwell)
et uxor   )
vs   ) Rule made absolute.
John McCown &   )
Elizabeth Campbell)

Eleazar Moberly)
vs   ) Debt. Dissmissed.
David Shelton)

Ordered that James Seal be allowed the sum of seven shillings for
wintering an estray cow. or heifer.

Patience McGraw vs William Willingham. Case. Judg^t by default writ
of inquiry to be executed.

County vs Joshua Badgers. Case Peter Curry swore to 10 days attendance
as an evidence on the above case.

Frederick Ansminger   ) The Defendant please plene administravit.
admor of Peter Ansminger) Debt. Judgement according to specialty. on
vs   ) the plaintiffs giving bond & security to
Benjamin May a dm^{or}) indemnify the Defendant from the original
of Briant Riley dec^d) specialty said to be lost
               James Craig, John Turner, John Gray

July Term 1794

Thursday 24th July 1794.
Court met according to adjournment.

Judges Present. James Craig, John Gray and John Turner Esq.^{rs}

Hawthorn vs Nealy. Case   Joshua Derham swore to 4 days attendance as an evidence in this cause.

Willingham vs Andrews. Case Joshua Durham swore to 12 days attendance John Haris to 20 days and John Parr to 8 days attendance as an evidence on this case.

State vs Rolly Hughes. Indt. for asst. &c. Ordered that the former Rule respecting the forfeiture of his recognizance be reversed and that the recogna. do lay over to next term.

State vs William Lathan. Bastardy. Recognizance discharged.

Robert Barkley vs John Smith. Case Dissd at plaintiffs Costs.

William Martin vs David Shelton. Debt. The cause was now called and the following Jury sworn.

Hugh Gamble. Obediah Henson. James Aikin. Peter Curry. Willm. Coggin. Benjn. Halsey. John Cubit. Samuel Craig. Andw. McDowel. Dudley Curry. Jno. Willingham. Quintin Craig.

Martin vs Shelton. Verdict. not received. The plaintiff suffers a nonsuit. Robert Moorman swore to 5 days attendance as an evidence on the above cause.

John Hennington) Case. The cause was now called and the same Jury
     vs   ) sworn except Samuel Alston in the place of John
Robert Walker) Willingham Verdict We do find damage in favor of
) the plaintiff L2:10/ Hugh Gamble foreman.

Admors. of Boyd vs John Buchanan. Debt. Judgement according to specialty and agreed that each party pays the own costs.

Thomas McClurken vs Exors of Alexr. Miller. Judgt. according to specialty subject to a plea of plene administravit.

Hugh McDaniel vs Robert Ewing & William Ewing. Debt. Judgement according to the specialty.

William Nelson vs James Phillips. Debt. Dismissed at defendants costs.

Hennington vs Walker. Jacob Pruebaker swore to 7 days attendance as an evidence Samuel Crosslin to 6 days. Jesse Kirkland 8 days. and Benoni Holly to 10 days in this case.

County vs Badgers. Case Jacob Gibson swore to 4 days attendance as an evidence.

Philip Hart vs Phillip Riley. Debt. Judge^{t} by default according to specialty.

John Sweetenburgh vs John Warren, Harris Freeman, George Lewey. Debt. The plaintiff nonsuited.

Obed Kirkland   ) On action of ditinus for a negroe boy slave named
pr his Guardian) Jacob aged about ten years. the same Jury sworn.
     vs   ) Verdict. We find in favour of the plaintiff fifty
John Winn Esqr.) pounds to be discharged on delivering of the said
admor of Joseph) negroe. Hugh Gamble Foreman.
Kirkland Esqr.   )

Minor Winn   )
   vs   ) Debt. The cause was now called and the same Jury
Heartwell Macon)   Sworn. We do find verdict in favour of the plaintiff
Junior   ) for the sum due on Heartwell Macons note with the
                     interest thereon.   Hugh Gamble   foreman

State   )
   vs   ) Eliz^h Hendricks pros^x Guilty. Fined L5 Sterlg.
Frederick Arrick)   and Costs.

State vs Samuel Crosslin. Mary Ingleman prosx. Guilty. Fined L 10
Sterlg. and Costs.

State vs John Sibley. Eliz^h Hendricks pros^x Guilty Fined L 5 Sterlg.
and Costs.

State vs Jesse Sibley. Eliz^h Hendricks prosx. Guilty. Fined L 10
Sterlg. and Costs.

State vs Saml. Crosslin. Eliz^h Hendricks prosx. Guilty. Fined L 10
Sterlg. and Cost ten pounds fine.

State vs Mary Owens. Eliz^h Hendricks prosx. Guilty. Fined in L 5
Sterlg. and Costs.

State vs John Hill. Eliz^h Hendricks prosx. Guilty. Fined L 5 and
Costs.

State vs John Willingham. John Haris prosr. Guilty. Fined in the sum
of 20/ and Costs.

Frizzle McTyre & Christ^r Ederington vs Henry Rogers. On appeal.
Ordered the Judgement be affirmed No defence being made by appellants.

                              James Craig
                              John Gray
                              John Turner

                         July Term 1794

Friday the 25th July 1794.
Court met according to adjournment.

Judges Present. James Craig, John Gray and John Turner Esqr.

James Craig vs Francis Palmer. Judgement according to specialty.

James Craig vs William Sims. Debt. Judgt. according to specialty.
Exon to be issued but not levied untill 26th January next.

Messrs Pickett)
and Briggs   ) Judge^t according to specialty against all but
   vs   ) William Strother. with respect to whom the cause
Kemp T. Strother)   lies over.
and others   )

John L. Bradford)
   vs   ) Arbitrated defendant pays costs.
William Nelson)

James Douglass   ) I acknowledge Judg^t on the within note. The
   vs   ) payments made to Robert Starke Esqr. and James
Daniel Brown   ) Douglass to be allowed on the Exon at the
Exor. of Jacob Brown)   return thereof or sooner.

                              D. Brown Exor or
                              Jacob Brown

                              104

Thomas Means vs James Hollis and Others. S. P. Decree according to specialty.

James Hanna vs George Watts. S. P. Decree for Eight pounds with interest from the 10th June 1792. the note cost by D. Brown Esqr.

John Burns vs Isaac Reynolds. S. P. The plaintiff nonsuited.

Judiah Seymour vs Shaddrack Jacobs, Isham Fair. Case Discontinued at plaintiffs Costs.

James Cameron vs Hugh Carson, Hugh Gamble, James McCreight. Debt. Judgt. according to specialty exon. to be issued but not levied for three months.

James Cameron vs James McCreight, James Barkley. Debt Jugt. according to specialty exon to issue but not levied for three months.

Robert Rabb vs Frizzle McTyre. Rule made absolute.

Jona^n Belton Surv^r)　　　The cause was now called and the following
of McCleod & Belton) Debt　Jury Sworn.
　vs　　　　　　　　　　)
William Roach &　　　) Hugh Gamble, James Aikin, Saml. Alston, Quintin
Thomp^n Whitehouse　) Craig, John Cubit, Peter Curry, Wm. Coggin,
　　　　　　　　　　　　　Obed^h Henson, And^w McCoule, John Hollis, Dudley
　　　　　　　　　　　　　Curry, Edwd. Martin. Verdict we do find for the
　　　　　　　　　　　　　plaintiff the amount of the note with interest.
　　　　　　　　　　　　　　　　　　　　Hugh Gamble foreman

Charles Johnstone vs Jesse Goyen. On attatt. The same Jury sworn the Tobbaco attached Condemned. Verdict in fav^r of the pltf according to the specialty.　　　　Hugh Gamble Foreman.

John Allen Thorpe vs Mr. Wm. Parkes. On appeal Judgt. reversed. James Davis swore to 5 days attendance. Joshua Durham swore to 15 days attendance as an evidence in this cause.

Willingham vs Andrews. Case. Jacob Gibson swore to four days attendance as an evidence.

John Bell Junr. vs John Bell Senr., John Robertson. Rule discharged.

John Means vs Spencer Brumett. On attachment. Dismissed.

Johnstone vs Goyen. Jesse Haris swore to 15 days. James Gamble to 2 days attendance as an Evidence.

John Hampton vs Dudley Curry. Debt. Judgement according to specialty confessed.

William Gibson vs Daniel Huger. Case. Continued at the plaintiffs costs. William England swore to 7 days attendance and David Goyen to 7 days attendance as an evidence in the above cause.

Heartwell Macon Senr.)
　vs　　　　　　　　　) On attachment same Jury sworn except Jacob
Robert Cooke　　　　　) Gibson Junr. in the place of Edward Martin.
　　　　　　　　　　　　Verdict. We do find a verdict in favour of
　　　　　　　　　　　　the plaintiff for the sum of fifty five
　　　　　　　　　　　　pounds Virginia money
　　　　Ordered a renditioni exponas issue　　　Hugh Gamble fore^n

Henry Myers vs Henry Rugeby. Case Abated by plaintiffs Death.

H. Macon vs Cooke. Thomas Wilkinson swore to 16 days attendance as an evidence in this cause and Robert Coleman to

Exors of Alexr. Miller)   Case. Same Jury sworn except Edward Martin in
          vs   )   the place of Jacob Gibson. Verdict We find
Minor Winn   )   for the plaintiff forty two pounds Stg.
                                                    Hugh Gamble foreman
                             Stay of execution granted untill the 1st day
                             of November next.

Robert Craig   )   Case. By consent of parties ordered that each
          vs   )   party do appoint an auditor and the said admors.
Admors of William)   appoint a third who shall examine the accounts in
Boyd. deceased   )   dispute and make a report at next term and that
                             the same be admitted in evidence at the trial of
                             the cause.

Fred^k Ansminger Exor of Ansminger vs Benjn. May admors. Debt.
Dissmissed.

Robert Starke vs Minor Winn. Debt. Judg^t according to specialty with
stay of execution untill the first day of February next. Exon to be
issued but not levied untill the time granted.

John Hornsby vs William Graves. On appeal Judg^t affirmed.

Jonathan Belton vs William Briant. Debt Judg^t according to specialty
by default.

Minor Winn vs James Rogers. On appeal Judgement affirmed.

Thomas Johnstone vs David Shelton & Elijah Majors. On motion of the
defendants attorney an appeal to the Circuit Court Granted.

Proceeded to Ballot for Petit Jurors to serve at next term when the
following Persons were drawn. John Broome. John Burns. Wm Cloud.
Joseph Helms. Barth^n Turnepseed. Joseph McMorris. Richd. Tidwell,
Jas. Arnet, Wm. Bonner, James Lendy, Thos. Lesly, Joh. Abra^n Jones,
Wm. Lathan, Maddern Leggo, Adam Blair, James Hunt, Mabry Helms,
Robt. Robinson, Quintin Hoy, Clement Arlege, Henry Haigood, Walter
Aikins, Isaac Arlege, Amos Arlege, Christ^r Brack, Thomas Hill, Saml.
McKee, John Alexander, John A. Thorpe, Moses Ayner, Andrew Allen.

Proceeded to ballot for Grand Jurors to serve at next term when the
following persons were Drawn Areo^s Liles. Robt. Adams. And^w Thomas.
Zack^a Kirkland. Albert Beam. John Bell. Hugh Milling. Thomas Means.
David McQuiston. James Brown. John Bell sen^r John Johnstone. John
Ogilvie. James Kincade. Minor Winn. Adam Hawthorn. William Thompson.
Ambrose Kirkland. Hick^s Peay. Mic^h Pickett. Henry Moore. John Means.
Darling Jones. Saml. Johnstone.

Ordered that the Clerk do have his books prepared for the inspection
of the Judges or any two of them when called on.

John Havis vs John Willingham. Case refered by Consent the award to
be made a rule of Court.

Adjourned to January term next.   James Craig
                                           John Turner.

                         January Term 1795

Friday the 16th day of January 1795
Court met according to adjournment.

Present. John Turner Esquire.

Adjourned untill Tomorrow at nine o'Clock.   John Turner.

                              106

January Term 1795

Saturday the 17th day of January 1795.
Court called according to adjournment.

Adjourned by the Clerk untill Monday next.   D. Evans   C. C.

January Term 1795

Monday the 19th day of January 1795.
Court met according to adjournment.

Present.   John Turner esquire.

Ordered that George Lott be appointed overseer on the road called the
mountain gap road in the place of Abraham Miller.

Ordered that James Lewis be appointed overseer on the road leading from
Winnsborough to Camden to begin at Dutchman's Creek from thence along
the same road to the County line.

Ordered that Isaac Knighton be appointed overseer on the road called
Jones's road from the ford of Dutchman's Creek down to county line in
the place of Robert Martin deceased.

Ordered that William Bonner be appointed overseer on the main road
from Winnsborough to begin at Moses Cockerills from thence up to the
Chester county line in the place of Samuel Caldwell.

Ordered that Daniel Huffman be appointed overseer on the Sandy River
road to begin at Moses Cockrills from thence to the county line.

                              John Turner.

January Term 1795

Tuesday the 20th day of January 1795.
Court met according to adjournment.

Present John Turner esquire.

Ordered that Thomas Starke. Charles Picket. John Boykin and Alexander
Irvin be appointed Commissioners to point out the best way for a Road
to lead from the Lower ford on Dutchmans creek into the road leading
from Winnsborough to Camden with power to appoint an overseer to
open and clean out the said road and that they do make a return of
their proceedings therein at the Court to be held on the second Monday
in April next.

Adjourned untill tomorrow morng. at 9 O'Clock.

                              John Turner

Wednesday 25th Jany. 1795.
Court called and adjourned untill Tomorrow Morng at 9 O'Clock.
                         D. Evans   C. F.

Thursday 22nd Jany. 1795
Court called and adjourned untill Tomorrow Morng. at 9 O'Clock.
                         D. Evans   C. C.

Friday 23rd January 1795.
Court called and adjourned untill Tomorrow Morng. at 9 O'Clock
                         D. Evans   C. C.

Saturday 24th January 1795
Court called and adjourned untill Tomorrow Morning at 9 O'Clock
                                        D. Evans C. C.

Monday 26th January 1795
Court called and adjourned untill Tomorrow Morng. at 9 O'Clock
                                        D. Evans C. C.

Tuesday 27th January 1795
Court called and adjourned untill the 16th day of July next.
                                        D. Evans C. C.

                        July Term 1795

Thursday the 16th day of July 1795.
Court met according to adjournment.

Judges present. John Turner, Arom[s] Liles.

Aromanos Liles produced his commission and was qualified as the law
directs and took his seat as one of the Judges for this county.

List of grand Jurors being called over the following Gentlemen
answered to their named and where sworn in (Viz)
                        John Woodward Foreman
        Charles Lewis   John Bell
        Charles Picket   Edward Martin
        Phillip Raiford   Phillip Pearson
        Robert Rabb   Roland Williamson
        Samuel Alston   Thomas Starke
        John King Junr   James Arthur

Joel Wilson and Thomas Goodrum where sworn in as Constables for this
County.

Ordered that Mr. James Millar be allowed 7/ for the wintering of a
steer tolled by him.

Ordered that Jesse Fort be allowed five shillings for the keeping of a
Heifer Tolled by him.

Proceeded to draw the grand and Pettit Jurors when the following where
drawn as grand Jurors for the next Court (Viz)

        John McCamey   William Rabb
        John McKinney   William M'Mooris Senr.
        Bartlee Smith D. C.   Wm. Miles Nevit
        James Rogers   Robert Reid
        Luke Rawls   Nimrod Mitchel
        Henry Rugeley   William Holley
        John Mickle   David Hamilton
        John Havis   Robert Hancock
        James McCreight   John Harvey
        David Shelton   John Ellison
        William Kirkland   Robert Moorman
        Benjamin Owens   James Gray
        Thomas Muse   Harris Freeman
        Eligah Haigood   Archibald McQuiston
        George Ashford   Alexander Gordon

                    Pettit Jurors

        James Hannah   Robert Tidwell
        George Arnet   John Richardson
        John Smith   Andrew McDowell
        Thomas Moberly   Thomas Sant
        John Mathews   William Joiner
        Reuben Starke   Nathaniel Harbin

                        108

Thomas Hill	Jesse Wilson
William Millar	Jesse Harbin
John Waugh	Daniel McCullough
Jacob Thorp	James Bishop
John Slone	John Long senior
William Neutreville	John Boyd
Austen Peay	John Hollis
William Boyd	Jacob Wright
Charles McWane	David Long
Richard Hopkins	Nathaniel Major
Leonard Taylor	Moses Wootten
John Tidwell	William Hendrix

Jonathan Brown petitioned the court that a Dedimus be granted him to take the renunciation of Dower from Mary McKinney to him Ordered accordingly and that the same be directed to Gardner Ford and Charles Picket.

William McTyre vs James Ederington. Case. Judgement by default.

Field Farren vs John Buchanan. Case Abated by death of plaff.

Pickett and Briggs vs K. T. Strother. Debt. Discontinued by letter from Mr. Mathis Atty.

Alexander Pervis vs Robert McTyre. Att. Dismissed.

John Crosby vs Henson Day. Case. Dissmissed.

David R. Evans vs Hugh Carson. Case. Dismissed.

Jonathan Belton vs William Ferguson. Debt Dismissed at Defd Costs.

Thomas Gladney vs Minor Winn. Dismissed at the defendant to pay clerk and Sheriff Fees.

Isaac Shellhouse vs John Allen estate. Award returned and made a Rule of Court.

Robert Brodie vs Hugh Smith. Dismissed.

Robert Brodie vs David Weir. Case. Dismissed.

Nathaniel Russell vs Musco Bowler. S. P. Settled.

John Adamson vs Joel Wilson. Debt. Judgement confessed according Specialty.

James Davis, Hugh Norville vs Jonathan Belton vs William Scott. Debt. Judgement by Default.

Jonathan Belton vs Aron Dukes. Debt. Judgement by Default.

Adjourned till tomorrow 9 O'Clock.   DE C.C.
                                   John Turner
                                   Aramanos Liles

July Term 1795

Friday the 17th day of July 1795.
Court met according to adjournment.

Judges Present. John Turner, Aromanos Liles Esq[rs]

James and William Owens now appeared in open Court and acknowledged themselves perfectly satisfied with the division they have made among themselves of the goods and chattles of John Owens deceased.

Grand Jurors sworn (Viz)
Bartlee Smith Edward Andrews Samuel Procter Robert Coleman.

The Citation on the Estate of William Morgan deceased was now produced
properly (certified letters of Administration was Ordered to Christian
Morgan who was sworn accordingly, he nominated.
                                    whom the court approved of

State vs Minor Winn Ju. Pet Sar^y Bill found

State vs William Rotten, Minor Winn Jur. Mis^{or} Bill found

State vs Archibald Douglass. Pet. Lar^y Bill found

State vs William Alexander. Swin^g Bill found.

State vs
Burbage Woodard. House Ste^g Bill found

Jonathan Belton vs Jesse Simmons. Debt. settled at defendants costs.

Ordered that the amount of a certain Roan Mare Tolled by James Hollis
and sold John Craig be given to Baxter Powel he having claimed and
proved the same his property within the time limitted by Law after
deducting all expences.

Jonathan Belton vs William Street. Att. The attachment dissolved at
plaff. Cost. William Scott swore to four days attendance.

State vs Samuel Simmons. Adultry. Ordered that the recognizance be
discharged.

State vs William Alexander. Swindling. The following Jury where
impannelled to try the same.

James Johnston Foreman. Samuel Arnet, James Hogan, Kador Coleman,
Frederick Arrick, Benjamin McGraw, Ephraim Butler, Enoch Butler, Hugh
Young, Lewis Haigood, Thomas Griggs Yarborough William Johnston. who
returned the following Verdict We find for the plaintiff L 6:10.
States Damage 107. James Johnstone foreman.

Jonathan Belton vs Samuel Oats, Henry Pettipool. Debt. Dismissed at
defendants Costs.

Jonathan Belton vs William Cason. Debt. Judgement confessed at the
Defendants Costs.

Jonathan Belton vs Laban Cason. Debt. Dismissed at Defendants costs.

Jonathan Belton vs Jesse Perry. Debt. Dismissed.

Jonathan Harrison Adam Pool and Walter Pool sworn in as Constables for
the county of Fairfield.

Jonas Bedford   )
Indorsee of Mumford Wilson) Debt. We acknowledge ourselves special
        vs   ) bail in this action for the sum of thirty
John Smith   ) five pounds sterling with interest and
                                costs of suit or to render the body of
                                the defendant in execution.

                                        James Barkley
                                        Samuel Richeyson

State vs David Gray. Ass^d & Battery. True Bill found John Woodard
Foreman.

State vs William Alexander. Ordered that the defendant be committed
to the common goal for the term of six months unless the fine and costs

110

be sooner paid.   John Turner
                                     Aramanos Liles

                        July Term 1795

Saturday the 18th day of July 1795.
Court met according to adjournment.

Judges Present. John Turner, Aramanos Liles Esqrs.

John Lucas vs Este of Ephraim Pettipool. Case. Ordered that it being
represented that the Plaintiff is out of the state if he does not
appear before the last day of court that a nonsuit be entered.

Henry Rugeley)
    vs   ) Case. The following Jury were sworn to try the writ
Henry Maskall) of inquiry Enoch Butler Ephraim Butler James Hogan
                Samuel Arnet Lewis Haigood Thomas Griggs Yarborough
                Hugh Young Kador Coleman Thomas Hodge William Johnston
                James Johnston William Ackin. Jury returned we find
                for the plaintiff L Fifty pounds and costs of suit
                                     James Johnston Foreman

Henry Moore produced his commission and was qualified as the law
directs and took his seat as one of the Judges for this county.

Elijah Jones vs Minor Winn. S. P. dismissed at equal costs.

James Douglass vs Minor Winn. Case. Dismissed at plaintiffs Costs.

State vs Hugh Gourly. Misd.ͬ A true bill. Jno Woodward. Foreman
Ordered that the defendant give in fresh security himself in 100 L
his security 50 L each.

State vs Martha Odear. Bastdy. Saith upon oath that John Lee is the
Father of her child. Ordered that a Bench Warrant be issued against
John Lee. The court fined Martha ODear L5 proc. but to give security
to Indemnify the county. but that the fine be not collected till
further Orders.

State vs Nicholas Ringer. Ordered that this cause be referred till
Monday morning Stealing.

State vs Robert Ross. Pettit Larceny. True Bill found J. Woodard. For.
Benoni Robinson was sworn in as constable for this County.

State vs Minor Winn Junr. Pet. Lary. This cause being called on the
following Jury where sworn and impannelled to try the same Enoch Butler
Ephraim Butler James Hogan Samuel Arnet Lewis Haigood Thomas Griggs
Yarborough Hugh Young Cador Coleman Thomas Hodge William Johnston James
Johnston William Aikin. The Jury returned a Verdict not Guilty
James Johnston Foreman.

Mary Aytcheson vs Phillip Pearson. S. P. Continued Trover

State vs Minor Winn, William Rotten. Misdeamaner. Noli prosequient
by order of court.

State vs William Adam. Pettit Larc.y True Bill found John Woodard
Foreman.

State vs William Adams. Hog stealing. True Bill John Woodard Foreman

State vs Robert Ross. Stealing. Robert Craig delivered the defendant
into the hands of the Sheriff in discharge of his recognizance. This
Bill continued and the deft was ruled to fresh securities.
Principal L 100 Stery. to 40 each.

                              111

State vs Rolly Hughs. Assa.^t Batty. Discharged for want of prosecution.

Jonathan Belton)
    vs   ) S. P. Judgement confessed
Isaac Reynolds)
    do   ) Debt Judgement confessed.
Elijah Hollis)

Jonathan Belton vs John Gladden. S. P. Judgement confessed.

State   )   This cause being called on the following Jury
   vs   ) Pet Lar.^y where sworn and impannelled to try the same
William Adams)   Enoch Butler Ephraim Butler James Hogan
                            Samuel Arnet Lewis Haigood Thomas Griggs
                            Yarborough Hugh Young Cador Coleman Thomas
                            Hodge William Johnston James Johnston William
                            Aikin. Guilty James Johnston Foreman.

Judges of Fairfield)
      vs   ) Debt. Indorsement for the penalty of the Bond.
Peter Sarrowe   ) Ordered that the Execution be issued for the
Frizzle McTyre   ) Arrears and fine & costs only...

State vs William Alexander. Ordered that the defendant be allowed ten
days to pay his fine in & giving Security for him. Shadrack Jacobs
William Paul was sworn in as constable for this County.

Judges proceeded to elect sheriff for the county of Fairfield when it
appeared that William McMorris was duly elected.

Mr. Wm. McMorris nominated Wm. McMorris Senr Jas. Kincaid Robt Rabb &
Alex. Kincaid as his securities whom the court approved of.

                            John Turner
                            Aramanos Liles
Adjourned to Monday next   Henry Moore
  at 9 O'Clock
         D. Evans C. C.

                  July Term 1795

Monday the 20th day of July.
Court met according to adjournment.

Judges Present. John Turner. Aramanos Liles and Henry Moore Esquires

State vs Jeremiah McDaniel. Horse Stealing. A true Bill. Jno.
Woodward Foreman.

State vs Wm. Street. Steal.^g a Waggon. No Bill. Jno. Woodward
Foreman.

State vs Penny Ginn. Pet Lary. No Bill. Jno. Woodward Foreman.

James Douglas vs Admors of Wm. Durphey. Case. Dismissed at Defts
Costs, no atty's Fees to be taxed.

Jonathan Belton vs Saml. Oates & Jesse Hevis. Debt. Judgment confessed for L 55.13.3 Interest and Costs.

Thos. Knighton, Indorsee of Chas. Pickett vs Garvis Gibson. Debt.
Judgement confessed according to Specialty. Exon to be issued, but
not levied, till ordered.

Jos: Gibson Senr. vs Harris Freeman. S. P. Dismissed at plts costs.

Allende Graftenreidt vs Dennis Crosby. Debt. Dismissed at Defts Costs

Phillip Burgin vs James McCreight. Case. Dismissed.

Mary Atcheson vs Phillip Pearson. Trover. Continued by consent of
Parties intered before.

Jonathan Belton vs Est. of Samuel Hollis. S. P. Judgement confessed
for the account with Int. Stay Exon till 1st March 1796.

Jno. Gilbraith et Na vs Jno Turner et Na. Case. The action withdrawn.

Thomas Meador appeared in open court and being duly sworn made Oath
that he was present and saw Samuel Mobley Sign seal and deliver a
certain sett of Titles to Job Meadors which have been since lost for
100 Acres of land part of 200 Acres of land Originally granted to Thomas
Meadows and to the best of his recollection the said Samuel Mobley
signed the receipt for the consideration Money and that the said Job
Meadors has been in possession of the said 100 acres of land ever
since.

James Hunt   ) Debt. The following Jury where impannelled and
   vs   ) sworn to try this cause. James Johnston Foreman
Charles Pickett) Ephraim Butler Enoch Butler Cador Coleman Samuel
                  Arnet Benjamin McGraw Hugh Young William Johnston
                  James Hogin William Aikins Thomas Griggs Yarborough
                  Lewis Haigood. Jury returned their Verdict. We find
                  the defendant clear James Johnston Foreman.

Exon Fincher) Ordered that the Deposition of Jno Fincher be taken
   vs   ) before Chas. Picket & W. S. Younge to be read in
Aaron Jones) evidence on the trial. The above by consent of parties
               and also agreed that if the Deft at next Court appears
and states on Oath a just & substantial defence, and that he cannot
have his Witnesses, he may be allowed a continuance.

State vs Nicholas Ringer. The same Jury where sworn to try this
Indictment. They brought in their Verdict We find the defendant
guilty Jas. Johnston Foreman.   Stealing

State vs Nich. Ringer. Stand in county court Exon Docket of Exons
returnable to Jan.ʸ term 1796.

John Wilson vs Meridith Taylor, Aron Duke. Case Dismissed at
defendants costs.

Jonathan Belton vs Aron Wooten. Debt. Settled.

State vs Nicholas Ringer. Corn Stealing. The defendant was brought to
the Bar to receive sentnece when the court Ordered that he received
ten lashes on the bare back within half an hour. That he gives security
for keeping the peace and good behavior for twelve months himself in
100 L and his securities in 50 L each. Ordered that Ringer be committed to Goal till his fees are paid.

State vs Nicholas Ringer. Cutting out a horses tongue. Ordered that
the prosecutors and Witnesses recognizances be continued next Court.

State vs Jeremiah McDaniel. Ordered that the recognizances be forfeited and a bench Warrant do issue against McDaniel and a Scire Facias
against his securities.

State vs Moses Hollis chaleos. Sc: Fa: William Johnston Isaac Gibson
and William Kennedy when excused by the court Moses Hollis Nimrod
Smith and Moses Smith who are fined 4 Dollars each and notice to be
posted on the Court House Door to appear in October Court, to make
their defence.

Elijah Jones vs Samuel Nelson. S. P. Judgement confessed according to specialty. Execution to be staid to January next.

State vs John McCown, John Willingham. Sc. Fia. Excused being under-age. Willingham Discharged.

State vs Racheal Tidwell. Sc. Fai. Recognizance Forfeited. Ordered that the bond be sent to Chester County and suit commenced against Robert Tidwell security for Racheal Tidwell's appearance.

State vs Mary Tidwell and others. Sci. Fai. Ordered the recognizance lie over till next court that the securities may have time to bring forward the Body of Mary Tidwell.

State vs James Adams Junr. et alias. Sc Fai. Rule made absolute.

State vs William Adams & others. Sci Fai recognizances Discharged, body being surrendered.

State vs Elijah Gibson et als. Sci Fai. Continued.

State vs John Shaver. Ass^t Bat^y. Discharged.

Phillip Raiford vs Abraham Gibson. S. P. Dismissed at plaintiffs costs. Thomas Richardson sworn to six days atten^d Quintin Craig swore to thirteen days attendance this action being brought by Chas. Johnston the costs to be paid by him.

Evans and Company vs Phillip Pearson. Case. Continued.

State vs Elizabeth Watts et alias. Sci Fai. Judgement on recognizance

State vs Burbage Woodard. Horse Stealing. Ordered that he enter into recognizance to appear at Camden Court at November next the witnesses also to be bound over.

State vs Geo: Ederington. Ass^t & Battery. Ordered that a bench warrant issue against Thomas Edrington. That he may be bound over to prosecute.

State vs Eliz Adams, Jordan Ginn, Burrell Lee. Bast^{dy} Recognizances forfeited Sc Fa to Issue.

State vs Jourdan Ginn. Bast^{dy} Continued.

State vs Samuel Alston. Bast^{dy} Defendant appears and continued. demands his Trial.

State vs Thomas Wright. Stealing. Dismissed.

State vs Robert Mannion. Charged with stealing the property of Levi Wooley within this district being brought into court and it appearing to the court from information that the said Robert Mannion had broke the common goal of Pinckney district and that a bill was found against him by the grand jurors for the said district Ordered that he be committed to Pinckney goal there to stand his trial and if he should be there acquitted in that case to be committed to Camden goal and that Levi Wooley be authorized to carry him to Pinckney goal and that he be empowered to press a sufficient guard for that purpose.

Aramanos Liles
Henry Moore

Adjourned till tomorrow morning
at 9 O'Clock
        D. Evans C. C.

July Term 1795

Court met according to Adjournment
Tuesday the 21st day of July.

Judges Present. Aromanos Liles, Henry Moore

State vs Hugh Gourly. Assault. In an attempt to Ravish. The following Jury were impanneled and sworn to try the same. James Johnston Foreman Ephraim Butler Enoch Butler Cador Coleman Benjamin McGraw William Johnston Samuel Arnet James Hogan Thomas Griggs Yarborough Frederick Arrick William Aikins Thomas Hodge. The Jury returned We find the Defendant Guilty. Jas Johnston Foreman. Judgement postponed till Tomorrow morning.

William Sibley vs Admia Dl. Dansby. Sum: Pro: Dismissed, Plaintiff to pay his own Attorney & Witnesses, and the Defendant to pay the rest of the Costs.

State vs Jennet Barton, Levi Mobley. For Suspicion of Murder. Ordered that all the persons bound to this County in this case do appear at next Camden Court and that the recognizances be returned there.

State vs Margaret Knowland. Bastardy Sc Fia vs Bail and Bench Warrant agt. Margaret Knowland.

State vs George Ederington. Asst. Batty. Dismissed at Defend. Costs.

William Gibson vs Daniel Hager. Case. Daniel Gowen swore to fourteen days attendance on this suit as an evidence. and William England to fourteen days.

William Gray vs Thomas Phillips. On attat. The same Jury were impanneled and sworn to Execute a writ of Inquiry Returned. We find for the plaintiff Twenty seven pounds Two Shillings and 8 pence sterling with Costs of Suit. Jas. Johnston foreman.

Jesse Havis vs Joseph Cameron. Case referred to Arbitration.

State vs James Smith. Basdy. Recognizance continued.

Allen de Graffenreidt vs Robert Moorman. Appeal. postponed.

Adjourned till tomorrow morning at 9 O'Clock
D. Evans C.C.

Aramanos Liles
Henry Moore

July Term 1795

Wednesday 22nd day of July.
Court met according to adjournment.

Judges Present. Aramanos Liles, Henry Moore.

Edward Maynard ats Isaac Arledge) Debt. Dismissed at plaintiffs costs.

James Shaw vs Smallwood Owens James Alexr. Watson) S. P. Judgement by Default

Exors of Thos Hughes Senr. vs Robert Moorman) S. P. Judgement by Default.

Richard Winn vs Jeremiah Taylor. S. P. Judgement confessed for five pds three shillings and 7/ Interest from 13th July 1794 and Costs.

William Gibson vs Daniel Huger. Case. Continued and Ordered peremtonly for trial the first day of next Court.

Heartwell Macon Junr. vs Thomas McClurken. Case Continued

Elijah Jones vs Francis McCall. Att. This cause being brought on the following Jury were impannelled and sworn to try the collateral issue James Johnston Foreman Ephraim Butler Enoch Butler William Aikin Cador Coleman Thomas Griggs Yarborough Adam Mabry James Hogan Hugh Young William Johnston Benjamin McGraw Samuel Arnett. The Jury returned verdict. We find the property to be Robert Craigs.
                                        Jas. Johnston Foreman

State vs Hugh Gourly. Assault. The prisoner was now brought into Court to receive Judgment Ordered that he be fined 10/ put in the Stocks for two hours and be imprisoned in the goal two weeks & stand committed untill the costs be paid or the deft shall swear out.

James Davis & William Nelson vs Hugh Norville. Attat. Dismissed at Defendants Costs.

Thomas Malone vs John Winn Junior and his securities. Upon Motion. The rule having been regular by posted, the court gave Judgmt against the Sheriff and his securities for Six pound three Shillings and seven pence and ordered that Execution Issue.

State vs Margaret Knowland. Basty Ordered that George Knowland recognizance be discharged he having delivered the deft into Court. The deft having sworn the child to James Smith the court fined her 5 L proc. not to be levied till Ordered.

Jesse Havis vs Joseph Cameron. Case. Referred to Arbitration.

Bartlee Smith vs James Hoy. Trover. Dismissed.

Bartlee Smith vs Quintin Craig. Trover. Dismissed.

John Woodard vs Robert Ellison. S. P. Dismissed at Defts Costs no attorneys fees to be taxed.

John Martin vs Robert Moorman. Debt. Judgement Confessed according to Specialty with costs of suit.

Raiford vs Geo: Harston. Slander. Dismissed on Confession, he paying L 1 damages and Costs of suit.

John Wilson vs Meredith Taylor. Case. Settled Each party pays his own Costs.

Admors. of L. Owens vs John McCamey. S. P. Continued.

Alexander Cameron vs John Winn Junior. Case Nonsuit.

John Smith vs William Gibson, Robert Ewing. Debt. Judgement by Nichil dicit.

Samuel Alston vs Hugh Gamble. S. P. Judgement according to Specialty.

Burbage Woodard vs James Rabb. Case Nonsuit.

Burbage Woodard vs William Nelson. Case Nonsuit.

John Graves vs Gardner Ford Admor. of Isaac Love. Debt Judgment Received.

Minor Winn vs John Bell Senr. Case. Ordered that a Commission do Issue to take the Evidence of Wade Hampton.

Elijah Jones vs Francis McCall. Attachment dismissed. Atta^t Edward McGraw swore to 4 days attendance.

Jona. Belton vs Turner Starke & Darling Jones. Debt Judgement by Nihil Dicit Stay Execution 6 Months.

John Foley vs Huston McWaters et als. Case. Ordered that a rule Issue against Andrew McDowle to show cause why an attachment should not issue for not attending at this Court as Witness.

John Smith vs Hesse Havis. Replevin. The same Jury were impanneled and sworn to try this cause Verdict for L 8 rent due from Jno Smith to Robert Auston. Judg^t for the same & costs & the goods replevied to be returned & sold.

Ordered that the Guard summoned to watch the prisoners in the goal be paid at the rate of 2/4^d apiece each night.

Robert Moorman vs William Martin. Attachment. Hartwell Macon Jnr. Guarninee swore said "There is a Ju-gement and Execution against me in the name of William Martin but whose property it is I know not"

Ordered Moses Cockerel Licence for retailing Spiritous Liquors, for six months.

Adj^d till tomorrow 9 O'Clock   Aramanos Liles
                    D. Evans   Henry Moore

                        July Term 1795.

Thursday 23rd day of July.
The Court met according to adjournment.

Present. Aramonas Liles, Henry Moore

Charles Johnston vs Jesse Gowen. Debt. Ordered that the Cow and Calf and 3 stacks of Blades levied on under this Attachment be sold to satisfy the Debt and Costs.

Brice Miller vs Joseph Singleton. On Attah^t Judgement by default.

Joseph Quarrel vs Samuel Lowry. On Attah^t Judgement by Default.

Andrew Patterson vs Samuel Parke. Debt. Judgement by Default.

Jonathan Belton vs Henry Saunders. On atta^t Judgement by Default.

John Foley vs Huston McWaters et als. Assault and false imprisonment Continued.

Robert Moorman) Attat. This cause being called on the following Jury
     vs   ) was impanneled and sworn to try the same James
William Martin) Johnston Foreman. Ephraim Butler Enoch Butler Thos.
                 Hodge Cador Coleman Thos. Griggs Yarborough Adam
Mabry James Hogan Frederick Arrick William Johnston Benjamin McGraw
Samuel Arnit   Mistrial

Gideon Kirk vs Admors of Thos. Baker. Debt. Judgement on Bond subject to a plea of plena administravit.

William Alexander vs Admors of Thos. Baker. Debt. The same Jury were sworn and impanneled to try this writ of Inquiry Verdict We find for the plaff L 16 Sterling with interest from the 18th Decr. 1786 from and costs to be levied of the future assets which may come to the hands of the Deft.   James Johnston Foreman.

Thomas Stone et uxor vs Obediah Henson. Case

```
Thomas Stone and wife)    Slander.  The defendant demurred generally.
        vs            )    The court gave Judgement for the plaintiffs
Obediah Henson        )    in the action on the dermurrer whereupon the
                           defendant moved for leave to plead not guilty
```
and the limitation act. to the action which motion was over-ruled. but
afterwards by consent of parties the cause was agreed to be left to
the Jury who returned the following Verdict. We find for the plaintiff
twenty pounds James Johnston Foreman.

Minor Winn vs Randolph Woodard. Case. Continued

Minor Winn vs Levi Moberly. Case. Continued.

John Foley vs Huston McWaters et als. Ordered that a commission do
issue. Directed to William Robertson Minor Winn and David R. Evans
to take the deposition of William Redan De bene esse.

Alexander Cameron vs Willm(?) Gibson. Debt. Nonsuit.

Daniel Mabry vs Robert Moorman. Debt. Nonsuit.

```
Robert Ellison)    Debt.  referred to Arbitration of David Read Evans
      vs       )    and Zachariah Canty and their award to be a rule of
Daniel Brown   )    Court to be returned and entered as a Judgment of
Robert Craig   )    this Court.
```

```
John Bell Junr.   )
       vs         )    Debt.  Ordered that the Process be amended by
Jno Bell & Admors)    striking out the names of the administrators
of Jno Robinson   )    from the suit.
```

```
Robert Craig      )    Case.  The same Jury were impanneled and sworn to
     vs           )    try this Cause  Verdict. We find the within
Admors of Wm Boyd)    account to be just with Interest.
                                        James Johnston, Foreman
```

Ordered that Robert Busby be admitted to Bail and that Sherard Busby
and Nathaniel Busby be accepted as such the principle in one hundred
pounds the Securities in 50 ₺ each.

Evans Winn & Co. vs Thomas Robertson. Case. Dismissed.

Ordered that the sum of four pounds the amount of sale of a Certain
Sorrell Horse sold as a stray be returned to James Lewis he having
proved the same his property agreable to law and to the satisfaction
of the Court.

```
William Boyd Junr      )
Exor of David Motte    )    Case.  The same Jury sworn to try the cause
     vs                )    who returned the following verdict.  We find
James Brown &          )    for the plaintiff thirty pounds with
Samuel Alston          )    Interest included.    James Johnstone, foreman
Admors of William Boyd)
deceased               )
```

Ordered that Joseph Chapman and Edward Moberly be appointed Overseers
of the road leading from Gladneys old place by Burr Harrison to
Chester County line which they are to put and keep in good repair.

```
Exor of David Motte    )    William Broom swore to 12 days attendance as
     vs                )    an evidence with(?) James Moore(?) in the
Admors of William Boyd)    above suit.
```

Jeremiah McDaniel vs John Jenkins. Nonsuit.

Jeremiah McDaniel vs Richard Dorkins. Nonsuit.

John Bell Junr.) The Same Jury when sworn and impanneled to try this
     vs   ) cause who returned the following Verdict. We find
John Bell Exr) for the Plaintiff one Shilling Sterling
of John Bell)   James Johnston, foreman

Jonathan Belton)
     vs   )   Debt   Judgement by Default
William McDonald &)
Susannah Arledge)

Owen Yarborough vs Susannah Arledge Excx Moses Arledge. Decree by
Default for ᴸ 4. 4. 9.

George Patterson) Case. The same Jury sworn to try the cause who
     vs   ) returned the following verdict We find for the
David Shelton   ) plaintiff ten pounds and five pence James Johnston
                   foreman.

Joseph Brevard) Sum: Pro:
     vs   ) Decree for Amount of the Note, Interest & Costs. Stay
Minor Winn   ) Exon. three months.

State vs Burbage Woodard. Felony. Ordered that the Deft. be Discharged

Adjourned till tomorrow   Aramanos Liles
9 O'Clock   Henry Moore
          D. Evans C.C.

                         July Term 1795

Friday July 24th
Court met according to adjournment.

Judges Present. Henry Moore, Arromanous Liles Esqrs.

John Lucas vs Estate of Ephraim Pettipool. Case. Nonsuit.

Admors of Samuel Hollis vs Henry Rugeby. Case. Commission to issue
to take the deposition of Robert Henry do bene esse.

Owen Yarborough vs Susannah Arledge Execx. of Moses Arledge. S. P.
Decree for L 4:4:9. & costs.

Jonathan Belton vs William McDonald, Susannah Arledge. Debt. Judgement
by default according to specialty.

Thomas Wright vs Robert Ross. Debt. Arbitrated by consent award
returned and made a rule of court. and this suit diss.d at Defts costs
as by award

George Boilstone vs William Briant. S. P. Judgement by Default
according to specialty.

David Read Evans   )
     vs   ) S. P. Decree for L 7:5 1 with interest
Thomas Robertson   ) from 1st November 1793 and costs of suit
& Hannah Robertson   ) Stay of execution three months.
admors. of John Robertson)
deceased   )

David R Evans vs Charles Lewis. Debt. Judgement according to
specialty.

Benjamin May Adm.ᵒʳ   )
of Bryant Riley Indorsee   )
of James Kennerly   )
     vs   ) Scire facias
Kemp Strother & others   )
Exors of William Strother)   Judgement received

                              119

Robert Barkley vs Alexander Young. Case. Dismissed at plaintiffs costs.

John Havis vs John Willingham. Case. Award returned ordered to be made a Rule of Court. Stay Exon three months.

Moses Camuck vs Robert Barkley. S. P. Decree according to Specialty Stay Exon three months.

Jas. Cameron vs John Winn Junr. and his securities. Rule on motion the notice having been regularly posted and the money proved to be paid the Sheriff. Judgment for 15. 19^S 2^P and Interest from the time of payment.

Robert Craig vs John Robertson. On appeal.

John Bell Junr. vs John Bell. On motion for new Trial. The same was denied by the Court.

On petition of Mary Tucker, Radford Tucker & Rebecca Tucker, orphans That Robert Tidwell be appointed guardian for the said Children and that the clerk be empowered to take a Bond from the said Robert Tidwell with two good securities in the sum of L 300 for his due a security with this court for his guardianship.

Ordered that so much of the rule respecting Robert Mannion as relates to Levi Wooley be recinded and that the name of Jesse Havis be inverted in the plea of Levi Wooley.

Ordered that a Bench warrant do issue against Levi Moberly and Jane Barton to bind them over to appear at Camden and that a Magistrate be directed to bind over all the Witnesses against the said Levi Moberly in a charge of Murder returned into this Court.

The Court having received information of a heinous Charge brought against Levi Moberly. and it being inconsistent that any person under such charge should remain in public office Ordered that the said Levi Moberly be and he is hereby suspended from being or acting in the office of Constable in the County of Fairfield. and that he be served with a copy hereof.

Aramanos Liles
Henry Moore

Adjourned till tomorrow
9 O'Clock
      D. Evans C.C.

July Term 1795

Saturday the 25th day of July 1795
Court was called according to adjournment.
Adjourned untill Monday morning 9 O'Clock.

D. Evans   C.C.

July Term 1795

Saturday the 25th, July.

None of the Judges attending this day to open Court, the Clerk adjourned the same by public proclamation, to Monday next, the 27th Instant, at 9 O'Clock.

D. Evans   C.F.C.

July Term 1795

Monday the 27th day of July 1795.
Court met according to adjournment.

Judges Present.   John Turner, Areomanus Liles and Henry Moore Esq[r].

William McMorris Junior having been elected sheriff for the county of Fairfield. now produced his Commission in open court and took the oaths of allegiance and office as prescribed by law.

Ordered that John McNeal be allowed the sum of six shillings for keeping a stray Heifer tolled by him and sold for the benefit of the County.

Ordered that James Weir be allowed the sum of ten Shillings for raising twelve pigs and sold for the use of the county.

Ordered that the late sheriff and his deputies do deliver up to the present sheriff all executions for Debts or costs remaining in their hands unsatisfied and other papers relative to the office of sheriff. and that the present sheriff do return a schedule thereof into the clerks office as soon as received.

Ordered that the presentments of the grand Jurors of this term be printed in the Columbia Gazette excepting Only such clauses as relate to the police of the county.

John Rabb was sworn in as Deputy Sheriff for the County of Fairfield.

Daniel Taylor was sworn in as a Constable for the County of Fairfield.

Ordered that Public Notice be given to all the overseers on leading or public roads in this county to put the same in good repair otherwise upon neglect and complaint made thereof to the court that they will be heavily fined.

Ordered that William Faris be appointed overseer to open and keep in repair the road leading from Samuel Caldwells to John Bells old place and from thence to the Chester County Line.

Ordered that the following persons be appointed overseers on the following roads that is to say --

James Cameron from the road leading from Winnsboro to Thomas Sents place and Samuel Gladney from thence to Cole Winns old place on little river Robert Ellison on the road leading from Winnsboro to John Stinsons place. and William Robertson on the road leading from Winnsboro to John Woodards place.

Ordered that the clerk do notify the Judges of Kershaw County that Minor Winn and Charles Picket esquires are appointed commissioners for this County to run out the line between Fairfield & Kershaw counties.

                    John Turner
                    Aramanos Liles
                    Henry Moore

                January Term 1796

Saturday the 16th day of January 1796
Court met according to Adjournment.

The waters being out and all creeks impassable none of the Judges attended therefore the clerk called the court and adjourned the same untill Monday the 18th.
                    D. Evans   C.F.C.

                January Term 1796

Monday the 18th day of January 1796
Court met according to adjournment.

Judges Present. John Turner, Areomanos Liles, Henry Moore Esq.[r]

Captain John Buchanan petitioned the court for a license to keep a house of entertaiment and retail spiritous liquors which was ordered accordingly with his giving bond and security.

Ordered on application that licenses granted to the following persons be rendered (VIZ) Samuel Johnstone, Samuel McKee, James Austin, William Langley, Claton Smith and Henry Hughey.

William Miller petioned the court for a license to keep a house of entertainment and retail spirituous liquors which was ordered accordingly with his giving bond and security.

Daniel Brown Esq.[r] the county attorney having neglected his duty. Ordered that Mr. William Smith be appointed to act pro temporary as county attorney.

Henry Moore produced his commission as one of the Judges of this court. And was qualified as the law directs.

The list of the grand Jurors being called the following gentlemen appeared and where sworn in (viz)

John Mickle Foreman	Henry Rugely
James Gray	William McMorris Sen.[r]
John Harvey	James Rogers
James McCreight	Archibald McQuiston
John Havis Senr	Robert Reid
Alexander Gordon	Luke Rawls

Benjamin Owens

John Foley) Ordered that a Rule Issue against
vs) Case. Samuel Arnet to show cause why an
Huston McWaters et als) Attachment should not issue against
him for contempt as not attending as
a witness in the above cause.

State) Asst.
vs) & True Bill Ordered that a Bench warrant do Issue
Thomas Stone) Batt[y] against the defendant.

State)
vs) Cutting out the
Nicholas Ringer) Tongue of a mare True Bill

William Clanton vs Isaac Reynolds. S. P. Decree according to specialty Interest & Costs.

James Lyon Admor of Joseph Lyon vs John Martin. Case. Abated by death of the plaintiff.

Quintin Craig vs Jere.[h] Taylor. Case. Dismissed

Quintin Craig vs Mere.[h] Taylor. Case. Dismissed.

State vs Jane Handley, Elij.[h] Hill. Bench Warrant. Ordered that the bench warrant be rendered.

State vs Mary Tidwell & others. Sci Fa. Time giving to produce Mary Tidwell by next court.

State) Lar[y] Ordered that the cause stand over till the last
vs) day of this term and that then if the evidence in
Robert Ross) behalf of the state does not appear that then the
defendant be discharged. also ordered that a Sci
Fa do Issue against Samuel Green the evidence in
the above case. and his securities and a bench
warrant against Samuel Green.

122

State vs Jese McDaniel & others. Sci Fa. Time given to the securities
to bring in the body of Jese McDaniel by next court.

Adjourned to tomorrow   John Turner
10 O'Clock   Aramanos Liles
                               Henry Moore

January Term 1796

Wednesday the 20th of January 1796.
Court met according to adjournment.

Judges Present. Henry Moore, John Turner, Areomanos Liles Esquires.

p^a9/4. The last will and Testament of Robert Coleman was produced
         proved and approved of and letters testamentary ordered to
         William Chapman and Ishia(?) Moberly. Executors of the within
         named and William Chapman was sworn in.

John Lewis vs James Craig. S. P. Debt. Decree for ten pounds. stay
Exon three months.

Thomas Parrot Junr. Indoree. of Ringer vs William Nelson. Sums Petn.
Debt. Decree according to Specialty Stay Exon. 3 months.

The Citation on the Estate of William Hill Deceased was now produced
legally published letters of administration where ordered to be granted
to Abel Hill Asaph Hill and Thos. Moberly. who were sworn in at the
same time the following persons were nominated as appraisers (viz0
Danel Mabry. Micajah Moberly Isham Moberly. Cullen Moberly. Job
Meadow whom the court approved of.

Ordered that the personal estate be sold giving a twelve months
credit with good security.

State vs Jane Handley. Thomas Handley. Asst. Batty. Bench Warrant
renewed.

State vs Catharine McClurken and others. Sci Fa. Dismissed.

State vs Elizabeth Adams. Bastdy. Recognizance forfeited Scire Facias
to Issue.

State vs Jourdan Ginn. Bastdy. Recognizance forfeited Scire Facias
to issue.

State vs Samuel Alston. Basy. Ordered that if the prosecutrix does
not appear by the last day of the term that the dependant be discharged.

Ordered that Charity Sweet be allowed the sum of 9 Shillings (including
three shillings paid the Magistrate) for wintering a steer.

State vs Jere.^h McDaniel. On Sci Fa.

State vs Jourdin Ginn & B. Lee. On Sc: Fa. Rule made absolute.

State vs Eliz. Adams Jas. Adams & Saml. Croslin. On Sc: Fa. Rule made
absolute.

State vs Eliz. Dabney. Basdy. Recognizances Forfeited.

State vs Silas Beard. Basdy Continued. Deft demanded his trial.

Robert Moorman vs Allen de Graffenridt. Appeal. Judgement confirmed
Wm. Hobson swore to two days attendance.

Allen de Graffenridt vs Robert Moorman. Sum pro open sect. 4.5.2 3/4
Judgement confessed Wm. Hobson swore to Six days attendance.

123

John Murphey vs Drury Bishop. Sun.^{y} process. Decree for plaintiff according to Specialty.

Robert Cook   ) Case. The following Jury were impannelled and
    vs   ) sworn to try the same (viz) John Tidwell John
Heartwell Macon Junr.) Hollis, Thomas Hill, William Boyd, John Stone,
                        John Smith, Leonard Taylor. Nathaniel Major.
Robert Tidwell Thomas Saint David Long and George Arnet. Jury returned their verdict We find for the plaintiff L 7.12.9 and costs of suit. John Smith Foreman.

William Gibson vs Daniel Huger. Case. Nonsuit.

William Robinson vs William Handley. S. P. Dismissed.

Jona Belton vs Hugh Carson. S. P. Decree for plt.

Admors. of Lewis Owens vs John McCamey. S. P. Continued

David Evans vs Francis Palmore, James Davis. S. P. note. Decree according to specialty.

On the presentment of the grand Jury Ordered that a Rule Issue against Thomas Nelson to show cause why he should not be fined for keeping a disorderly house. and retailing Spirituous liquors contrary to law. and that Mary Watson be summoned as an Evidence.

John Folley   ) Case. The same Jury were sworn and impanneled to
    vs   ) try the same Jury returned We find the defendant not
Huston McWaters)   guilty John Smith foreman. Samuel Arnet swore to
& others   ) 9 days attendance and Andrew McDowle swore to 20
                     days.

Charles Pickett vs John Byrd. Attat. Discharged.

Admors. of J. Hollis vs Henry Rugely. Case. Continued.

State vs John Ammons. Indt. for Horse Stealing Jas. Moody Pros.^{r} No pros. nor witnesses appearing. Ordered that John Ammons be discharged from confinement.
                        John Turner
                        Aramanos Liles
                        Henry Moore

                    Thursday. January 21st 1796.

Court met according to adjournment.

Judges Present. John Turner, Henry Moore and Areomanos Liles Esquires

Thomas Starke vs John Mickle & wife. Case. Dismissed.

Ordered that the administrators of Henry Hails Deceased have liberty to dispose of his goods and chattels at twelve months credit taking good security.

Robert Craig vs John Robertson. Appeal. Judgement confirmed.

James Kincaid vs Samuel Parks. Attat. Judgement by default.

John Bell Exor of Hugh Donnelly. vs Joseph Cameron. Case Dismissed at defts costs.

Joseph Quarrell vs James Lowry. Attat. Continued.

Brice Miller vs Joseph Singleton. Attat. continued.

Minor Winn vs Randolph Woodard. Case. Contd. at pltfs costs.

Minor Winn vs Levi Moberly. Case. Contd. at plaintiffs costs.

James Rogers vs Isaiah Coleman. Appeal from Magistrates Judgement.
The Judgement reversed.

James Rabb vs Thomas Parrot. Rep.n Judgement for Plaintiff.

Jesse Ginn vs John Tidwell. Case. The following Jury where impanneled
and -worn to try this cause (viz) John Smith foreman John Richardson
Robert Tidwell Thomas Hill William Boyd John Slone Leonard Taylor.
Nathaniel Major. Thomas Saint David Long. George Arnet. Daniel
McCullock who returned the following Verdict for the defendant.
John Smith Foreman.

State vs Nicholas Ringer. Cutting out the tongue of a mare. Ordered
That the prosecutor and the Evidence be bound over to next Camden court
as well as the Defendant.

Adjournment till tomorrow   John Turner
10 O'Clock   Areamanos Liles
                                   Henry Moore

                       January Term 1796

Friday 22nd January 1796
Court met according to adjournment.

Judges present. John Turner Areomanus Liles, Henry Moore.

Thomas Means vs Darling Tidwell on attachment. On motion that the
Defendant be ruled to special Bail. the defendant being called made
default thereupon Ordered that the property attached be sold.

Admors. of Milling vs Richard Winn. Debt. Nonsuit.

Ordered that James Arther be allowed five pounds for the attendance
on and burying William Craig a pauper only deducting the amount of
Craigs property on a fair valuation to be certified by Henry Moore.
Esqr.

Jesse Ginn)   The following evidence swore to their attendance
    vs   ) Case   (Viz)
John Tidwell)   Eli Tidwell 3 days
                               John Stevens 3 do.
                               John Tidwell Junr. 2 days
                               Obediah Henson 4. do
                               Simon Tidwell 3. do

Frederick Arrick vs John Bagwell. Case. The following Jury were
sworn and impannelled to try this cause (viz) John Smith Foreman John
Richardson Robert Tidwell Thomas Hill John Slone Leonard Taylor,
William Miller Daniel McCollouck George Arnet. Nathaniel Major. Thomas
Saint David Long who returned the following verdict We find for the
plaintiff L 2.5.0 & Costs. Zich: Kirkland Swore to 5 days Attendance
John Smith foreman   Sam: Croslin 23D^S Jesse Sibley 4.
                      days, Jno. Croslin 4 D^S

John Adair   ) Debt. John Ellison entered himself as a Security
    vs   ) for Costs, in behalf of plaintiff.
Alex^r Kennedy &)
James Craig   ) John Atckison was appointed Constable in the room
                    of William Paul.

John Adair   ) Debt. The same Jury except William Boyd in the room
    vs   ) of William Miller were Impannelled and Sworn to try
Alexr. Kennedy &)) the same who returned the following Verdict. We find
Jas. Craig   ) for the plaintiff according to specialty
                                       Jon^o Smith foreman

                          125

George Knowland vs Jeremiah Cockerill. S. P. Trover. Dismissed at plaintiffs costs.

Martha Johnstone vs James Kincaid. Continued at plaintiffs costs.

Exors of Thomas Hughs vs David Shelton. Debt. The same Jury returned their verdict we find for the plaintiff according to specialty and cost of suit.   John Smith foreman

Francis Sumer vs Havis Feeman. Debt. The same Jury returned We find for the plaintiff according to Specialty and cost of suit.
                                        J. Smith Foreman

One application to the court by the friends of the children of William Colhoun deceased showing that their mother Catherine Colhoun was married to Patrick McConnell desireing that the Judges would take some method to secure the property left them by their Father. whereupon the court appointed Patrick & Catharine McConnell late Colhoun and James Hindman their guardian and that they should give bond in three hundred pounds penalty with two good securities for the due performance of the trust reposed in them they proposed James Arthur and George Beasely as securities whom the court approved of.

Mary Aytckeson vs Phillip Pearson. S. P. Trover. The same Jury returned we find the possession of the property not being sufficiently proved the Court ordered a nonsuit to be entred

Jas. Rabb swore to ten days Attendance Thomas Dent. swore to fifteen days. do. being two hundred miles and four ferrages.
                                        John Turner
                                        Aramanos Liles
                                        Henry Moore

                    January Term 1796

Saturday 23rd January 1796.
Court met according to adjournment.

Judges Present. John Turner. Areomanos Liles and Henry Moore.

On application of Thomas Nelson for a license to keep a tavern and retail spiritous liquors. Ordered that the same be granted on his giving security.

Ordered that John Gwin, William Johnson, and John Johnson be commissioners to inspect and examine that part of the road now leading by John Gwin and coming into the old road between sd Gwins and Thomas Means and that the commissioners give their opinion in Writing at April court. next. whether it should be continued where it was heretofore.

James Murdock was appointed Overseer in the room of Levi Moberly.

The citation on the Estate of John Harrison was returned certified Ordered that letters of Administration be granted to Minor Winn Esquire John Wilson and David Read Evans securities whom the court approved of.

Joseph Bradley vs John Wilson. Dismissed.

Miner Winn vs Levi Moberly. John Richardson swore to 11 days attendance in this suit.

Exors. of Samuel Neal vs Jono Winn Junr. & securities. Rule. Decree for L6.3.3. and cost of suit.

State vs Archibald Douglass. Stealg. Corn. The following Jury were impannelled and sworn to try this cause (viz) John Smith foreman,

John Hollis, Robert Tidwell, Daniel McCullock, Nathaniel Major, William
Boyd, John Richardson, John Slone, Thos. Saint, George Arnet, David
Long, Thomas Hill who returned the following Verdict Defendant not
Guilty.   John Smith, Foreman

State vs David Gray. Asst. Batty. The same Jury was sworn & returned
their verdict We find the defendant Guilty of the assault.
                    John Smith foreman

George Harson appeared in open court and acknowledged the signing
sealing and delivery of a conveyance to James Hendrix of a tract of
land containing twenty two Acres being part of a tract originally
granted to John Sibley situated on the waters of Mill Creek and Little
River.

Admors. of Milling vs Richard Winn. Ordered by consent of the Defts
Attorney that this cause be reentered on the Docket.

Ordered that the Rule made last court for Suspending Levi Mobley from
the office of Constable be now discharged.

William Yarborough was appointed Constable and took the oaths prescribed
by Law.

Joshua Durham vs William Nelson. Debt. The same Jury was Impannelled
and sworn to try the same, and brought in their Verdict, We find for
the plaintiff Seventeen pounds and Costs of suit.
                    John Smith. Foreman

State   )   Hugh Ronalds swore to 9 days attendance
  vs   )   James Dickson Swore to 2 days Do
David Gray)   Thos. Rousham Swore to 6 days Do
              Robt. Phillips Do. 6 Do. Do.

Thos. May vs Jno L. Dabney. Att.ᵗ Decree for Ten pounds

Ordered that the perishable property in the hands of Thorpe Parrot be
sold and that a rule issue against Jacob Gibson to show Cause why an
attachment should not issue against him for not appearing as a garnishee
in this cause being duly summoned.

John Smith vs Saml. Pearson, James Pearson. Debt. Ordered that a
commission issue to take the deposition of the subscribing witness
to the bond in this case.

Robert Barkley vs Francis Papp. Appeal. Judgt. Affirmed

James Dodds vs Andrew Boyd. App.¹ Judgement confirmed.

John Campbell vs James McMullin, Samuel McMullin. Debt Judge.ᵗ by
Default.

Heartwell Macon Junr. vs William Martin, David Shelton. Attat. Judgt.
by Default.

Jonathan Belton vs Thomas Jones. Debt. Judge.ᵗ confessed for forty
pounds one shilling with interest from 10th June 1795 according to
specialty.

Josiah Knighton and Thomas Knighton were appointed overseers on the
road leading from John Goodrum to Boilstones in the room of John and
William Hollis.

Proceeded to draw the grand and Petit Jurors when the following were
drawn as grand Jurors for the next court. (viz)

Richard Winn	Charles Lewis	Jacob Lewis
Bartet Smith	Thomas Starke	John Mickle
Jno. Bell Senr.	Alexr. Gordon	Robert Rabb

James Brown	William Kirkland	David Quiston
James Rogers	Areo⁶ Liles	David Hamilton
Albert Beam	David Shelton	John King
Hezekiah Ford	John Andrews	William Shether
John McCamey	George Ashford	Luke Rawls
Zack. Kirkland	William Watson	Alexr. Kennedy
Edward Martin	William Thompson	Chas. Picket

Petit Jurors

James Lucas	Alex. Cameron	Darling Jones
Joseph Arledge	Alexr. McEwen	Shadrack Jacobs
Jacob Summerland	Irtheo Mobley	John Badgers
John Neily	John Turner Tay^r	Meredith Taylor
Edmund Tidwell	Robert Barkley	John Trap
William Pinks	William Trap	Jacob Turnepseed
Jeremiah Taylor	William Pennet	Jno. Armstrong
Thos. Johnstone	Andrew Younger	James Porter
William Kennedy	Asaph Hill	John Harris
Abraham Mayfird	Zack. Hill	Andrew McQuiston
Thos. Mickle	Wm. Morgan Junior	Nickreal Henning
James Henning	John Kelly	David Thompson

Robert Miller and Robert Rabb now produced the citation on the Estate of Daniel Miller deceased. property certified.

Ordered that the administration be granted they proposed James Rogers and William McMorries as securities whom the court approved of Administrators Sworn.

State vs David Gray. Asst. Batty. The defendant David Gray was fined six Dollars and to have three months to pay the same in.

Adjourned to next Court   John Turner
in course   Aramanos Liles
                               Henry Moore

July Term 1796

Saturday the 16th day of July 1796.

None of the Judges attending this day to open court the Sheriff adjourned the same till Monday next the 18th Instant at 9 O'Clock.

July Term 1796

Monday 18th day of July 1796.
Court met according to adjournment.

Judges Present. Areomanos Liles, John Turner

James McCreight and Barthelomeus Turnepseed petitioned the Court for a Licence to keep a Tavern and retail spirituous liquors ordered accordingly.

James Rabb was appointed overseer in the room of John Ogilvie on the road leading from Thomas Means to Columbia being from the forks of the Road going to Shireys Ferry and from thence to James Wards.

Admors of Lewis Owens vs John McKemie. S. P. Referred to the arbitration of James Beard (Carpenter) and Colonel John Pearson with leave fro them to chuse an umpire.

Jonathan Bratton vs Samuel Oaters, Jesse Havis. On motion ordered that the sheriff be allowed to sell the property of the Defendant Samuel Oates taken under execution at the house of said Samuel Oates on

128

the first Saturday in Sept? next giving due and legal notice thereof.

The list of the Grand Jurors being called over the following gentlemen
appeared and were sworn in (viz)

Thomas Starke Foreman   William Thompson
Robert Rabb   William Kirkland
George Ashford   John Brown
John Andrews   Alex? Gordon
Alex? Kennedy   Charles Pickett
David Hamilton   Zach Kirkland

Jonathan Belton vs William Miller. Debt L 15. Judgement confessed
for L 41"8" 11. to be paid January next the residue in January 1798
L 16"4"5 and Interest thereon from the 11th April 1794 and Interest
on the whole from this day.

Jonathan Belton vs William Miller & Isaac Arledge. S. P. Debt.
Judgement confessed stay Exon. for one half untill January 1797.
and the other half untill January 1798.

Jesse Havis vs Joseph Cameron. Case Settled defts pays costs.

James Stone vs Obediah Henson. Slander Nonsuit.

Jonathan Belton vs Henry Sanders. Attat. Docketed this court by
mistake their having been a Judgement obtained last court.

Chris? Bowler vs James Stone & Thomas Stone. Case Judg? by Default.

Thomas May vs John L. Dabney. Attat. Jacob Gibson sworn as Garnishee
That he has neither money nor property of any kind of the Defts.

John Sanders vs Exors of Nathan Sanders. Case. Ordered that a
commission do issue to examine Henry Sanders in the State of No.
Carolina as a witness.

Robert Tidwell vs William Sims Junr. Debt. Settled.

The list of Petit Jurors being called over the following gentlemen
appeared and where sworn in viz.

               Meredith Taylor, foreman
James Porter   Zachariah Hall   Jere? Taylor
Robert Barkley   Andrew McQuiston   John Neely
William Pinks   John Turner   John Kelly
David Thompson   William Kennedy

                       John Turner
                       Aramanos Liles

July Term 1796

Tuesday 19th of July 1796.
Court met according to adjournment.
Judges Present. John Turner and Arreomanos Liles Esqrs.

Ordered that Benjamin McGraw be appointed Overseer in the place of
Shadrack Jacobs on the road leading from Shirers ferry to Thomas
Means.

State vs John Lee. Bench Warrt. Ordered that the bench warrant be
renewed.

State vs James Andrews, Quintin Craig, Robert Craig. Asst. Batty.
True Bill Ordered that a bench Warrant do Issue against Robert Craig
Traversed till next court.

State vs Elizabeth Dabney, John L. Dabney. Sc fa on recogee. Rule
made absolute.

State vs John Craig. Sc fa. Ordered that he be discharged from his recognizance on paying his costs.

Ordered that William Randal be allowed six shillings for the Wintering of a Stray Steer.

Robert Ellison vs Heartwell Macon, Robert McTyre. Case. The following Jury where impanneled and sworn to try this cause (VIZ) David Thompson foreman, Meredith Taylor, Jeremiah Taylor, Edmund Tidwell Robert Barkley Wm. Pinks Andrew McQuiston John Betty John Turner Shadrack Jacobs William Kennedy John Nealey We find for the plaintiff L 9"18"4 and costs

David Thompson Foreman

Minor Winn by Samuel Gladney vs Enoch James & Joseph James. S. P. Judgement confessed for nine eight shillings and six pence Stay of Exon. untill 14th Novr. 1796.

Minor Winn by) In this case Benjamin May Security for the appearance
Samuel Gladney) of Enoch James came into court and surrendered the
vs   ) body of the said Enoch James in discharge of his bail
Enoch James   ) bond. and John Barker acknowledged himself special
& Joseph James) bail in this action for the sum of nine pounds eight
              shillings and six pence with costs of Suit or to
              render the body of the defendant Enoch James in
              Execution.   John Barker

Lewis Denkins vs James Craig. Case. Judgement confessed accordingly to note and costs to be in Sheriffs hands but not served for three months.

Jonas Bedford) Whereas now at this day to wit on the nineteenth day
vs   ) of July in the year of our Lord one thousand seven
John Smith   ) hundred and ninety six the said John Smith being in
              the custody of the sheriff of the said county of
Fairfield came into court and confessed Judgement for the sum of thirty five pounds with interest from the twenty third day of May one thousand seven hundred and ninety five according to the note and the said John Smith being unable to pay the same and claiming the benefit of the acts of the general assembly made for the relief of Insolvent Debtors and having taking the oaths prescribed and required by the said acts. It is ordered that the said John Smith be discharged from the custody of the said sheriff no good cause being shown to the contrary on motion of Wm. Smith Defts. Atty.

Minor Winn by) Burr Harrison came into court and delivered the body
Samuel Gladney) of Joseph James in discharge of his bail bond and
vs   ) John Baker acknowledged himself special bail in this
Enoch James   ) case for the sum of nine pounds Eight Shillings and
Joseph James) Six pence and costs of Suit or to render the body of
              the said Joseph James in Execution.
                                 John Barker

Bruce Miller vs Joseph Singleton. Attat. Judgement by Deft. at last court. Continued.

Thomas Nelson vs Henry McCoy. App^l Settled by consent of parties.

William Starke vs Exors of John Graves. Debt. Continued.

John Turner
Aramanos Liles
Henry Moore

July Term 1796

Wednesday the 20th day of July 1796
Court met according to adjournment.

130

Judges Present.   John Turner, Arramanos Liles and Henry Moore, Esquires.

The Last will and testament of Marcellus Littlejohn was produced proved and approved of and Letters Testamentary was thereupon ordered to be granted to Thomas Robertson and Jonathan Harrison Executors named in the said Will who were qualified accordingly.

Minor Winn vs John Bell Senr. Case. The following Jury where impanneled and sworn to try this cause (viz) David Thompson foreman, Meredith Taylor, Jeremiah Taylor, Edmund Tidwell, Robert Barkley, William Pinks, Andrew McQuiston, Jimpsey Porter, John Turner, Shadrack Jacobs William Kennedy and John Nealy who returned the following verdict we find for the Defendant.   David Thompson foreman.

State vs James Thomas. Horse Stealing. Ordered that a bench warrant do issue against the Defendant.

Christopher Ederington vs Daniel Mabry. Case. James Davis came into court and acknowledged himself security for the costs of the plaintiff he living out of the State.   James Davis

Christopher Ederington vs Daniel Mabry. Case. Continued.

State vs William Hollis. Asst. Batty. Noli Prosequi

State vs John Lee. Bench Warrt. to be renewed.

William Martin vs Heartwell Macon Junr. fi fa. Ordered that the sheriff do pay over the monies recovered in this case to Samuel Mathis attorney on record.

Robert Moorman vs William Martin. Attat. Dismissed.

Minor Winn vs Randolph Woodard. Case. Continued untill tomorrow.

Exors of Aron Fincher vs Aaron Jones. Debt. The same Jury were impanneled to try this issue who returned the following verdict. We find for the plaintiffs amount of Note and Interst.
                                        David Thompson foreman

Admors of Saml. Hollis vs Henry Rugeley. Case. The same Jury were impannelled to try this Issue who returned the following verdict we find for the plaintiff four pounds twelve shillings and six pence in full above all accounts.   David Thompson

State vs William Randal. Inds. Convent an Estray. True Bill

State vs Richard Wood otherwise Richard Adams. Break of goal. True bill.

State vs Amos Beal Barker and Arthur Yarborough. Indc.^t Stea§ Money. No Bill

State vs James Smith. Bastdy. The court fined James Smith and Margaret Nowland the sum of three pounds ten shillings each and Costs of Court Eighteen months given them to pay the fine in on giving good security.

State vs Richard Wood otherwise Richard Adams. Breakg Goal. Ordered that a Bench Warr^t do issue against the defendant.

Martha Johnston vs James Kincaid. Case. The same Jury were sworn and impanneled to try this Issue. who returned the following Verdict we find for the defendant with cost of suit. David Thompson foreman. John Bell swore to four days attendance on the above suit.

Jonathan Belton vs Robert Ewing & William Ewing. Debt. Settled.

131

John Smith vs James Peirson & Samuel Peirson. Debt. Dismissed each party paying half the whole costs.

James Lewis vs John Bradley. Case. The same Jury were sworn and impannelled to try this issue who returned the following verdict we find for the Plaintiff Eight pounds five shillings.

David Thompson

Zachariah Lewis swore to 5 days attendance in the above
John Turner
Aramanos Liles
Henry Moore

July Term 1796

Thursday the 21st day of July 1796.
Court met according to adjournment.

Judges Present. John Turner. Areemanus Liles and Henry Moore Esquires.

Jonathan Belton vs William Street. Debt on note.

William Street vs Jonathan Belton & Nathaniel Ford. Debt on attachment Bond.

William Street vs Jonathan Belton. Case Malcious Prosecution.

The above three cases referred by Consent to the Arbitration and award of James Craig, Darling Jones and John Boykin. the arbitrators to meet at the house of James Lewis on the twenty sixth day of September next. and that the said arbitrators have power to adjourn from time to time or untill such times afterwards as they shall appoint for the purpose of arbitrating the above causes and making their award. which award is to be returned at January term next and made a rule of Court. And ordered that the Evidences be subjoined to attend at the time & place of arbitration.

Minor Winn vs Randolph Woodard. Case dismissed.

Minor Winn vs Levi Moberly. Case Dismissed.

Isham Shurling vs James Alexr. Watson. Debt. Judgement accoring to specialty.

Minor Winn vs James McCreight. Case. Continued under a pereramtory order for trial next court.

Heartwell Macon Junr. vs Robert Cook and John Means. Debt. On motion ordered that the plaintiff have leave to amend his writ by inserting therein the name of John Winn Junr. otherwise called John Winn Junr. Sheriff of the County of Fairfield it being sworn to have been agreed to by the Parties Continued

J. Heartwell Macon Junr. acknowledge myself security for the Costs in the above suit John Winn named plaintiff residing out of the state, if the suit is adjudged against plaintiff. H. Macon Junr.

Robert Craig vs Robert Ross. Attat. Dismissed at defts costs.

Richard Davis vs John Stokes. Attat. Nonsuit.

John Leslie vs Henry McCoy. Reptn. Nonsuit.

Jonathan Belton vs Whitehouse Cason. Debt. Settled.

Samuel Crosslin vs Robert Boyd. S. P. Trover. Dismissed.

Agness Brown vs Jonathan Bannes. Slander. settled.

Jesse Havis vs John Long. Debt. Judgement confessed for L 10" s 18"
D 2 1/4.

Simeon Theus &)	DEILON.	The following Jury were impanneled and
John G Guignard)	DEBT.	sworn to try this cause (VIZ) David
vs)	L 1500.	Thompson foreman Meredith Taylor Jeremiah
Charles Lewis)		Taylor Edmund Tidwell Robert Barkley
Robert Ellison)		William Pinks Andrew McQuiston James Porter
Samuel W. Yongue)		John Turner John Kelly William Kennedy
Robert Craig)		and John Nealy who returned the following

verdict we find for the plaintiffs twenty
pounds seventeen shillings and five pence.
David Thompson. foreman

Christopher Bowler)	Case	Ordered that the Judgement by default
vs)		be set aside.
James Stone)		
Thomas Stone)		

Robert Forsythe)		
vs)	S. P.	Decree for Eight pounds ten shillings with
John Bradford)	Trover	cost of suit.

Robert Rabb as)	Case.	The same Jury were sworn and impanneled to
Guardian of)		try this issue. who returned the following
James Powell)		verdict we find for the plaintiff nine pounds
vs)		and eight pence half penny with interest
John Ogilvie)		from the 7th March eighty three

David Thompson fore[n].

Robert Rab as Guardian)
of James Powel) On motion of Mr. Starke attorney for the
        vs   ) Defendant that this cause was not cognizable
John Oglivie   ) in and without the jurisdiction of this court
                   and on that ground the party praying an
appeal Ordered that the same be granted - he proposing Jacob Gibson
and Thomas May for his Security of whom the court approved.

                        Aramanos Liles
                        Henry Moore

                  Friday 23rd of July 1796

Court met according to adjournment.

Judges Present. John Turner, Areomanos Liles, Henry Moore Esq[rs]

Thomas Means vs John L. Bradford. Debt. Judgement accordingly to
specialty.

John Tolley vs Admors of Durphey. S. P. Decree for L 3"6"10.

John Means vs Minor Winn. Debt. Judgement confessed according to
specialty stay Exon. four months.

Nicholas Peay vs William Starke. Debt. Judgement according to
specialty stay Exon. four months.

Wm. Nelson & Lewis Owens vs Phillip Pearson. S. P. Decree according
to Specialty with Interest and costs.

David Thompson vs Duke Wm. Harris. Attat. continued by affadavit pltf
paying costs.

Thomas Means vs Darling Tidwell. Attat. decree for L 6"1"2.

Trea^s of So. Carolina) Debt. The following Jury were sworn and
       vs   ) impannelled to try this issue (viz)
John Winn et alias   ) David Thompson foreman Meredith Taylor
Jeremiah Taylor Edmund Tidwell Robert
Barkley William Pinks Andrew McQuiston James Porter John Turner John
Kelly William Kennedy and John Nealy. who returned the following
verdict we find for the plaintiff sixteen pounds one shilling and nine
pence.   David Thompson Fore^n

Heartwell Macon Junr vs William Martin and Thomas Shelton. Attat
Judgement by default.

Samuel Mathis Esquire the garnishee summoned in this case appeared
and made Oath that at the time he was summoned garnishee he had not
neither has he had at any time since any money goods or chattels debts
or Effects or anything else to his knowledge of or belonging to the
above named defendants in his hands. therefore Mr. Mathis is not to
be required to attend at next court.

Jonathan Belton vs Randal Simmons. Debt. Judgement confessed for L 18
Eighteen pounds two shillings and nine pence with interest from the
11th February 1792.

William Langley vs Littleton Raines. Debt. Judgement confessed for
twenty three pounds twelve shillings with Interest from the 28th
December 1795.

Thomas Blakeney vs James Alexr. Watson. SP. Decree by default
according to specialitywith Interest and costs.

Heartwell Macon vs William Martin & Thomas Shelton. attat. Writ
of Inquiry executed and the following verdict returned we find for the
plaintiff fourteen pounds with costs of suit.
                           David Thompson fore^n

Rebeccah Steel   )
Ex^x William Steel Exor.) S. P. Decree by default accordingly to the
of Joseph Steel   ) speciality Interest and costs.
       vs   )
John Smith   )

James Douglass vs Hugh Gamble, Hugh Carson. S. P. Decree according
to speciality Interest and costs stay Exon. four months.

James Workman vs Hugh Gourley. Case. Judgement by default.

John McMorries vs Thomas May. Debt Judgement confessed accordingly
to the speciality.

Henry Haygood vs David Dunn. Debt. Judgement confessed for twenty
eight pounds one shilling and ten pence with interest from the 12th
April 1796 being first credited for 17/1 Indorsed on the back of the
speciality.

Jonathan Belton vs Littleton Raines. S. P. Judgement according to
speciality Stay of Exon. till the 1st of November.

Wm. Brown & Co. vs James Wilson. Debt. Judgement confessed for twelve
pounds fifteen shillings and ten pence with Interest from the 24th
July 1792 being first credited with one pound Eight Shillings dated
12th Sep^t 1794. Endorsed on the back of the note.

Wm. Brown & Co. vs Edward Morgan. Debt. Judgement by default accordingly to the speciality.

Wm. Brown & Co. vs Smallwood Owens. Debt. Judgement by default
according to speciality.

Wm. Brown & Co. vs Charles Johnston. S. P. Judgement confessed according to speciality with Interest and costs.

Wm. Brown & Co. vs William McDonald. S. P. Judgement confessed according to Speciality with Interests and costs.

William Fearys Admor. of Mary Lewis vs Eliz[h] Wilson. Trover. This case refered by rule of court to Stafford Curry James Turner and William Bonner to meet at the house of Captain Moore on Monday the 25th of July and their award to be a rule of court.

Margaret Richardson vs James Craig. Debt.

On the application of Hugh Milling Esqr. acting admor. of John Milling. Ordered that a negroe fellow by the name of Abraham belonging to the estate of John Milling be sold on the first Saturday in September next at Winnsboro on a credit untill the first day of December 1797.

Margaret Richardson vs James Craig. Judge[t] confessed according to the Specialty with interest and cost. Exon to be stayed untill January next.

James Kincaid vs Thomas Ederington. Assn. Judgement by default.

Robert Craig vs Alexr. Purvis & James Purvis. Appeal Judgement Confirmed.

Thomas Rousham vs Sarrah Flowers Adm[x] of Joshua Flowers. On appeal Ordered that the magistrates Judgement be reversed.

Minor Winn vs John Bell. On motion of Mr. Starke plaintiffs Attorney ordered that an appeal be granted to the Circuit Court Camden district the pltf proposing William Cato as security whom the court approved of.

Phillip Pearson vs Robert Craig. On appeal. Ordered that the magistrates Judgement be reversed.

State vs Lyles Beard. Bastdy. Ordered that the defendant be discharged from his recognizances.

Proceeded to draw the grand and Pettit Jurors when the following were drawn as grand Jurors for next Court. (viz) William McQuiston Rolling Williamson, Benjamin Owens, John Woodard, Ambrose Kirkland, Reuben Harrison, Phillip Pearson, John Pearson, Hugh Milling, Battee Smith, Isham Moberly, Robert Hancock, Samuel Alston, Job Owens, James Arthur Robert Reed, Samuel Proctor, Edward Andrews, Arch[d] McQuiston, Elisha Haggood.

Petit Jurors.

David Martin, Hugh McQuiston, Crispin Morgan, James Becket, Robert Moore, John Mansel, John Walker, David McDill, Samuel Barker, William Malone, Alexander Brunt, John Shane, Stephen Smith, William Sandeford, Edward McGraw, Champ Taylor, Downy Bishop, William Moberly, Benjamin Scott, John Stanton, John Steward, James Owens, Andrew Walker, Morris Weaver, John Stinson, Robert Shurley, John Smith, Samuel Robertson, Robert Boyd, William Broom.

James Workman vs Hugh Gourley. Case. On motion of Mr. Smith the Judgement by default in this cause was set aside.

Ordered that James Workman be bound over to prosecute Richard Wood alias Richard Adams for breaking Goal.

State vs Peter Larowe & Frizzle McTyre. Bastdy. Ordered that the sheriff pay to Kesiah Forst. the money in his hands levied on Larowes property deducting her fine and fees.

Chr. William Smith was by the unaminous voice of the court appointed
States Attorney for this County.
                                    John Turner
                                    Aramanos Liles
                                    Henry Moore

                        January Term 1797

Monday the 16th day of January 1797.
Court met according to adjournment.

Judges Present. John Turner and Areomanus Liles Esq.r

Court adjourned untill tomorrow 10 O'Clock.

                                         John Turner
                                         Aramanos Liles

                        January Term 1797

Tuesday the 17th day of January 1797.
Court met according to adjournment.

Judges Present. John Turner and Areomanos Liles Esqrs.

The Office of Clerk being become vacant by the decease of David Evans
-he Court proceeded to Elect one whereupon Mr. Samuel Wharter Younge
was appointed. Who appeared in Court & was qualified accordingly.

Ordered that the personal Estate of Jacob Gibson deceased be sold at
a credit of twelve months on giving bond and good security.

State vs Henry Hartin & Hugh Hartin. Lar^y Defendant comes into court
and demands his Trial.

Proceeded to draw the grand and Pettit Jurors for next court when the
following were drawn as Grant Jurors (viz)

Minor Winn   William McMorries   John McKinney
Chas. Montgomery   John Johnston   Micajah Picket
John Harvey   John Bell   James Hart
William Holley   Harris Freeman   William M. Newitt
John Havis   Robert Coleman Junr.   Phillip Reiford
William Johnston   Benjn May   Robert Moorman
Anderson Thomas   Adam Hawthorn

                        Pettit Jurors

John Watson   John Pear   Wm. Richardson
Alexr. Robertson   Alexr. Roseborough   Robert Lathan
John McCole   Adam Beazely   Richd Woodard
John Lightner   Shadrack Wooley   John Bishop
James Nealy   Enoch Seal   John Robinson
James Rabb   William Robinson   Henry Saunders
James Rutland   Simon Mott   John Tidwell
Charles Johnston   Michael Leaner   Adam Pool
John Brunt   Thomas Meador   Lewis Perry
William Paul   Isaiah Coleman   Henry Pool

William Boner resigns being Overseer on the road leading from Winnsborough to Chester Court House Ordered that Hugh Mardough be appointed
in his room.

The Citation on the Estate of William McKey was now returned duly
certified and Letters of Administration was thereupon ordered to be
granted Mariane McKey who proposed Captain John Boykin and Jese Havis

Secureties, the Administratrix was worn in accordingly who with the
securieties to be bound in the Sum of fifty pounds. the appraisers
named, James Rutland Kador Coleman, Charles Coleman Wm. Moon & Ralph
Jones any three of whom are to act.

Ordered that Susannah Knox widow of Dr. James Knox be appointed Guardian
to her three children to wit Robert Knox Matilda Knox and Eliza Knox who
appointed William Lewis Cap Wm. Watson Micajah Picket securities whom
the court approved of and thereupon ordered that Letters of Guardianship be granted, and that a Bond be taken in the penal sum of one
thousand pounds.

Jonathan Belton vs William Street. Cope. Postponed

William Street vs Jonathan Belton & Nathaniel Ford. Debt. Postponed.

William Street vs Jonathan Belton. nel pros. Postponed

Ordered that a commission do issue directed to Isaac Dubythe John
Cashace and Joseph Brevard Assn. to take the Examination of Reuben
Patterson of Kershaw County or to any two of said Justices, Jaid
Patterson being a witness on the first of the above names.

Brice Miller vs Joseph Singleton. Attacht. Dismissed.

Samuel McAdams	)		
James Johnston	)	Jumy	Judgement confessed with stay of
vs	)	process	Execution untill the first day of
Samuel Johnston	)		May
Exor of James Gordon	)		
& William Graham	)		

State vs Elizabeth Adams, Jourdin Gin & Burrill Lee. Ordered that
Jourdin Ginn be discharged from his Recognizance upon payment of
costs/

State vs Jeremiah McDannal. Lary. On Motion Ordered that James
Lucus and Thomas Hendricks the Baile of the said Jeremiah McDanniel
be permitted to surrender him to the Sheriff and that they be
discharged from their recognizance upon payment of Cost.

John Blake Indorse of Hugh Carson vs Elijah Jones. Debt. Hugh
Gambell enters himself Security for Costs in this case The plaintiff
living out of the State.   Hugh Gamble

The last will and testament of Jacob Bonny was produced proved and
approved of and Letters Testamentary was thereupon ordered to be
granted to Sarah Boney and Jacob Boney executors named in the said
Will, and that a Dedimus do issue to Burrell Cook to qualify said
executors.

Christopher Boler vs James Stone & Thomas Stone. Case. Nonsuit.

The citation on the Estate of John McBride was now returned duly
certified and letters of Administration was thereupon to be granted
to Henry McBride and James Rogers who appointed Morris Weaver and
Creighton Buchanan as Securities whom the court approved of, the
administrators were sworn in accordingly and appointed Andrew Cameron
John Cameron Henry Akison Archibald Poule and David Camack apprentitus
any three of whom are to act.

Adjourned till tomorrow at 10 O'Clock   John Turner
                                               Aramanos Liles

January Term 1797

Wednesday the 18th day of January 1797.
Court met according to adjournment.

Judges Present. John Turner and Aromanus Liles Esq^{rs}

Isaac Arledge vs William Street. S. P. Dismissed.

Ordered that the Commissioners appointed on the Road from John Gwinn
to Thomas Means, do proved agreeably to their report thereon.

Samuel Adams   )
James Johnston   ) Sum On motion of Mr. Evans Ordered that the
       vs   ) Pro plaintiff have leave to amend the process
Samuel Johnston   )   by striking out the name of William Graham
Exor. of James Gordan)   and that the Judgement stand as confessed
                           by Samuel Johnston according to specialty
                           subject to the plea of plane Administravit

State   ) Bill The following Jury were sworn and impannelled
  vs   ) In^{t} to try this cause, (viz) John Smith foreman
William Randell)   James Owins, Christion Morgan, Hugh McQuiston,
                      John Walker, David Martin, Morris Weaver, John
                      Stenson, Samuel Robinson, John Stanton, Edward
                      McGraw.

and Andrew Waugh. who returned the following verdict. Guilty
                              Jno. Smith foreman

The Last Will and Testament of Dennis Burns was produced proved and
approved of, and Letters Testamentary was thereupon Ordered to be
granted to James Laughton and William Berry Executors named in said
Will. who were qualified accordingly.

On the petition of Henry Rugely by his Clerk Thomas Starke for a
Licence to retail a Licence to retail spiritous Liquors, for one year
Ordered that the same be granted.

David Thompson vs Duke. W. Harris. Attach^{t} The court not agreeing
the cause stands over.

Ordered that John Willingham be Overseer to keep the road in repair
from near James Oglivies to the Columbia Road near Widow Kinstows,
as laid out by the former Commissioners.

Ordered that Kalb Doud be allowed the sum of fourteen Shillings for
keeping an estray.

Robert Ellison vs Daniel Brown & Robert Craig. Debt. Discontinued

State vs Mary Tidwell, Jesse Havis, Jesse Gwinn & Robt. Craig.
Sci fa. on Recog. The same Jury were sworn and impanelled to try
this cause. who returned the following Verdict. We find the within
Recognizance to be the deed of Mary Tidwell Jesse Gwin Robt. Craig &
Jesse Havis.   Jno. Smith foreman

State vs James Andrews, Quintin Craig & Robt. Craig. Asst. Baty.
Settled. Defendant to pay Costs.

State vs William Randall. Leonard Miles appeared and swore to five
days attendance as a Witness, William Haigwood also swore to four
days attendance in the above cause.

David Thomson vs Duke. W. Harris. Debt. Richard Bolan appeared and
swore to three days attendance as a witness in the above cause.

James Cameron vs John Winn & Robt. Craig et alias. Debt Rule.

Adjourned till tomorrow at 10 O'Clock
                            John Turner
                            Aramanos Liles

January Term 1797

Thursday January 19th 1797

Judges Present. John Turner. Aromenus Lisles Esq.^{rs}

State vs Henry McBride. Ordered that his recognizance be continued.

Heartwell Meacon [Macon] vs Thomas McClurkin. Ordered that a commission do issue in this case to take the Deposition of John Woodward.

Joseph Quarrel vs James Lowry. Att. Judgement by default according to Specialty. Ordered that the House and Lott levied on be sold and the money be returned into this court.

Tresurers of	)	Debt. The following Jury were sworn and impannelled
So. Carolina	)	to try this Cause, (viz) John Smith foreman
vs	)	Christian Morgan, John Walker, John Stenson, John
John Winn Junr	)	Stanton, Edward McGraw, Hugh McQuistion, David
Charles Lewis &c.	)	Martin, Morris Aleavor, Samuel Robison Andrew

Waugh, and James Owens who returned the following Verdict. We find for the plaintiffs forty one pounds five shillings with Interest from Novr 2nd, 1793. John Smith foreman

Christopher Ederington vs Daniel Mayberry. Case. The same Jury were Sworn and impannelled to try this cause who returned the following Verdict. We find for the Defendant. Jno. Smith foreman

Leaticia Hutchison vs Mrs. Walker. Debt. Ordered that the Execution be reviewed.

Court adjourned till tomorrow at nine O'Clock.

John Turner
Aramanos Liles

January Term 1797.

Friday the 20th January 1797
Court met according to Adjournment.

Judges Present. John Turner & Aromanos Liles Esq.^{rs}

Zachariah Kirkland resigns being an Overseer on the road leading from Winnsborough to McCords Ferry, from the Grunpon one mile above Cedar Creek to the County Line, in the room of whom, Ordered that Capt. John Smith be appointed.

State vs John Lee. Ordered that an alias Bench Warrant do issue.

State vs Jeremiah McTannal. Ordered that the Sheriff do convey To. McDannal to the District Goal, at Camden.

Ordered that a Rule do issue against each of the following persons, (viz) Samuel Ware, Hartwell Macon Junr. Frank Macon, John Macon, George Lemley, William Adams, George Adams, Shadrack Jacobs, William Alexander, Henry Nelson Barit Woolley, George Lestir, Edmund Mayfield Samuel Young, William McCrory, Andrew Younge, Enoch Butler, James Butler, to appear at next Court July Term, to show cause why they should not be fined for non attendance to work on the Roads.

James Cameron vs John Winn Junr. & his Securities. Rule. Ordered that this cause stand over until next Court under a peremtory rule to come to trial at that Term.

John Winn	)	Debt. The following Jury were sworn and empannelled
vs	)	to try this cause (viz) John Smith foreman Chrispin
Robt. Cook &	)	Morgan, John Warker, John Stenson, John Stanton,
John Means	)	Edward McGraw, Hugh McQuiston, Morris Weaver, Samuel

Robison, Andrew Waugh, James Owens, David Martin. The issue not being made up in this case before the Jury were sworn and impannelled, Mr. Stark one of the Attorneys for the Defendants moved for a Nonsuit which was overruled by the Court and the cause ordered to proceed upon this grounds, that the practice of the Attorneys in this court does not usually extend to making up their proceedings in full and one of the attorneys of the Defendants having ordered the Jury to be sworn without giving previous notice that he meaned to deviate from their usual practice in this case... Whereupon the Jury returned the following Verdict. We find for the plaintiff forty pounds and Interest according to Law. John Smith Foreman. On Motion Ordered that an appeal be granted in the above cause, on Joseph McDannal proposing himself Security, of whom the Court approved.

Joseph Cameron vs Willm. McCarmick & Rosanah his Wife. Case dismissed. Jesse Havis proved attendance of 12 days as witness in this cause.

State vs William Randall. Mis^n Fined five pounds sterling to the informer.

On the complaint of Thomas May, Ordered that the appointment of John Willingham as an Overseer on the Road from Oglivies to Columbia Road, be suspended untill the intermediate Court, and that Capt. Andrew do report the sense and wishes of the neighbouring Inhabitant with respect to said road to said Court.

Court adjourned till tomorrow at 9 O'Clock

John Turner
Areamanos Liles.

January Term 1797

Friday Saturday the 21st day of January 1797. Court met according to Adjournment.

Judges Present. John Turner and Arreomanos Liles Esquires.

James Kincaid vs Samuel Parks. Debt on Attat. Dismissed at Defts. costs by agreement.

Owen Yarborow vs Thomas G. Yarborow. Case. Nonsuit.

State vs James Thomas, George Thomas Junr. Recognizance forfeited.

William Faris Adm^r Mary Lewis vs Elizabeth Wilson. Trover. Award returned in favor of the plaintiff for four pounds sterling.

Ordered that the same be made a rule of Court.

James Howard & Ann Howard Admors. of Heli Howard deceased vs Maddern Lego. Sum^{rs} & Petition. Decree according to specialty.

James Howard & Anne Howard Admrs. of Heli Howard deceased vs Charles Bradford. Writ Debt. Judgement confessed according to specialty.

Ordered that A Rules do issue against each of the Juries both grand and petit. who have failed to appear at this court, to appear at next Court and show cause why they should not be fined.

George Harson vs Richard Hopkins. Case. Dismissed at plaintiffs Costs.

Elizabeth Bartin vs James Steward. Trover. Judgement by default.

Jonathan Belton vs Thomas Ferril. Sum & pet^n Decree for nine pounds Sixteen shillings Ster^g

Jonathan Belton vs Solomon McGraw. Debt. Decree by default according to Specialty.

William Langley vs John Mickle & wife. Debt. Judgement by default.

John Turner vs John Carter. Debt. Judgement confessed according to Specialty.

William Boyd vs Jesse Ginn & Robert Randel. Sci fa. Judgement revived. Rule made absolute against Robert Randel.

Daniel Brown vs William Starke. Debt. Judgement by Default.

James Workman) Case. The following Jury were impannelled and sworn
   vs   )   to try this cause, (viz) John Smith foreman,
Robert Barkley)   Chrispin Morgan, John Walker, John Stenson,
                  John Stanton, Edward McGraw, Hugh McQuiston,
Morris Weaver, Samuel Robison, Andrew Waugh, James Owens, David Martin, who returned the following verdict: we find for the Defendant, John Smith foreman. James Cameron proved attendance 6 days as a witness in this cause.

Jeremiah Cockral vs Arthur Clerk & Guerard Duntye. Debt. The same Jury were empannelled and Sworn to try this cause. Who returned the following Verdict, we find for the plaintiff thirteen pounds four shillings and four pence, and Interest. Jno. Smith, foreman.

William Johnston vs Robert Phillips. Debt. Nonsuit.

Jesse Havis vs William Durant. Attach.^{t} Ordered that John Havis constable do return the proceedings in this cause to the next court, and that a rule do issue for this purpose, and that James Rowe do return the attachment Bond it being paid to be now in his possession.

Court adjourned till the next Court in course.   John Turner
                                     Aramanos Liles

July Term 1797

Monday 17th July 1797
Court met according to adjournment.

Judges Present. John Turner, Aromanos Liles, Richd Winn Esq.^{rs}

James McQuiston appeared in open Court and acknowledged that he signed sealed and delivered a Release to James Blair for two hundred Acres of Land, in Fairfield County.

Fairfield County vs Wm. McQuiston et als. Sci fa. Reubin Harrison, excused for Non attendance, as a grand juror last court.

John Boykin Indorsee of Elizabeth Mickle vs John Mickle. Debt. Judgement confessed according to specialty, Stay of Execution till first January 1798.

James Rogers appeared in open court, and acknowledged that he signed sealed and delivered a Lease and Release to David Campbell for one hundred Acres of Land, in Camden District.

Ordered that Bartholamen Turnepseed be appointed Guardian, to Henry Lewey and Catharine Lewey, who nominated, Phillip Rayford and Samuel Richardson Securities of whom the Court approved, to be bound in the sum of two hundred and fifty pounds sterling, and that letters of guardianship be granted accordingly.

Mary Funderburg appeared in open court and acknowledged that he signed sealed and delivered a Deed of Gift unto Thomas Mobley for a Negroe Boy named Phillip.

141

Fairfield County)
    vs   ) sci fa
Thomas Stone &)
Isaac Knighton)

Isaac Knighton excused, he having showed
to the Court that he was not an overseer
at the time, the information was lodged.
Rule stands over against Thomas Stone.

Isaac Knighton appointed Overseer on the new road from Dutchmans
Creek to Sauneys Creek.

The Citation on the Estate of Burrel Burge was returned duly certified
and Letters of Administration, order to be granted to William Nettles
Junior, who nominated James Hart and William Nettles Senr. Securities
of whom the Court approved, to be bound in the sum of one thousand
pounds sterling, the administrator qualified in, and appointed Reuben
Harrison, Zachariah Nettles, Richard Burge, John Boykin, Alexander
Erwin Appraisers.

Court adjourned till Tomorrow at 10 O'Clock

                    John Turner
                    Aramanos Liles
                    Richard Winn

July Term 1797

Tuesday the 18th day of July 1797.
Court met according to adjournment.

Judges Present. John Turner, Aromanos Liles, Genl Richard Winn Esqrs.

Samuel Weldon appointed Overseer in the room of James Cameron resigned,
on the Road leading from Winnsboro to Col^n Winns place on little river,
as far as Sants old place.

The list of the Grand Jury being called over, the following Gentlemen,
appeared, and were sworn in (viz)

Minor Winn	William McMorris	Charles Montgomery
John Harvey	John Bell	Harris Freeman
John Havis	Robert Coleman	Phillip Rayford
Ben^n May	Robert Moorman	Anderson Thomas
Adam Hawthorn	John Johnston	Willm. Johnston
James Harte.		

The list of petit jurors being called over, the following Gentlemen
appeared, and answered to their names (viz).

Alexander Robinson	Adam Beasley	James Nealy
James Rabb	William Robinson	John Tidwell
William Paul	John Watson	John Pear
Enoch Seal	Charles Johnston	Thomas Meadors

The Inventory and appraisement of the Estate of Henry Rugely was
returned by the Executors, Ordered that the same be recorded, also
ordered that such part of the personal estate of Henry Rugely
(excepting Negroes, cattle, horses, plantation tools and also such
part of said Estate as is not immediately perishable) be sold at
public Vendue on a credit until the first of January next, giving
twenty days previous notice, and taking Bond and Security for all sums
above five shillings.

Thomas Graffin)
    vs   )
John Turner)

Case. The following Jury were impannelled and Sworn
to try this cause (viz) James Rabb, Alexander
Robinson, Adam Beasely, James Nealy, William Robinson,
John Tidwell, William Paul, John Watson, John Pear,
Enoch Seal, Charles Johnston, Thomas Meadows who returned the following
Verdict; "We find for the Defendant." James Rabb foreman. Thomas
Goodrum, proved nine days attendance in the above cause. Wm. Porter
proved, two days attendance, in the same.

State vs Heartwell Freeman & Mark Mitchell. Stealing. A True Bill
against Freeman not a true bill against Mitchel   M. Winn Foreman.

State vs Henry McBride. mis demeanor. A True Bill M. Winn Foreman.

James Norton vs William Ready. Debt. Abated by the death of the
plaintiff.

Ordered that a Tavern Licence be granted to Joseph Woodward for the
Term of three months.

James Owens Junr. vs John Owens. Case. Continued generally at
Defendants Costs.

Thomas McCulley Assignee of Samuel Johnston vs Robert Hill & James
Craig. S. P. Judgement confessed according to Specialty, Stay of
Execution six months.

John Saunders vs Exors. of Nathan Saunders. Case. The same Jury were
empannelled and sworn to try this cause. who returned the following
Verdi-t. "We give our Verdict in behalf of the Defendant." James Rabb
foreman.

Inventory and appraisement of the Estate of William Mackey deceased
was returned, Ordered that the same be recorded.

Alexander Bookter vs Robert Moorman. Debt. Judgement confessed for
nine pounds eight Shillings and eleven pence three farthings, with
Interest from the fourth day of April 1794 until paid, stay of
Execution three months.

Inventory and appraisement, also, a Bill of Sale, of the, estate of
Mosley Collins deceased was returned, Ordered that the same be recorded.

William Starke vs Exors. John Graves. Debt. John Tollason proved
attendance as an Evidence in this Cause, two days, and rode eighty
miles.

John Oglevie produced an Account against the Estate of William Powel,
Ordered that the same be refered to the Clerk, to report upon the
several charges.

Inventory appraisement and Bill of the Sale of the Estate of James
Ward deceased were returned, Ordered that the same be recorded.

Adjourned untill tomorrow, 10 O'Clock.   John Turner
                                                Aramanos Liles
                                                Richard Winn

                          July Term 1797

Wednesday the 19th day of July 1797.
Court met according to adjournment.

Judges Present. Genl. Richard Winn, John Turner, Aromanos Liles Esqrs.

State vs John Stewart. per.y Defendant discharged from his
Recognizance.

State vs John Smith et als. Asst. fals. impr. Defendants John Smith
Aaron Smith Reuben Johnston, Jesse Rawls and Hardy Miles, discharged
from their Recognizance.

State vs John Smith. keep the peace. Defendant discharged from his
Recognizance.

The Reports made upon the Road leading from James Oglesvies over
Gibsons ford by Wm. Daniels to the Columbia Road, not appearing to

that Court agreeable to Order, - Ordered that a Rule do issue to John
Pearson, Burrel Cook & Adam Hawthorn to examine said road, and report
to next court, if sd. road be rendered impassible or whether a better
way can be pointed out.

On the Road leading from Chester Court House to Charleston, Captain
Durham appointed Overseer on the same from Dutchmans Creek to the
Woolf-pitt, and Jesse Perry from the Woolf pit to the Charleston Road.

Ordered that Hugh Milling Esquire do certify to the Judges at next
Court, his proceedings in a certain Attachment bind before him, at the
Suit James Norton against Thomas Roseman, wherein Judgement was given
against John McCoy as Garnishee, and that in the meantime all
proceedings on the said Judgement be stayed.

Hartwell Meacon [Macon] vs Thomas McClurkin. Case. Discontinued.

Evans Winn & Co.) Case. The following Jury were empannelled and sworn
    vs   ) to try this cause, (Viz) James Rabb, Alexr. Robinson
Phillip Pearson) Adam Beasley, James Nealy, William Robison, John
                   Tidwell, William Paul, John Watson, John Pear,
Enoch Seal, Thomas Meadows, Adam Pool. Who returned the following
Verdict, "We find for the plaintiff, nine pounds eighteen shillings
and three pence 1/2 with Interest from the 1st Jany. 1786, and Costs
of Suit, Subject to a Discount of a Sum, paid by Mr. Cato to Major
Winn, in behalf of the defendant.   James Rabb. Foreman.

Phillip Rayford vs Abraham Gibson. fi fa for costs. On motion ordered
that the Execution in this case be set aside as it was obtained and
issued against the express Order of this Court.

Hugh Milling appeared in open Court and acknowledged that he signed
Sealed and delivered to Thomas Means a Release for a Lott of Land in
the Town of Winnsborough, No. 102.

John Whitehead vs James Johnston. Case. Abated by Death of the
Defendant.

John Taylor vs Reuben Harrison. Debt. Settled.

On Motion ordered that a Rule do issue to Samuel Alston Esquire to
certify his proceedings up to this court, in the case William Hardrise
against Andrew Boden, on appeal.

Captain John Grey appeared in Court, and took the usual Oath, as
Administrator on the Estate of Doctor Daniel Cockron deceased.

Ordered that the personal Estate of Doctor Daniel Cockran be sold by
the Administrator on a Credit of nine months, taken Bond & Security
for all Sums amounting to ten shillings and upwards, giving twenty
days previous notice.

Minor Winn vs James McCreight. Case. The same Jury were empannelled
and Sworn to try this cause. "We find for the Defendant" James Rabb.
Foreman. William Robinson proved attendance three days in the above
cause as a witness.

Jonathan Belton) Case. The same Jury were empannelled and sworn to
    vs   ) try this cause. who returned the following Verdict,
William Street) "We find for the plaintiff the sum of fifteen pounds
                   fourteen shillings and seven pence." James Rabb.
Foreman. Willm. Scott proved nine days attendance as a witness
in this case.

Ordered that William Miller have a Tavern Licence for one year from
this date.

Adjourned till tomorrow 10 O'Clock   John Turner
                                            Aramanos Liles

July Term 1797

Thursday the 20th Day of July 1797.
Court met according to adjournment.

Judges Present. John Turner, Aromanos Liles, Esquires.

William Starke vs Exors John Graves. Debt. Dismissed.

William Street vs Jonathan Belton. Debt. Continued at plaintiffs
Costs.

William Street vs Jonathan Belton. mal. pro. Continued at plaintiffs
Costs.

Edmund Tidwell vs Wm. Hornsby & Jos. Strange. Debt. Judgement
according to Specialty.

Elizabeth Bartin vs James Stewart. Trover. Ordered for Judgement set
aside and Cause continued.

Basil Pourie [Powell?] vs Bartlee Smith. Debt. Judgement for fifteen
pound sixteen shillings and ten pence, with Interest from the 9th
March 1795. Stay of Levey three months.

John Blake vs Elijah Jones. Debt. Judgement according to specialty,
with Interest and Costs, Stay of Levy three months.

Jonathan Belton vs Isaac Williams. S. P. Settled.

Darling Jones vs Jno. Mickle admors of Joseph Mickle. S. P. Settled.

John Majors vs Willm. Ewin. Case. Settled each party to pay their
own cost.

Henry Hampton vs Adm^X Henry Hale. Debt. Dismissed at Defendants
costs.

Darling Jones admor of Dony Muse vs Admors. Jos. Mickle. S. P.
Settled.

Benjamin Hutchison & Co. vs Littleton Rains. Judgement confessed
according to specialty, no levy for three months.

James Blair vs Maberry Helms. Case. The following Jury were empannelled to try this cause (viz) James Rabb, Alexander Robison, Charles
Johnston, Adam Beasley, James Nealy, William Robison, John Tidwell,
William Paul, John Watson, John Pear, Enoch Seal, Thomas Meadows. who
withdrew and brought in the following Verdict "We give a Verdict in
behalf of the Defendant" Jas. Rabb foreman.

Edmund Tidwell vs Wm. Sorseby & Jos. Strange. Robert Tidwell proved
Attendance as a Witness two days.

John Feaster Overseer, on the Road from Means Store to Dunkers Meeting
House, and Jacob Feaster from thence to Johnstons Ferry on Broad
River.

John Ealey, Overseer on the Road from Means Store to Shireys Ferry.

James Craig appeared in open court and acknowledged that he signed
sealed and delivered to Thomas Wright a Release for two hundred Acres
in Fairfield County.

Minor Winn vs James McCreight. Case. Robert Barkley appeared in
open court and swore to six days attendance as a witness in this case.

John Saunders vs Exors. Nathan Saunders. Case. George Lott swore to two days attendance as a witness in this case.

Thomas Graffin vs John Turner. Case. George Lott, swore to two days attendance, as a witness in this case.

William Hardridge vs Andrew Boden. Appeal. Ordered a new trial before the Magistrate.

Ordered that a Tavern Licence be granted Hugh Murdock for one year, commencing this day.

James Brown Indorsee) S. P. The same jury were sworn to try this
of John Burns   ) cause, who returned the following Verdict.
    vs   ) We give our Verdict in behalf of the Defendant
William Millar   ) Jas. Rabb Foreman.

William Hardridge) Magistrates on new trial, reported, "Upon hearing
    vs   ) the alligations of both parties, it is our opinion
Andrew Boden   ) that Mr. Hardridge had no right of action agst.
                   Boden and therefore adjudge the plaintiff pays
                   the cost.
                                    H. Milling
                                    W. Robertson
                                    S. Alston

John Blair vs Mary Helms. Thomas Goodrum swore to eleven days attendance as a witness in this case. Jesse Gladden, swore to six days
attendance on a subpa̱ from the Defendant, and three days on a subpia
from the plaintiff, in all nine days, as a Witness.

Robert Rabb appeared in Court and Qualified in as administrator of the
Estate of John Marple deceased.

Adjourned till Tomorrow 10 O'Clock.   John Turner
                                               Armamanos Liles

                        July Term 1797

Friday the 28th day of July 1797.
Court met according to adjournment.

Judges Present. John Turner, Aromanos Liles & Genl. Richard. Winn
Esquires.

Charles Lewis vs Benjamin Burke. Guerard Duntze enters himself Special
Bail for the Defendant. Guerard Duntze.

Whereupon Guerard Duntze, produced Benjamin Burke in Court and delivered
him in Discharge of his Bail piece.

Ordered that a Citation issue to the Administratrix of the Estate of
Henry Hale to show cause at next Court why John Tidwell & Isaac Gibson
should not be released from their security-ship.

Minor Winn vs James McCreight. Alexander McHenry, Swore to six days
attendance as a Witness in this case on a Subpa̱ from the ptf. at Jany.
Court ninety six.

State vs John Watts. As̱ Discharged from his Recognizance upon payment of Costs.

Charles Lewis) Debt. The following Jury were empannelled and sworn
    vs   ) to try this cause (viz) James Rabb, Alexander Robison,
John Burke &) Adam Beasley, James Nealey, Willm. Robison, John
Benjamin Burke) Tidwell, John Watson, John Pear, Enoch Seal, Thomas
                 Meadows, Isaiah Coleman & Adam Poole. "Who returned

the following verdict "We give our Verdict in behalf of the plaintiff for four pounds."   Jas. Rabb. Foreman.

David Thomson vs Duke Wm. Harris. Att^t Decree for the Defendant. Jacob Gibson swore to eight Days attendance in this Case as a witness.

John Bell   ) Case. Mr. John Brown moved to set aside the
    vs   ) Venire, on the following grounds (viz) because,
Admors. John Robison) returned on a day not in Term, 2nd, because not
                        returned on Oath, 3rd because no return had
actually been made, Which were overruled by the Court, and the Cause ordered to be tried. Whereupon the same Jury except Isaiah Coleman in whose place Wm. Paul were empanneled and sworn to try the same. Who retired and returned the following Verdict, "We find for the plaintiff forty nine pounds five Shillings & four pence half penny.
                                    Jas. Rabb foreman

William McMorris swore to nine days attendance as an evidence in this case.

Samuel Robison appeared in Court & swore in as a constable for this County.

Daniel Huffman vs William Smith. S. P. The Defendant discharged from his Bail Bond.

Charles Lewis vs Benjamin Burk. The defendant claimed the privilege of insolvent debtors and having produced a schedule of his Effects, and Debts was admitted to take the Oath appointed by Law, in such case, and thereupon was Discharged.

Adjourned till Tomorrow 8 O'Clock.   John Turner
                                            Aramanos Liles
                                            Richard Winn

July Term 1797

Saturday the 22nd Day of July 1797.
Court met according to adjournment.

Judges Present. Genl Richard Winn, Aromanos Liles, Esquires.

Proceeded to draw the Grand and Petit Jurors for next Court, when the following Gentlemen were drawn as Grand Jurors (viz)

James Brown	Jesse Beam	George Boilstone
David Long	John Bell Junr.	Thomas Means
Willm. Bell Junr.	Willm. Chapman	Robt. Lathan
James Kincaid	Jonathan Belton	John King Senr.
James Lawhorn	John King Junr.	Albert Beam
Thomas Johnston	Ephraim Liles	Dennis Burns
Roling Williamson	Moses King	

Petit Jurors

George Harson	Jacob Curry	John Porter
Moses Dukes	Nathan Cook	George Dockins
Thomas Goodrum	Thos. Griggs Yarborough	Willm. Holms
Edward McGraw	Thomas Gladney	Jesse Gladden
Abner Smith	Thomas Hill	Saml. Oates
James Butler	John Elsey	James Blane
John McDaniel	Willm. Craig	Stephen Gibson
James Cameron	Dudley Curry	Peter Currey
John Harris	Andrew Brand	Saml. McKinstry
Saml. Brand	Abraham Nealand	James Aikins

147

Inventory Appraisement and Bill of the Sale, of the Estate of Alexander
Turner deceased, were returned Ordered that the same be recorded.

Jonathan Belton) On Motion for a New Trial, The Court were of opinion
    vs   ) that no new trial ought to be granted, but that on
Willm. Street) sufficient vouchers, or proof produced by Mr.
               Street, the Charge by Donavin, be allowed in Belton's
               account.

Judges of Fairfield County)
      vs   ) Debt. Dismissed at Defendants Costs.
Willm. Dansby, Thos. Parrot)
& Willm. Cato   )

Jesse Havis vs James Rowe. S. P. Stands over under a peremtory rule
to come to trial next Court and payment of Costs.

William Dearon vs John Havis. Repn. Stands over under a perremtory
Rule to come to Trial next Court and payment of Costs.

James Cameron vs John Winn Junr. et als. Rule. Judgement for fifteen
pounds nineteen Shillings and two pence with Interest from the
Sixteenth day of July 1795, and Attorneys fees, one pound.

Bill of Appraisement of the Estate of Joseph Frost deceased, was
returned by the Administrator, Ordered that the same be recorded.

Admors of McCorkle vs Admors of Milling. Sci fa. Judgement revived,
Subject to the assets that may come in the hands of Administrators.

Ordered that Administrator of the Estate Joseph Frost have Liberty to
sell the personal Estate on a Credit up till January next, giving
twenty days previous notice. and take Bond and Security for all sums.

Benj.[n] Boyde vs Admors DeUrphy. Sci fa. Judgement revived.

Rule vs Hugh Milling Exy.x to certify proceedings up to next court, in
the Case, Norton vs Rousana, set aside.

Francis Coleman vs John Winn Junr. et als. Rule, on two Executions
Francis Coleman against David Shelton, Judgement for twenty four
pounds seventeen shillings & eight pence. on Execution Francis
Coleman against William Rabb, Judgement for L 4.11.8.

Ordered that rules do issue, to the overseers on the road from Winnsborough by Conl. Winns to Spuries Ferry. and from Williomons to
Columbia, from Winnsborough cross Crumptons Ford to Shiries Ferry,
from Winnsboro to Ammors ferry----- to show cause at next Court why he
should not be fined.

State vs Henry Hartin and Hoy. Hartin. petit larceny. Discharged
from their Recognizances.

William Langley vs John Mickle et unos. Settled.

Charles D. Bradford vs David James. Settled at Defendants costs.

State vs James Thomas, George Thomas Junr., George Thomas Senr.
Rule to issue to show cause why their Recognizance should not be
forfcited.

State vs Andrew Gibson et als. Rule to issue, to show cause why they
should not forfeit their Recognizances.

State vs Christopher Ederington et alias. Rule to issue to show
cause why they should not forfeit their Recognizances.

Fairfield County vs Wm. McQuiston et als. Rule. The whole excused
upon payment of Costs.

Fairfield County vs Saml. Ware et als. Rule. The whole Excused upon payment of Costs.

James Austen vs James Rogers. S. P. Continued untill next Court.

Overseers Appointed, (viz).

Elisha Haigood on the new road from Minor Winns cross little Cedar Creek to the old Columbia Road and big Cedar Creek. John Trapp, from big Dedar Creek to the County Line. Calebb Powel, on the Columbia road from Roland Williamsons to its Junction with the Columbia Road. James Barklay on the Road from Winnsborough to John Campbells.

David Martin from John Cambells to John Atckisons. William Johnston from John Atckisons to Crumptons Ford.

Adam Hawthorn from Crumptons to Shiries Ferry, on the road from Winnsborough to Shiries Ferry.

On the road to Ammons Ferry, James Nelson from Shiries Ferry Road to Mill Creek. and John Andrews from mill Creek to Badgers.

Robert Mooreman on the road from the Chester Line to Chapmans, William Chapman to Rockey Creek. Phillip Rayford from Rockey Creek to means' Road leading to Oglevies Ferry.

William Moon, on the Road from the Charleston Road to Roaches place, James Porter from Roaches place to Dutchmans Creek. Quinton Hoye from Dutchmans Creek to Mainyards. Guardian Ford from Mainyards to Sawneys Creek.

George Selby vs John Stanton. S. P. Judgement confessed for L 9.3.7. Stay Execution till 16 Jany. next.

John Wallace vs Dudley Currey. S. P. Decree by Default according to Specialty.

Jonathon Belton vs John William Climings. Debt. Judgement confessed for L 30, 10, Interest from 20th Jan. 7, 1797.

Lewis Perry vs Jeremiah Taylor. Case. Judgement by Default.

Thomas Means vs Heartwell Meacon Junr. Det. Judgement confessed for L 11.17 - Interest from the 6th February 1797 Stay of Execution till 16th Jany. next.

Jonathon Belton vs John Saunders. Debt. Judgement confessed for L 40. with interest according to note.

Ordered that a Tavern Licence be granted Samuel McKee for six months.

Ordered that John Buchanan be appointed Treasurer of the County of Fairfield and he be authorized to receive of Samuel Whorter Yongue late Treasurer of the said County all the Money now in his hands, belonging to the County, or that he may hereafter receive together with all the papers Books Bonds Notes and Accounts relative to said office, and that said Buchanan do receit said Yongue for all such money papers books accounts &c, so received, under the Authority of this Court. And that all lawfull Steps be taken to collect all monies due or to become due to the County and to pay the same to General Richard Winn, and to no other person, without a Special Order of Court (Untill a certain Bond is discharged which has been long since given by the Judges to Mr. James Brown for building the Court house in the Town of Winnsborough) you are further directed to call on the Sheriff of the County and his Deputies, as well as all other persons for all such money that is now in their hands or shall come into their or either of their hands as the property of the County. and to pay the same as first directed taking Receits for all such money so paid. and that the said John Buchanan do give bond with security for the faithful

performance of his Office as Treasurer, and that he be further Bound
to settle with the County every six months if called upon. Ordered
that Wm. McMorris Sheriff and his Deputies do without delay, pay into
the hands of John Buchanan Treasurer all money he or they now have or
hereafter may have in their hands as property of the County. Also that
said Sheriff do make up his Accounts as the law has pointed out and
report the same to the Court.

John Buchanan Treasurer is directed to call on the Executors of the
Estate of David Evans deceased for all such money due by him to the
County of Fairfield.

Ordered that James Smith be appointed Overseer on the Pinkney Road,
from Gladneys old place to Harrisons and Jonathan Harrison on said
road, from Harrisons to Chester County Line.

Ordered that Samuel Alston, and James Man be appointed Commissioners
to examine the nearest and best way for a road to run from the
Columbia Road near the long Meadows by Kinslows, into the said Columbia
Road.

Adjourned untill the next court in course.   Richard Winn
                                                Aramanos Liles

                        January Term 1798.

Friday 16th January 1798.
Court met according to adjournment.

Judges Present. John Turner, Aromanos Liles Esqrs.

Proceeded to ballot for Jurors to serve at next Court July Term 1798.
when the following were, drawn.

David Andrews	Edward Andrews	William Arledge
Hugh Milling	Joseph Arledge	David Grey
Reuben Starke	Charles Montgomery	James Rogers
William McMorris Senr.	Daniel Mayberry	Jonah Mobley
Henry Moore	Hugh Montgomery	George Ashford
Minor Winn	Zachariah Kirkland	David McGraw Jun.
James Long	Micajah Pickett.	

                        Petit Jurors

Joab Oen [Owen]	Moses Hollis	Adam Mayberry
George Lightner	John Sibley	James Robison
Simeon Cameron	William Cloud	Thomas Muse
Adam Robison	David Row	Samuel Owen
Robert Hood	Anthony Polurh	Elijah Hollis
George Hodfrey	William Fearis	James Rutland
Obediah Henson	James Man	Samuel Dods
Austen Smith	John Guymn	Burrel Cook
Zachariah Nettles	Moses Knighten	Alexander Rosebrough
Benjamin Owens	John McEwen	Benjamin Hattsa (?)

Zachariah Kirkland appeared in open Court and acknowledged the Signing
Sealing and Delivery of a Release to Francis Lee for three hundred and
fifty Acres of Land Situate in Fairfield County.

George Smyth appeared in open Court and acknowledged the Signing
Sealing and delivery of a Release to Francis Lee for one hundred and
ninety seven Acres of Land, Situate in Fairfield County.

Gen.[1] Richard Winn)   Atth. James Coldwell Senr. and James Coldwell
    vs   )   Junior, summoned as Garnishees, appeared in open
John McCombs   )   Court and upon Oath declared that they had not at
                      the time of being summoned, any Money, goods, Debts

or any other property belonging to said John McCombs, in their hands or possession.

Daniel Huffman vs William Smyth. S. P. The Defendant appeared in Court and Confessed Judgement according to Specialty.

Minor Winn appeared in Open Court and acknowledged the signing sealing and Delivery of a Release for fifty two and one half Acres of Land, to Quinton Craig.

Adjourned untill Tomorrow 10 O'Clock.   John Turner
                                                    Aramanos Liles

January Term 1798

Wednesday the 17th day of January 1798
Court met according to adjournment.

Judges Present. John Turner, Aromanos Liles Esquires.

Bill of the appraisement of the Estate of Elijah Beam was returned, ordered that the same be recorded.

Ordered that the Administratrix of the Estate of Elijah Beam have Liberty to expose to sale the personal Estate thereof, on a Credit of twelve months, taking Bond and Security for all Sums above five shillings, and giving fifteen days previous Notice.

Ordered that George Hallsey be appointed a Constable to serve in this County, who appeared in Court and took the Oath of said Office as prescribed by Law.

Admors. Lewis Owens vs John McKemie. S. P. Nonsuit.

John Reid vs Minor Winn. Debt. Continued.

James Austen vs James Rogers. S. P. Settled.

Survivors of Evans Winn & Co. vs Thomas Parrott. S. P. Abated by Defendants Death.

John Egleston vs Guerard Duntze. Debt. Judgement confessed fourteen pounds ten shillings and six pence half penny.

Ordered that Wm. Burten be appointed Overseer on the road from the Chester Line to the Red Post, and Alexander Galloway from the Red Post to Thomas Means Store.

Alexander Robertson appeared in open Court and acknowledged the signing sealing and delivery of a Bill of Sale fro a Negroe woman.

Jonathan Belton vs James Craig. Debt. Judgement confessed according to Specialty.

State vs Elijah Gibson, Lewis Gibson, Abraham Gibson. Sci fa. Continued untill next Court.

State vs Richard Wood. B. W. Abated.

State vs James Thomas, George Thomas Senr. & George Thomas Junr. Sci fa. Rule made absolute.

Proceeded to call over the list of the petit Jurors when the following persons appeared and answered to their names.

George Harson	Thomas Goodrum	Edward McGraw
James Cameron	Thos. Yarborough	Thomas Gladney

John Elsey	Jesse Gladden	Samuel Oates
John Harris	Abraham Nealand	Samuel McKinstry
James Aikin		

Ordered that the Administrators of the Estate James Alexander Watson
have leave to expose to sale, the personal property thereof, on a
Credit of twelve months, taking Bond and security for all sums above
five shillings, and giving fifteen days previous notice.

Lewis Perry) Case. The following Jury were empannelled and sworn
   vs) to try this cause - Viz, Samuel Oates, George Harson,
Jeremiah Taylor) Edward McGraw, James Cameron, Thomas Grigs Yarborough
                Thomas Gladney, John Elsy, Jesse Gladden, John Harris
Abraham Nealand, Samuel McKinstry, and James Aikin, who returned
the following verdict - We find for the plaintiff thirty seven dollars
and one half with Interest -- Saml. Bates foreman.

James Kincaid vs Hartwell Freeman. S. P. Judgement confessed for
seven pounds Six Shillings and Seven Pence.

NcRa Canty & Co. vs Admors of Jas. Knox. Debt. Judgement confessed
for the amount of the account filed with a stay of execution for
eight months.

Burd Owen appeared in Court and acknowledged the signing sealing and
delivery of a Release to Jesse Ginn for one hundred acres of Land

John Starke vs Hartwell Macon. sc fa on sum p.

Jonathan Belton vs Henry Rugeby. sc fa on S. P.

Isham Shurley vs James A. Watson. sc fa on Debt.

Joseph Brevard vs Minor Winn. si fa on S. P.

Thomas Blakeney vs James A. Watson. si fa on S. P.

John Adamson vs Joel Wilson. si fa on Debt.

Samuel Webb vs Agness Brown. si fa on S. P.

Samuel Webb vs Agnes Brown. si fa on S. P.

Ordered that the Sheriff do return the above mentioned Executions into
the Clerks Office tomorrow with a full and particular return on Oath
made on each of them.

Daniel Brown vs John Owins. Case. Samuel Johnston appeared in Court
and enters himself Special Bail for the Defendant.

Adjourned till tomorrow at 10 O'Clock.   Saml. Johnston
                                      John Turner
                                      Aramanos Liles

January Term 1798

Thursday the 18th day of January 1798.
Court met according to adjournment.

Judges Present. John Turner, Aromanos Liles Esquire.

John Egleston vs Guerard Duntze. Case. Judgement confessed for
eighteen pounds nine shillings and eight pence.

Ordered that Christopher Thompson have Licence to retail Liquors and
keep a house of Entertainment for one year.

Benjamin Harrison produced in Court Affidavits proving a Bay Horse tolled by Willm. Pannell before Archibald McQuiston and Sold last January Court to John Gwinn, to be his property whereupon Ordered that the Treasurer do pay over to said Benjamin Harrison the Sum of two pounds two shillings, being the sum said horse was sold for Deducting fees.

Arthur Clarke & Co. vs Adam Poole. S. P. Settled at pltfs costs.

The Citation on the Estate of Mary Martin deceased, was returned duly certified whereupon Ordered that Letters of Administration be granted to William Martin the person named in said Citation, who proposed Jesse Havis, and Josiah Knighton as his Securities of whom the Court approved to be bound in the Sum of fifty pounds, the said Martin took the oath as administrator of said Estate.

Admors of Milling vs Richard Winn. Case Discontinued.

The Citation on the Estate of Thomas Parrott Senior deceased, whereupon Ordered that Letters of Administration be granted to Thomas Parrott Junior, who proposed Major Winn and William Cato as his Securities of whom the Court approved, to be bound in the Sum of three hundred pounds sterling the said Thomas Parrott was qualified as Administrator and a Didimus to Issue to Benjn. May to qualify, Wm. Cato. Joshua Durham, Phillip Pearson, Thomas Nelson and John Barker or any three of them, as appraisers.

James Neiley vs John Winn Junr. Case. Layed over under a peremtory Rule to come to Trial the second day of next term.

William Street vs Jonathan Belton & Nathl. Ford. Debt. The following Jury were empannelled and sworn to try this cause viz. Samuel Oates, James Aiken, Edward McGraw, James Cameron, Thomas Griss Yarborough, John Harris, Abraham Nealand, Samuel McKinstry, James Buttler, Jacob Curry, and Thomas Gladney. who returned the following Verdict. We find in behalf of the Defendants Samuel Oates foreman.

Ordered that the Executors of the Estate of Henry Rugeby deceased have Liberty to expose to sale the personal property of said Estate, on a Credit till the first day of January 1799. Taking Bond and Security, and giving, twenty days previous Notice.

State vs Hartwell Freeman. p. L. The above named Jury were empannelled and Sworn to try this cause, who Returned the following Verdict. Guilty, but we recommend him to Mercy.

Ordered that John Pacell be appointed a Constable in the room of John Sloan.

Arthur Clerk & Co. vs Henry Crew. Debt. The Defendant confessed Judgement according to Specialty with Interest & Costs of Suit and the Bail is ordered to be released from his Bail Bond.

William Johnston vs Robt. Shurley and John Shurley. S. P. Judgement confessed according to Specialty.

Ordered that Frank Harrison be appointed Overseer on the Road leading from Winnsborough to Hancocks Ferry as far as Mill Creek, in the room of Robert McCreight.

Ordered that the Administrator of the Estate of Thomas Parrott Senior have Liberty to Expose to Sale the personal Estate thereof Giving twenty Days previous Notice, on a Credit of twelve months, for all Sums above five shillings, taking Bond and Good Security.

James Owens Junr. vs John Owens. Case. The same Jury were empannelled and Sworn to try this Cause. Who returned the following Verdict we find for the Defendant. Saml. Oates foreman.

Patrick McConnel and Catharine McConnell late Catharine Calhoun, by their own voluntary act, relinquished all their Right to the Administration of the Estates of James Calhoun and William Calhoun deceased in favour of William McMorris Senior and Alexander Kincaid. Whereupon Ordered that Letters of Administration be Granted to the said William McMorris Senior and Alexander Kincaid, on all and Singular the Goods and Chattles Rights and Credits of said Deceased who were qualified accordingly, having given Bond for Two hundred pounds, with William McMorris Junior and James McMorris Securities.

Adjourned till tomorrow at 10 O'Clock   John Turner
                                      Aramanos Liles

January Term 1798

Friday the 19th Day of January 1798
Court met according to adjournment.

Judges Present. John Turner, Aromanos Liles Esquires.

James Kincaid vs Ephraim Lyles. S. P. Judgement confessed According to specialty.

Richard Bowlen vs David Thompson. Debt. William Thompson enters himself special bail.   William Thompson

Treasurers of So. Carolina) Debt. The Same Jury which served
         vs   ) yesterday were empannelled to try this
John Winn Junr. Securities) Cause who returned the following Verdict
                             We find for the plaintiffs the sum of
twenty seven pounds sixteen shillings and two pence with Costs of Suit
Samuel Oates foreman.

Daniel Gourn vs William Deason. Rep^n. The same Jury were empannelled to try this cause, who returned the following Verdict. Viz. We find in favor of the Defendant. Saml. Oates.

James Owens vs John Owens. Case. Samuel Lacey, John Ray, David Owen and Henry Harden, each, Sworn to one days Attendance in this Suit as Witnesses and each rode sixty miles.

Burd Owen appeared in Open Court and acknowledged the Signing Sealing and Delivery of a Release for one hundred and fourteen Acres, lying in Fairfield County.

Jonathan Belton vs William Rogers. S. P. Dismissed at Defendants Cost

William Rayford appeared in Court and took the Oath prescribed by Law to the Office of Constable, being appointed by Order of Court in the Room of Thomas Parrott Junr.

Gavin Curry vs William Fearis. Case. The aforesaid Jury were empannelled being sworn generally to try this Action, who returned the following Verdict, Viz. --- We find in favor of the plaintiff L 4.
                                   Saml. Oates

William Street vs Jonathan Belton & Nathaniel Forde. Debt. Josiah Knighton Swore to his Attendance as a Witness duly Summoned nine days, in this Action.

Adjourned till Tomorrow 9 O'Clock   John Turner
                                       Aramanos Liles

January Term 1798

Saturday the 20th Day of January 1798.
Court met according to adjournment

154

Judges Present. John Turner, Aromanos Liles Esquires

Gavin Curry   ) Case. John Turner, Robert Kilpatrick, Thomas
    vs   ) Kilpatrick, Andrew Walker, Stafford Curry, Joseph
William Fearys) Currey, and Robert Patterson, each Swore to four days
                   Attendance as Witnesses duly summoned in this cause,
                   and John Turner swore to three days Attendance.

On application. Ordered that a Citation do issue Enternable to July
Court next. to Summons the kindred & Creditors of William Ball deceased
to show cause why administration should not be granted to James
Rhodes and William Rhodes on the Este of the said William Ball.

Ordered that Depotistation issue to three Justices of the Peace in the
State of North Carolina to take the depositions of Witnesses touching
what they may know of James Rhodes and William Rhodes being the heirs
at law of William Ball deceased.

James Kincaid vs Thomas Parrot. Judgement Confessed according to the
note with interest & Costs. Execution not to be levied for twelve
months.

James Kincaid vs Thomas Parrot & William Cato. Judgement confessed
according to specialty with Interest & Costs Execution not to be
levied for twelve months.

Arthur Clerk & Co. vs Nathaniel Smith. S. P. Decree for three pounds
seven shillings with costs of Suit.

Jonathan Sutton vs Minor Winn. S. P. Decree according to specialty.

Arthur Clarke & Co. vs Minor Winn. Debt. Settled at defendants costs.

Arthur Clarke & Co. vs Samuel Nelson & Catherine Nelson. S. P. Decree
for four pounds four shillings & two pence with costs.

State vs Hartwell Freeman. pet. lar. The prisoner was brought to the
Barr to receive sentence. Ordered that he receive seven lashes on the
Bare, Back, to be put in Execution on the Sixteenth day of Aprill
next.

Elizabeth Barten vs James Steward. Trov.ᵣ Nonsuit.

Moses Dukes vs Edward Sims. Case. Nonsuit.

Elijah Hollis vs Admors. Saml. Hollis. S. P. Dismissed at pltfs
costs.

Whereas Valentine Rachael has been for some time absent from this
state and is supposed to be dead and hath left a child and some
property within the Limits of this County, Therefore Ordered that
Thomas Willingham be appointed Guardian of the said Child, and that
he give Bond and Security in the Sum of one hundred pounds for the
faithful discharge of his Trust, Said Willingham proposed Edward
Willingham and Jesse Havis as his Securities of whom the Court approved

Henry Nelson) Case. The following Jury were empannelled being Sworn
    vs   ) Generally, to try this Cause, Viz. Samuel Oates, James
Jean Weare   ) Aikin, Edward McGraw, James Cameron, John Elsy, John
                Harris, Samuel McKinstry, James Butler, Thomas Gladney,
Jesse Gladden, Abraham Nealand, Jacob Curry. ---- Who returned the
following Verdict, Viz, WE find for the plaintiff ten pounds damage
Saml. Oates Foreman.
Isom Jean proved three days attendance. Thomas Nelson proved 5 days
attendance.

William Rabb vs Thomas Nutterville. Lease. Referred to James Davis
John Barker Minor Winn and Guerard Duntze, who have liberty to choose

an Umpire in case they do not agree, and their Award to be a rule of Court...Edward Willingham proved four days attendance as a Witness in this Cause.

Treasr. Faird. County vs Walter Poole & Adam Poole. S. P. Judgement confessed according to Specialty, with costs. Stay of Execution till Seventeenth April next.

Arthur Clerke & Co. vs Robert Berkley. S. P. Decree for two pounds sixteen shillings and ten pence, with costs.

James Brown vs Littleton Raines. S. P. Nonsuit.

James Workman vs Hugh Gourley. Case. Continued under a peremtory Rule to come to trial next Court.

Thomas Rauch vs Thomas Nelson. Debt. The same Jury were empannelled to try this cause - who returned the following Verdict - We find for the Plaintiff award and to Specialty. Saml. Oates.

Arthur Clarke & Co. vs Samuel Oates. Debt. Judgement confessed according to Specialty, Stay of Execution six months.

Arthur Clarke & Co. vs James Craig. Asst. Judgement confessed for eight pounds thirteen shillings and eight pence, Stay of Execution three months.

William Rook vs Thomas Dent. Atth. on noto. Judgement by Default.

Duke W. Harris vs David Thompson. sci fa. Ordered that the Execution to much of the respect the costs of Jacob Gibson shall not be levied, until he makes it appear that he was duly summoned.

Adjourned until the next Court in Course.   John Turner
                                                   Aramanos Liles

July Term 1798

Monday 16th day of July 1798.
Court met according to adjournment.

Judges Present. John Turner, Esquire.

Proceeded to ballot for Jurors to serve at next Court January Term 1799, when the following persons were drawn---Viz---

Grand Jurors

Gardner Ford	Harris Freeman	James Grey
William Foote	Charnel Durham	John Oglivie
James Nelson	Morris Weaver	Robt. Moorman
Reuben Harrison	Joseph McMorris	Saml. Dunning
Robert Martin	James McMorris	Basil Wherter
Moses Hill	Bartlett Smyth	Chas. Pickett
Nicholas Peay	John Bell M. C.	

Petit Jurors

Thomas Richardson	Willm. Richardson	Henry Hartin
Robert Randell	Kador Coleman	Andw. Young
James Bright	Willm. Millar	Saml. Gladney
Chris.ᵗ Brach	Saml. Owens	Fredrick Carish
Henry Ederington	Patrick Gladney	James Graves
James Mobley	Willm. Ewin	David Martin
James McCreight	Lemuel Perry	Henry Crumpton
Henry Poole	Robert Shurley	Adam Poole Jun.

| James Hanny | Francis Ederington | Jacob Turnipseed |
| James Owens | Willm. Ferguson | Antony Seale |

Adjourned till tomorrow 10 O'Clock.   John Turner

July Term 1798

Tuesday the 17th Day of July 1798.
Court met according to Adjournment.

Judges Present. John Turner & Aromanos Liles Esquires.

John Bell appeared in Court and acknowledged the Signing, Sealing and delivery of a Release to William Bell for three hundred & fifty four Acres in Fairfield County.

Proceeded to call over the List of Grand Jurors, when the following Gentlemen appeard, and were Sworn in (viz)

Minor Winn, fore.[n]	Henry Moore	James Long
Edward Andrews	Charles Montgomery	Daniel Mabry
William Aldrige	Wm. McMorris	James Rogers
Josiah Moberly	David McGraw	David Grey
Hugh Milling		

The Last Will and Testament of Thomas Bell deceased was produced in Court, proved, and approved of, whereupon Ordered that Letters Testamentory be granted to James Craig and William Bell, Executors named in said Will, they having taken the Oath, prescribed by Law.

The Last Will and Testament of Joseph Cameron deceased, was produced in Court proved and approved of, whereupon Ordered that Letters Testamentary be granted to Andrew Cameron, and John McEwin.

two Executors named in said Will, Henry Moore, having refused to act as such, the said Executors were qualified in as usual---- John Harvey, David Wears, Alexander McEwen, Andrew McDowell, James Barber, were nominated appraisors.

The Last Will and Testament of James Andrews deceased was produced in Court, proved and approved of, whereupon Ordered that Letters Testamentary, be granted thereon to Mathew Andrews, and Edward Andrews, Executors named in said Will, who were qualified in as Exors.

John & Elijah Hill, Orphans, appeared in Court, and made Choice of Thomas Meadows as their Guardian, whereupon ordered that Letters of Guardianship be granted to the said Thos. Meadows, on all Singular the Goods & Chattels of said Orphans. Who proposed Joseph McDaniel, and William Alsup as Securities of whom the Court approved.

Elizabeth Hill, John Hill, and Mary Hill, orphans, appeared in Court, and made Choice of Abell Hill, under the appointment of the Court, as their Guardian. Whereupon Ordered that Letters of Guardianship be granted to the said Abell Hill, on all and Singular the Goods and Chattels of the said Orphans. who propose Joseph McDaniel, and William Alsup as Securities of whom the Court approved.

Henry Funderburgh, appeared in Court, as an Orphan, and made Choice of Richard Hill, as his Guardian. Whereupon Ordered that Letters of Guardianship be granted to the said Richard Hill, on all and Singular the Goods and Chattels of the said Orphan who proposed Thomas Meadows and Joseph McDonald as Securities of whom the Court approved.

State vs David Noland. Misn. Nel pros

The Last Will and Testament of John Cork deceased was produced in Court, proved by the Oaths of Wm. Tennon & James Hindmon, ordered that the same be recorded.

Jonathan Belton vs Thomas Stark. Sci Fa on Bail bond. Judgement.

State vs Andrew Gibson, Jacob Gibson & William Gibson. Sci Fa on
Recog. Ordered that their Recognizances be forfeited so far as to pay
the Costs and that Executors do Issue _____ for Costs only.

State vs Joseph McDaniel Senr., Joseph McDaniel Junr., Jacob Minks.
House Break^g Ordered that the Defendants be bound over to appear
at the Superior Court of Camden District on the 19th Novemr next to
stand their trials.

The Citation on the Estate of Albert Beam was returned duly certified
whereupon Ordered, that Letters of Administration be granted to Sarah
Beam, the person therein named, that a Dedimus do Issue to Mosey Hill
Esquire, to qualify said Administratrix, and to see her Administration
Bond duly executed, and to take sufficient Securities, to qualify
appraises &c. to be appointed also by him -- the administratrix to be
bound in one hundred and fifty pounds.

Margaret Robertson vs Samuel Cork. Case. Dismissed at Defendants
Costs.

State vs Shadrick Jacobs. Asst. Baty. A true Bill.

State vs Margaret Rush, Nancy Penny, Sarah Penny, Ann Penny, Samuel
Penny. Asst. Baty. Not a true bill. and. Discharged from their
Recognizance.

State vs Phill^n. Holcom & Walter Poole. Swin^g a true Bill.

State vs Theophilus Williams. Steal^g Not a true Bill. and discharged
from his recognizances.

State vs John Thompson. Asst. Baty. A true Bill.

State vs John Thompson. Asst. Baty. A True Bill.

State vs Thomas Fearis. Asst. Baty. A true Bill.

Proceeded to call over the List of the petit Jurors, when the following
persons appeared, were empannelled and Sworn generally to try all
causes of a civil nature, which may come before them this term (viz)

Thomas Muse	John McEwin	Simon Cameron
Elijah Hollis	George Godfrey	Adam Mabry
Benjamin Owens	John Sibley	Moses Hollis
Zachariah Nettles	Obediah Henson	James Rutland

Ordered that Moses Hill Esquire, do have William Alexander bound over
as a Witness in behalf of the State, against Shadrick Jacobs to appear
at next Court.

State vs Thomas Fearis. Asst. Batty. The above named Jury were Sworn
to try this Bill of Indictment. who brought in the following Verdict,
Viz, "We find Thos. Fearis Guilty.   Thomas Muse Fore^n.

State vs Thomas Stone. Asst. & Baty. Noli prosqui

James Cameron vs John Winn & Securities. Sci Fa. Ordered that the
Sheriff do return the Execution into Court on Thursday next his
return to be on Oath.

Generale Richard Winn appeared in Court, and took the Oath of office,
as one of the Judges of the County of Fairfield, being previously
appointed by the Assembly and Commissioned by the Governor for that
purpose.

Adjourned till Tomorrow at 9 O'Clock.   John Turner   Richard Winn
                                             Aramanos Liles

July Term 1798

Wednesday the 18th Day of July 1798
Court met according to adjournment.

Judges Present. John Turner Aremanos Liles, and General Richard Winn, Esquires.

Daniel Brown vs John Owens. Case. Settled at Defendants Costs.

Patience McGraw vs Willm. Willingham. Case. Nonsuit.

William Dunkin vs Admors of James Winn. S. P. Dismissed at pltfs Costs.

William Rabb vs Thomas Nutterville. Case. Abated by Death of plaintiff.

James Kincaid) Case. Ordered that a Commission do issue, directed
     vs   ) to John Moore, William Scott, Joseph Dickson, John
Swanson Lunford) Reid, Joseph Grimes, Esq^{rs} or any three of them
                  of the State of North Carolina. Lincoln County to
take the Examination of Demsy Thain, a Witness, in the Above Cause.

McRa Canty & Co. vs Littleton Rains. Debt. Judgement by Default.

William Denton appeared and acknowledged a Release to Thomas Means, for one hundred acres in this County.

Samuel Owen vs Bartlee Smyth. Debt. Judgement confessed, Stay of Execution three months.

David Thompson vs the same. Debt. Judgement confessed. Stay Exon. three months.

James Kincaid vs the same. Debt. Judgement confessed. Stay of Execution three months.

James Kincaid vs William Hardage. Case Settled.

The same vs The Same. Debt. Settled.

Jonathan Belton vs Exors. Usley Pettipool. S. P. Decree for L 6 -18

Ordered that William Ewin be allowed four shillings and eight pence for keeping an estray.

James Neiley) Case. The same Jury who served yesterday were
     vs   ) empannelled to try this Cause, who returned the
John Winn Ju^{r}) following Verdict (viz) "We find for the plaintiff
                 nine pounds with Costs of Suit. Thomas Muse foreman.

State vs James Hutchison. Asst. Baty. A true Bill.

State vs William Denton & William Marshaw. Killing a Guelding. A True Bill.

State vs James Andrews. Hog Stealg. Not a true Bill.

Ordered that William Fant be appointed a Constable in the room of William Rayford resigned, who appeared in Court and took the Oath of Office, as appointed by law.

Ordered that William Paul be appointed a Constable in the room of John Paul, who appeared in Court, and was Qualified for that purpose.

State vs Christopher Ederington, Jamed Davis & John Barker. Sci fa on Recog^{s} Discharged from their Recognizances upon payment of Costs.

159

James Kincaid vs Shadrick Jacobs. Debt. Judgement confessed according to Specialty, Execution to be Lodged but not Levied untill January next.

Ordered that Stephen Dumas be appointed an Overseer on the road from Enoch Grubs to Johnstons Ferry, in the room of Enoch Grubs resigns.

The Citation on the Estate of William Rabb deceased was returned into Court duly certified, whereupon Ordered that Letters of Administration be granted to John Rabb and William Rabb the persons therein named, who proposed William McMorris Senr. and William Dansby as Securities of whom the Court approved, to be bound in the sum of five hundred pounds sterling, the Admors named.   William McMorris Senr. William McMorris Junr., Robert Rabb--- appraisers. a Decimus to Benjn. May Esqr. to qualify Admors & appraisers.

David Shelton vs James Martin. Appeal. Judgement of Magistrate affirmed.

Ordered that Mes.^r James Kincaid and John Bell be appointed Commissioners to lay out a new Road from Cromptons Ford on Little River to join or go into the Columbia Road at or near Mr. David McGraws plantation, which Road you are to take the nearest and best way and you are to proceed to Lay out the same as soon as possible.

State vs Thomas Fearis. Asst. Baty. The defendant, fined in the sum of ten pounds Sterling to be paid within six months giving note and good Securities to be bound to his good behavior for two years, himself in the penal sum of fifty pounds, and two good securities in the sum of twenty five pounds each and to remain in the Custody of the Sheriff until the above sentence and Order be complied with.

Adjourned untill tomorrow 9 O'Clock.   John Turner
                                            Aramanos Liles
                                            Richard Winn

                          July Term 1798

Thursday the 19th Day of July 1798.
Court met according to adjournment.

Judges Present. John Turner, Aromanos Liles and General Richard Winn Esquires.

Ordered that Muscar Bolar have a Licence to retail Liquors and keep a Tavern for one year.

William Street vs Jonathon Belton. nell prof. Nonsuit.

James Lewis, having given Security for the Indemnification of the County, relative to the maintainance of two base born Children, begotten by him upon the Body of Alex Stripberry, Ordered therefore, that he be liberated from his Confinement.

Richard Bolen vs Samuel Parkes. Debt. Judgement confessed for eleven pounds, each party to pay equal costs.

State   ) Asst.   The following Jurors were empannelled and Sworn
  vs   ) &   to try this Bill of Indictment (viz) Thomas
John Thompson) Batty. Muse, foreman. Elijah Hollis, Benjn. Owens.
                       Zachariah Nettles, John McEwen, George Godfrey,
John Sibley, Obediah Henson, Simeon Cameron, Adam Maybry, Moses Hollis.
James Rutland, Who returned the following Verdict (viz) We find the
prisoner John Thompson guilty of an assault. Thomas Muse fore.^n

State vs John Thompson. Asst. & Batty. The same Jurors were empannelled and sworn to try this Bill of Indictment, who returned the

                              160

following Verdict (viz). We find the defendant John Thompson guilty.
Thos. Muse fore[n].

State vs John Faulkner. peace. The defendant appeared in Court. in obedience to his Recognizance.

Jesse Jinkins vs Bird Owens. S. P. John Owens appears in Court and enters himself Special Bail in this Case.

<pre>
                                              his
                              John   I   Owens
                                             mark.
</pre>

Ordered that Letters of Administration on the Estate of William Bale deceased be granted to John King Senr. who proposed Major Winn and Jesse Havis as his Securities of whom the Court approved, to be bound in the Sum of two thousnad pounds Sterling.

State   ) Miss[n]. The same Jury were empannelled and sworn to try
  vs   ) this Bill of Indictment. who returned the following
Henry McBride) Verdict. Not Guilty.   Thos. Muse fore[n].

Adjourned till tomorrow 9 O'Clock.   John Turner
                                       Aramanos Liles

July Term 1798

Friday the 20th Day of July 1798.
Court met according to adjournment.

Judges Present. John Turner, Aromanos Liles, and General Richard Winn Esquires.

Robert Rabb vs Robert Miller. Debt. Judgement confessed for two hundred Dollars, Execution to be stayed four months.

State vs George Thomas Junr., George Thomas Senr. Ordered that the Defendants be discharged from their recognizances and that he pay the Costs.

Robert Gamble Indorsee of Minor Winn vs John Bell. Debt. Judgement confessed according to Specialty. Stay of Execution three months.

James Austen vs Guerard Duntze. Case. The same Jury who served yesterday were empannelled and sworn to try this issue. Who returned the following Verdict. (viz) We find for the plaintiff two pounds, with Costs of Suit.   Thos. Muse fore[n].

Survivors of Evans Winn & Co. vs Thomas Parrott. Sci fa. Dismissed at Defendants Costs.

Survivors of Evans Winn & Co. vs Thomas Parrot. Sci fa. Judgement revived for Seven pounds twelve shillings and six pence, with Interest from 1st Feby. 1791. Stay execution till 19th July next.

In Obedience to a Writ of Mandamus issuing from the Justice of the Court of general sessions of the peace &c holden at Camden on the 19th day of April last commanding the Judges of the County Court of Fairfield to annul and revoke the Letters of Administration granted by them to Robert Rabb on the Estate of John Marple decd. and grant the same to Northrup Marple Brother of the deceased. Ordered thereupon that the Letters of Administration granted by this Court to Robert Rabb of the Estate of John Marple deceased unadministered on by Thomas Marple late of the County of Fairfield deceased be annulled and revolked, and that the same be granted to Northrup Marple, on his taking the usual Oath, and giving Security as required by Law. Whereupon the said Northrup Marple nominated James Kincaid and William McMorris Senr. as Securities, of whom the Court approved, to be bound in the Sum of one thousand pounds Ster[g] and the Oath of office was administered to the said Thomas Marple.

The Last Will and Testament of Hugh Gamble, late of this County deceased, was produced in Court, proved and approved of by the Court, and Letters Testamentary thereupon ordered to be granted to Agness Gamble Widow of the deceased and John Bell and Nathan Majors Executrix and Executors named in said Will, the aforesaid Executors appeared in Court and took the Oath of Executorship prescribed by Law.

Ordered that John King senior appointed Administrator on the Estate of William Ball deceased, have untill the first day of September next to execute a Bond for due Administration of said Estate, and that a Dedimus do Issue to Charles Pickett Esquire, to the said Bond duly executed and to qualify said Administrator.

The Citation on the Estate of Charles Palmer deceased, was returned into Court duly certified, whereupon ordered that Letters of Administration be granted unto James Kincaid who proposed William McMorris Senr. and Alexander Kincaid Securities of whom the Court approved, to be bound in the Sum of twenty pounds, the Administrator appeared in Court and took the Oath, of Administration prescribed by law.

State vs John Thompson. Asst. The defendant to be imprisoned ten days, and fined in the sum of five pounds. payable in three months.

State	) Asst.	The defendant, to be imprisoned twenty days,
vs	) &	and fined in the sum of ten pounds payable in
John Thompson)		ten months to be bound to the peace and good-

behavior, for two years, himself in the sum of one hundred pounds and two good securities, in the sum of twenty five pounds each.

James Kincaid vs John Foote. Case continued at Defendants Costs.

William Rabb vs Northrup Marple. Slan.r Dismissed.

James Austen vs Guerard Duntze. William England swore to eight days attendance as a Witness in this cause Jesse Havis proved ten days attendance as a witness in the same.

Ordered that John Brunt be appointed an Overseer on the Road, from the Negroe Burning to Gibsons New Ford on Little River --- and David Andrews from Gibsons New Ford on Little River to the Columbia Road by Ulay of James Daniels old place.

James Neily vs John Winn. Case. Nathan Majors proves Attendance as a Witness five Days in this case.

Ordered that, in compliance with the request of the Grand Jurors, such parts of their presentments as appear to require legislative interference, particularly the first, third, and fourth of their presentments, be sent forward by the Clerk to the Legislature of this State at their next Session.

Ordered that the Clerk do write to the Overseers on each of the Roads presented by the Grand Jury this court, enforming them, that unless they immediately proceed to put the several roads under their care in good repair they will be proceeded against as the Law directs, and that unless the Defaulters make good excuses to the Overseers, where Default may happen, the Overseers are to return them to the Court, ensuing.

Ordered that Daniel Harris be appointed an Overseer on the Road from Winnsborough to John Gambles old place James Marr on the road from Dutchmans to Sauneys Creek and George Reddish on the road from Lees Mile to Strothers Ferry in the room of John McKenny.

Ordered that the Road from Robert Kilpatricks to John F. Taylors, be considered a publick road and that James Arthur be appointed an Overseer thereon.

Jesse Havis vs James Rowe. S. P. The same Jury were empannelled to
try this Cause who, returned the following Verdict. (viz) We find for
the Defendant with Costs of Suit.   Thos. Muse fore.[n]

                         John Turner
                         Aramanos Liles
                         Rich[d] Winn

                    July Term 1798

Saturday the 21st Day of July 1798.
Court met according to Adjournment.

Judges Present. John Turner, Aromanos Liles, Esquires.

James Workman vs Hugh Gourley. S. Case Dismissed.

James Hoye vs Thomas Hathcork. S. P. Settled at plaintiffs Costs.

Trea[r] of Fairfield vs Richd. Dunkley & Johnston Stanton. S. P.
Judgement according to Specialty

George Noland vs Andrew Cameron. Stan[n] Settled at Defendants Costs.

John Hampton vs John Wallace. Sci fa. Dismissed at Defendants Costs.

Jonathan Belton vs John Jenkins & Cordal Hogan. S. P. Judgement by
Default according to Specialty.

John Smith vs John Cameron. S. P. Dismissed at Defendants Costs.

William Hughs vs Guerard Duntze. S. P. Judgement confessed according
to Specialty.

Jonathan Belton vs William McDonald. Debt. Judgement by Default
according to Specialty.

Jonathan Belton vs Thomas Muse & Daniel Muse. Debt. Judgement
by Default according to Specialty.

John Adamson vs Joel Wilson. Sci fa. Judgement revived.

Elijah Jones vs James Craige. S. P. Judgement by Default.

Elijah Haywood vs Kemp T. Strother. Debt. Judgement according to
Specialty.

David McCradie & Co. vs Guerard Duntze. Case. Judgement by Default.

Thomas Means vs John Carter. S. P. Decree for Six pounds seventeen
shillings and two pence.

Jesse Havis vs John Smith & Hugh Carson. Debt. Nonsuit.

Francis P. Vaughon Exi[r] of Wm. Vaughon vs Roling Williamson. Debt.
Judgement confessed according to Specialty. Stay of Levey four
months.

John Faulkner vs Robert Berkley. S. Case. The same Jury who served
yesterday were empannelled to try this Cause who returned the
following Verdict (viz) We, find for the plaintiff one pound and costs
of suit.

Samuel W. Yongue vs Robert Berkley. Case. Dismissed at equal Costs
Eleazer Jones proves Attend[e] Days in this suit as a witness.

Daniel Gowen vs Wm. & Benj[m]. Deason. Case. Dismissed.

                         163

John Faulkner vs Robert Berkley. Case. Capt. Wm. Robison swore to three days attendance as a Witness in this cause. John Yarborough, Elizabeth Yarborough and Arthur Yarborough, each swore to four days attendance in this suit.

William England vs James Wilson. William England proves attendance nine days as a Witness in this suit.

Ordered that a Tavern Licence be granted to Joseph McCork for the year.

Ordered Tavern Licences to Guerard Duntze, and James McCreight for one year their former Licences expiring this Date.

Adjourned till the next Court in Course.   John Turner
                                                  Aramanos Liles

                    Fairfield County Court

Wednesday the 16th January 1799

Neither of Judges attending this Day, the Court was adjourned untill tomorrow at 10 O'Clock.   Saml. W. Yongue C.C.

Thursday the 17th January 1799.
Court met according to Adjournment.

Judges Present. John Turner, Richard Winn Esqrs.

Proceeded to ballot for Grand and petit Jurors to serve at next Court July Term 1799. When the following persons were drawn Viz.

                    Grand Jurors

Abraham Miller, Walter Aiken, Robert Armstrong, Robert Eckles, Isaac Arledge, Alexr. Kincaid, Adam Hawthorn, Edward Lovejoy, Hugh Young, William Strother, Thomas Shannon, Barthalmew Turnipseed, Nathaniel Ford, John Woodward, Jesse Ford, Phillip Pearson, Robert Rabb, Littleton Rains, Benjamin May, Darling Jones

                    Petit Jurors

Ephraim Butler, Enoch Butler, John Hollis, Newton Foote, John Elliott, Isham Dansby.

Walter Poole, Guerard Duntze, Ezekill Frazer, Jarvis Gibson, Caleb Frazer, George Free, Saml. McMullin, Hartwell Macon, Edward Mobley, Wiley Bishop, Richard Mansil, James Roseborough, Stephen Dumas, Saml. Fant, John Feaster, Saml. Alkins, Canon Cason, Wm. Ederington, James Caldwell, Josiah Knighton, George Beasly, John Brown, Andrew Blain, David Wear.

James Bell and William Robertson petitioned the Court for a Licence to keep a Tavern and Retail Liquors, Ordered that the same be granted.

On application, Ordered that a Tavern Licence be granted to David Patton for one year.

The Citation on the Estate of Robert Hancock was duly returned, certified, whereupon Ordered that Letters of Administration be granted to Lucy Hancock, John Morris and William Harper, who proposed Minor Winn John Pearson and James Kincaid as Securities to be bound in the sum of seven hundred and fifty pounds Sterling, a Dedimus to issue to Benjamin May to qualify Said Administrators and the appraisers, Viz, Philip Rayford, Phillip Pearson, William Woodward, Aromanos Liles, and William Nevit ---- and see the bond duly Executed.

Proceeded to call over the List of Grand Jurors who were to serve at this Court when the following persons appeared and were Sworn in as

such. Viz. Moses Hill foreman. Gardner Ford. William Foote.
Robert Martin. Nich.^{S} Peay. Harris Freeman. Charnel Durham.

Joseph McMorris, James McMorris, James Green, Robert Moorman, Basil
Wheat, Charles Picket.

Ordered that James Richey be appointed an Overseer in the room of
Hugh Murdock.

Elijah Jones vs James Craig. S. P. Judgement confessed for seven
pounds eighteen shillings & eight pence.

Peter Crim vs James Craig. Debt. Judgement confessed according to
Specialty with interest & Costs Stay Execution three months.

Proceeded to call over the List of Petit Jurors to serve at this Court
when the following persons appeared, were empannelled and sworn to
try all causes of a civil nature which might come before them this
Term (Viz)

David Martin for^{n}., Thomas Richardson, Chris. Bras., Henry Ederington,
James Mootey, Willm. Richardson, Kador Coleman, William Miller,
Robert Shirley, Willm. Ferguson, Henry Hartin, Henry Poole.

Richard Brown vs Austen Peay Exor. of John Ellison. Debt. Judgement
confessed for the ballance due on the Note, Stay Execution till next
Court.

State vs William Denton & William McShan. Killing a Guely. The
above Jury were empannelled and Sworn to try this Cause, who returned
the following Verdict. Guilty. David Martin foreman.

The last Will and Testament of Richard Neily was produced in Court,
proved, and approved of whereupon Ordered that Letters Testamentary
be granted unto Ann Neily Surving Executrix named in said Will who
appeared in Court and took the usual Oath, prescribed by Law.

David Montgomery appeared in Court and made Choice of Theophalus
Wilson as his Guardian, Whereupon Ordered that Letters of Guardianship
be granted to said Theophelus Wilson, who proposed James Craig and
Charles McDaniel as his Securities, of whom the Court approved, to be
bound in the Sum of two hundred pounds.

Ordered that Charles Montgomery be appointed an overseer on the road
from Crumtons to Shireys Ferry.

Ephraim Pettipool and Thomas Pettipool Orphans appeared in Court, and
made choice of William Pettipool, as their Guardian; Whereupon Ordered
that Letters of Guardianship be granted unto the said William Pettipool, as guardian of the said Orphans who proposed Charles Pickett and
John Kelley as his Securities of whom the Court approved to be bound
in the sum of two hundred pounds.

Ordered that Francis Lee be appointed an Overseer on the Road leading
to Columbia, on that part, from Cedar Creek by Capt. Kirkland to the
County Line.

Adjourned untill 10 O'Clock tomorrow.   John Turner
                                               Richd. Winn.

                    Fairfield County Court

Friday the 18th Day of January 1799.
Court met according to adjournment.

Judges Present. John Turner and Richard Winn Esqrs.

The following Gentlemen viz. Moses Hill, William Robertson, Nicholas Peay, John Mickle and Daniel Mabry, appeared in Court and took the usual Oaths of Office, as Justices of the Peace, for the County.

Charles Pickett Esqr. appeared in Court and took the usual Oaths of Office, as a Justice of the Peace for this County.

John L. Bradford vs Mary Ward Admrx. of James Ward. Debt. Judgement confessed according to Specialty. Joshua Durham proved three days attendance as a Witness in the above suit.

James Kincaid vs Thomas Ederington. Case. Abated by Death of Defendant after inter___ Judgement.

John Martin vs John Hill. S. P. Settled Defendant paid Debt & Costs.

John Oglevie vs Northrup Marple. Case. I enter myself Special Bail in this action, to surrender the Body of the Defendant in Execution. Thos. Parrott

James Gamble vs Thomas Farrel & Thomas Neily. Debt. Judgement by Default.

John Havis Junr. vs John Havis Senr. Case. Refered to Minor Winn and Henry Moore with leave to choose an Umpire, and their award to be a rule of Court.

John Means vs Joseph Stanton. Sci Fa. Judgement revived.

James Kincaid vs John Wilson Junr. & Nimrod Mitchell. Sci fa on Bail. Judgement.

James Kincaid vs Enoch James. Debt. Judgement confessed for sixteen pounds 8/6. Interest from 4th February 1797.

Minor Winn vs John Woodward. Sci fa. Judgement revived.

Edward Martin and Elijah Jones appeared in Court and took the Oaths of Office as Justices of the Peace for this County.

Charles McDaniel appeared in Court and took the Oath of Office as a Constable for this County being appointed thereto by the Court.

The Last Will and Testament of Peter Limley was produced in Court, and proved by the Oath of Basil Wheat, Ordered that Letters Testamentary be granted to Milley Limley and George Limley Executor named in said Will, A Dedimus, to issue to.

Moses Hill, Esqr. to qualify said Executors.

State   ) Asst.   The following Jurors Viz. David Martin,
   vs   ) &   Thomas Richardson, Christopher Bragg, Henry
Shardrick Jacobs) Batty.   Ederington, James Motey, Henry Poole, William
                           Richardson, Kader Coleman, William Ferguson,
Henry Hartin, James McCreight and Samuel Owen, were empannelled and
sworn to try this cause, who returned the following Verdict. Guilty.
                          David Martin foreman

Jonathan Belton vs Jesse Martin. Debt. Judgement confessed according to Specialty with Interest & costs.

Ordered that John Graffin have a Tavern Licence granted him for one year.

State vs Thomas Stone. Sci Fa. Dismissed.

State vs James Hutchison. Asst. & Batty. The same Jury, except James McCreight, in the room of whom, Robert Shirley, were empannelled, and

Sworn to try this Cause. who returned the following Verdict. Guilty.
David Martin foreman

James Barkley Ind.^e)
Robert Ellison   )   Judgt. confessed for L 9:1:1 1/2 Jany.
         vs   )   Debt.   1792 Subject to the plea of plene
Charles D. Bradford   )   Administratrix & Stay of Exon. ten
Executor of   )   months.
Isaac Lowe   )

Samuel Alston appeared in Court and took the Oaths prescribed by Law,
as a Justice of the Peace.

James Kincaid vs Swanson Lunsford. Case. Cotninued at Defendants
Costs under a peremtory rule for trial at next court.

State vs Shadrick Jacobs. Asst. & Batty. Fined in thirty dollars,
to remain in Custody of the Sheriff until paid, or give good security
to the same within six months and Costs to be paid immediately.

State vs James Hutchison. Asst. The defendant fined in the Sum of
fifteen Dollars, to be paid within six months. Costs to be paid
immediately.

State vs William Denton & William McShan. Kil^g a Guely. The Defendants fined in the sum of twenty pounds, to be paid within twelve
months and give good Security, or remain in the Custody of the Sheriff
until paid, also the costs to be paid immediately.

Adjourned until Tomorrow at 10 O'Clock.   John Turner
                                                  Richard Winn

                        Fairfield County Court

Saturday the 19th January 1799.
Court met according to adjournment.

Judges Present. John Turner. Esquire.

Ordered that a Tavern Licence be granted to John Curry for six months.

Executrix of Wm. Vaughon vs Roling Williamson. Sci fa. Ordered that
William McMorris Sheriff do show cause on Monday next why he should
not pay over the monies on this Execution Attorney.

William Hughes vs Guerard Duntze. Sci fa. Same rule.

On application of William McMorris Senior and James Kincaid, Securities
of Northrup Marple Administrator of the Estate of John Marple deceased,
to be released from their Securitiship. Ordered that the said
Securities be released as aforesaid, from this time forth only, and the
said Northrup proposing James Berkley and James Davis as new Securities
for his Due Administration of said Estate, the Court approved of them
and Ordered that they should be bound in the sum of one thousand
pounds.

William Kirkland vs Thomas Jones. S. P. Continued at Defendants
Costs under a preremtory rule to come to trial next Court.

William Paul vs James Davis. S. P. Judgement confessed according
to specialty.

William Kirkland vs Thomas Jones. S. P. William Clanton swore to
nine days and James Perry to four days attendance as witnesses in this
suit.

State vs Chesley Mathis. Noli prosequi entered by leave of the court.

The last Will and Testament of Sarah Bennet was produced in Court and proved by the Oath of Jesse Kirkland a subscribing Witness, and there being no Executor appointed or named in said Will Ordered that Letters of Administration with the Will annexed, be granted unto William Kirkland, who proposed Jesse Kirkland as Security, to be bound in the sum of five hundred pounds, the Administrator was Qualified in accordingly

Adjourned until Monday next at 10 O'Clock.   John Turner

                    Fairfield County Court

Monday the 25th January 1799.
Court met according to adjournment.

Judges Present. John Turner & Richard Winn Esquires.

Ordered that a Tavern Licence be granted to Peter Tidwell for six months from this date.

Jesse Havis &   )
John Harvey   ) Debt. Judgement confessed for thirteen pounds
    vs   ) nine shillings and nine pence half penny. being
James McCreight &) the principle and interest due on said note.
Alexr. McHenry   )

John King Junr.) S. Case. Settled, each party to pay their own costs.
    vs   ) John Bell proved four days attendance as a witness in
Simeon Tidwell) this suit.

Ordered that a Tavern Licence be granted to Andrew McDowell for one year from the Date of his permit.

James Kincaid) Case. The following Jury were empannelled being sworn
    vs   ) generally, to try this cause. Viz. David Martin
John Foote   ) fore.ⁿ Christopher Brock, James Mootey, Henry Poole,
        William Richardson, Kader Coleman, Robert Shurley,
William Ferguson, Henry Hartin, James McCreight, Samuel Gladney and
William Ewen, who returned the following Verdict. We find for plain-
tiff seven pounds fourteen shillings & six pence.
                            David Martin foreman

Ordered that John Rabb have a Licence for one year from this date.

Benjamin Boyde vs Minor Winn Admor. of Jas Winn. Debt. Judgement confessed for nine pounds thirteen shillings and four pence. with Interest from the second day of January 1796.

Ordered that Daniel McCullock have a Tavern Licence granted him for one year from the 8th January Instant the Date of his permit.

William Johnston) S. Case. The same Jury except James Mootey in the
    vs   ) room of whom Thomas Richardson, were empannelled,
Robert Phillips) being sworn generally, to try this Cause, who
                   returned the following Verdict. We find for the
                   Defendant with Costs of Suit. David Martin foreman

Ordered that Hugh Berkley be allowed five shillings for keeping an Estray Calf and that John McCants be allowed seven shillings for keeping an Estray colt.

Robert Rabb   )
    vs   ) S. P. The Council for each party having gone
Northrup Marple)   through their Arguments. the Court defered
                        their decision until tomorrow

Adjourned till tomorrow at   John Turner   Richard Winn
10 O'Clock.

                           168

Fairfield County Court

Tuesday the 22nd Day of January 1799.
Court met according to adjournment.

Judges Present. John Turner and Richard Winn Esqrs.

James Williamson et uxor. vs Alexander Irvin. Debt. Abated by
Defendants Death.

Ordered that James Austen have a Tavern Licence granted to him for one
year from this date.

Henry Dancer vs George Robertson. Asst. Ordered that an Attachment
do issue.

David Hamilton appeared in Court and took the Oaths of Office, as a
Justice of the peave for this County.

James McCreight vs Admors. John Milling. Case. Judgement confessed
for fourteen pounds seventeen shillings and eight pence, subject to
the plea of plene Administravit.

Alexander Blair)   Debt. The following Jury viz. David Martin, Henry
        vs   )   Poole, William Richardson, Kader Coleman, William
Roling Williamson)   Ferguson, Henry Harten, James McCreight, Saml.
                     Gladney, Thomas Richardson, James Mootey, Burd
Owens, Thos. Fant. were empannelled and sworn generally. to try this
Cause who returned the following Verdict. We find for the plaintiff
L 10. 7. 4 with Interest.   David Martin foreman

Robert Rabb vs Northrup Marple. S. P. The Court being divided in
Opinion, the cause stands over.

Arthur Clerk & Co. vs Obed Kirkland. Debt. Judgement confessed
according to Specialty, Stay Exon until next Court.

McRa Canty & Co.)   Debt. The same Jury except Bird Owen and Thomas
        vs   )   Fant in the room of whom Chirstopher Brock and
John Mickle   )   William Ewen were empannelled being sworn generally
                     to try this cause, who returned the following
Verdict. We find for the plaintiff according to Specialty with one
cent Damages & Costs of Suit.   David Martin foreman.

Robert Rabb vs Northrup Marple. Debt. Continued at Defendants Costs
under preremtory Rule to come to trial next Court, and that a
Commission do issue to take the Examination of David Marple a Witness
in this Cause.

Executrix of Vaughon vs Roling Williamson. Sci fa. The Sheriff having
tendered paper money into Court which the pbs. Attorney would not
receive, Ordered that he have time to change said paper money into
hard money.

Jeremiah Corkral vs James Smith & James Andrews. S. P. Decree
according to Specialty stay Exon. four months.

Isham Fair vs Benjamin McGraw. S. Case. Nonsuit.

William Lacey Asee of Edward Lacey vs James Craig. Debt. Nonsuit.

James Hutchison vs Stephen Splaun. S. Case. The Same Jury were
empannelled, being sworn generally to try this Cause. who returned
the following Verdict. We find for the plaintiff nine pounds with
Costs of Suit.   David Martin foreman.

Jesse Jenkins vs Burd Owens. S. P. Samuel Owens proved six days
attendance at last Court and five days at this Court as a Witness in
this Suit and rode 20 miles going and coming each court.

169

David Grey vs Admor. Hesther Cook. Case. Thomas Fant proves 4 Days
Attendance as a Witness in this Suit.

Gavin Curry vs William Fearis. Sci fa. On motion of Defendants
Attorney. Ordered that the Bill of Costs be retaxed, so far as
relates to the Costs acrued July Term 1797. The cause being postponed
that Court by Agreement at plaintiff costs.

Joseph Laney vs James Phillips. S. P. Decree for seven pounds with
Costs of Suit.

John Faulkner vs Robert Berkley. Slander. The same Jury were empannelled, being Sworn generally, to try this Cause--who returned the
following Verdict. We find for the plaintiff five shillings and
Costs.   David Martin fore.[n]

Jesse Jinkins vs Burd Owens. S. P. Bail released, and Decree for
six pounds six shillings with Costs of Suit.

James Hutchison vs Stephen Splaun. Appeal. Magistrates Judgement
reversed.

John Faulkner) Slander. The following persons Viz. James Cameron
    vs   ) proved five Attendance Joshua Harrison, Benjamin
Robert Berkley) Harrison and Arthur Yarborough each six, and Henry
                 Page two days, as witnesses in this Suit also Alex-
ander McHenry proved five days Attendance as a Witness in this suit.
William Paul proved five days Attendance in this Suit.

                              John Turner
                              Richard Winn

                         July Term 1799

Tuesday the 16th Day of July 1799.
Court met according to Adjournment.

Judges Present. John Turner, a Genl. Richard Winn Esqrs.

On application of Davis Austen, Ordered that he have a Licence to keep
a Tavern and retail Liquors for one year. from the 5th June last the
Date of his permit.

John Smith appeared in Court and took the Oath of Office, as a
Constable for this County.

Ordered that the Executors of the Estate of George Martin deceased
have Liberty to expose to sale the personal property thereof, agreable
to the Will, giving twenty Days previous Notice, and on a Credit of
eighteen Months for all sums above five shillings.

Jacob Gibson appeared in Court and acknowledged the Signing Sealing
and delivery of Conveyance of 144 Acres of Land to Jesse Ford.

Isaac Arledge appeared in Court and took the Oath of Office as a
Constable for this County.

The Last Will and Testament Alexander McDowell was produced in Court
and proved by the Oath of David Read Evans a subscribing Witness
Whereupon Ordered that Letters Testamentary be granted to Alexander
McKain, Jane McDowell and James McDowell Executors named in said
Will who appeared in Court and were qualified in, accordingly.

The Citation on the Estate Michael King was returned into Court duly
certified, Whereupon Ordered that Letters of Administration be
granted to John King the person named in said Citation, Who is to
administer with the Will annexed and the Testater being in the State
of North Carolina, the original Will was proved and lodged in the

170

Secretaries Office of that State An authenticated Copy of the same, is
ordered to be filed in the Office of the Clerk of this Court. he
naming John Hollis Moses Hollis and William Robertson to be bound in
the sum of three thousand pounds five hundred sterling. John King
Josiah Knighten, Thomas Stark, Nicholas Peay and Moses Knighten were
appointed as appraisers.

The last Will and Testament of Robert Brown was proved, and approved
of and Letters Testamentary Ordered to William Kirkland, Executor
named in said Will, who was qualified accordingly.

Proceeded to ballot for Grand and petit Jurors to serve at next Court
Viz. January Term 1799. When the following persons were drawn Viz.

Grand Jurors

John May	James Russel Junr	James Barber
Thomas Parrot	James Pearson	John Waw
Thomas Stark	John Mickle	Phillip Rayford
John Havis Sen.	Alexander Kenedy	Andrew McQuiston
Willm. McDaniel	Jacob Gibson	Willm. Robertson
Kiah Ford	Thomas Robison	James Andrews
David Shelton	Elijah Haywood	

Petit Jurors

Edward Briant	John Barber	Andrew Boyd
John Briant	Willm. Boyd	James Armstrong
James Beaty	Adam Beasley	Elijah Majors
William Nutterville	Saml. Frazier	James McDowell
Robert Richardson	David Boyd	Benjn. Jones
John Reyns	Thos. Robison Junr.	Tobias Taylor
Willm. Johnston	Willm. Beard	James Arthur
John Brunt	John Allen	Willm. Alsop
John Alexander	James Alcorn	Chris^t Attison
Henry Attchison	Robert Barber	Saml. Richardson

Court Adjourned untill tomorrow 9 O'Clock   John Turner
                                              Richard Winn

Wednesday 17th Day July 1799

Court met according to adjournment.

Judges Present. John Turner, Genl. Richard Winn and Aromanos Liles
Esquires.

Bartholamew Turnipseed applied for a Licence for to keep a Tavern &
Retail Liquors, ordered the same to be granted for one year.

Samuel Laughan vs Robert Berkly. Debt. Hugh Berkley appeared in
Court and enters himself Special Bail. Hugh Berkley.

David Read Evans vs Lewis Collie & Levi Moberly. Judgement confessed
according to Specialty with interest and cost Stay of Exon three
months.

David R. Evans vs Elijah Ivey. S. P. Dismissed by agreement on
Defendants paying all costs.

The Last Will and Testament of John Andrews was produced, and proved
by the Oath of John Wallace Whereupon Ordered that Letters Testamentary be granted to Phobe Andrews and John Bell Executors and
Executrix named in said Will. Who were Qualified in as such.

Proceeded to call over the List of Petit Jurors, when the following persons, appeared, were empannelled and sworn generally Viz. John Brown foreman, Ephraim Butler, Enoch Butler, Walter Pool, James Caldwell, Ezekial Frazier Richard Mansil, Saml. Fant, George Free, Edward Mobley, James Roseborough, and William Ederington.

David R. Evans vs John Winn Junr. Att. Judgement according to Specialty.

The Court proceeded to ballot for a Sheriff for this County, the Former Sheriff William McMorris' time now having expired. When upon casting up the Votes, it appeared that Hugh Milling Esquire was unamanously elected.

Teh Court also proceeded to ballot for a Corner for this County. When upon casting up the Votes it appeared that Mr. John Bell was unamanously elected.

James Kincaid vs William Cato. Debt. Judgement confessed according to note with Interest & Costs. Stay of Exon six months.

John Bell vs Phillip Raiford. S. P. Referred to Joseph Wood & William Rook & in case of disagreement the Arbitrators to have leave to Chuse an umpire & their award to be a Rule of Court.

State	)		The foregoing Jury except Walter Pool, in
vs	)	Swind-	the room of whom David Wear, were empan-
Phillimon Holcom)	ing.	nelled and Sworn to try this Bill of Indict-
Walter Poole	)		ment, who returned the following Verdict.

Viz. We find the Defendant Guilty for eight pound ten, with costs of Suit.
John Brown foreman

Ordered that the Administratrix of the estate of Thomas Graffin deceased, have Liberty to expose to Sale the personall thereof upon a Credit of twelve months, for all sums above five shillings, taking Bond and good Security, and giving twenty Days previous notice.

Samuel McKinney vs David Smith. Case. Refered to the Arbitration of Capt. Jesse Havis and Mr. James Barber with leave to Chuse an umpire upon Disagreement their Award to be a rule of Court.

State vs Andrew Hancock. Killing a Mare. James Brown and Samuel McKinstry, who were bound for the appearance of the Defendant, Surrendered the Body of said Hancock into Court, in Discharge of their Recognizance.

State vs Andrew Hancock and Wife. Stealg. John Brown and Saml. McKinstry, Surrendered the Bodies of Defts as above.

Ordered that, the Sheriff take the aforesaid Andrew Hancock and Wife into Custody.

Ordered that Josias Wood have a Tavern Licence for one year from the 14th June last.

Alexander Kincaid vs James Powel. Attacht. The same Jury were empannelled and sworn to try this Cause who returned the following Verdict. Viz. We find for the plaintiff according to the Note with Interest and Costs of Suit. John Brown foreman

Thomas Parrot vs Alcorn Yarborough. William Cato who was common bail or bail to the Sheriff, came into Court and entered himself as special bail in discharge of his common bail or bail to the Sheriff. Wm. Cato.

William Kirkland vs Thomas Jones. Judgt. confessed according to Note with interest & cost Exon not to be levied for six months until first January next.

Sion Coates, and Willm. Clanton proved their attendance as Witnesses in this Suit, Coates six days, and Clanton three Days and rode 25 miles coming and going from Winnsboro.

State vs John Baulkner. Asst. Daniel Harris and George Harris Securities for the Defendant appeared in Court and Surrendered the Body of said Faulkner in Discharge of their Recognizances. Ordered into the Custody of the Sheriff.

Capt. Hugh Milling appeared in Court and proposed Mr. Thomas Means, and James Berkley as his Securities for the Due performance of his Duty as Sheriff of Fairfield County of whom the Court approved and they entered into Bond, accordingly.

Adjourned untill tomorrow 9 O'Clock   John Turner
                                          Aramanos Liles

Thursday the 18th Day of July 1799

Court met according to adjournment.

Judges Present. John Turner, Aromanos Liles.

Phillip Pearson vs John Oglevie. Debt. Judgement confessed according Specialty.

Hartwell Macon vs William Martin & Thomas Shelton. Att. On motion, Ordered that the Verdict in the case so far as relates to Thomas Shelton be set aside, it appearing to the Court that the said Thomas Shelton was not a party to the suit.

The security of Ann Lashley administratrix of Thomas Lashley having given notice to the said Ann to appear and show cause why they should not be released from their bond, wherein they were securities for her administration of the Estate of the said Thomas.

Ordered that the said Securities be released from their said bond, and the Administratrix proposing John Stenson and Thomas Gladney Junr. as new Securities, they were approved of by the Court, and entered into Bond accordingly.

John McCreights Licence continued one year from this date.

James Kincaid vs Swanson Lansford. Case. The same Jury who served yesterday, were empannelled being Sworn generally, to try this Cause. Who returned the following Verdict. Viz. We find for the plaintiff L 19.10 & costs,   John Brown foreman.

The last Will and Testament of William Holmes deceased was produced, and proved by the Oath of William Davidson, the Executors named said Will James Rogers and Charles Montgomery, declining to act, the Court, Ordered that Letters of Administration with the Will annexed, be granted to Mary Holmes the Widow of the deceased, who proposed James Rogers and James Mootey Securities of Whom the Court approved to be bound in the Sum of one hundred pounds. The administratrix was qualified in, and nominated Mr. James Rogers, James Davison, James Davis, Charles Montgomery and William Thomson appraisers.

Jonathan Belton vs John Lucas. Attaht. Judgement by Default according to Specialties.

Debt proved by Zackriah Thompson. Witnesses for plaintiff.

James Kincaid vs Swanson Lunsford. Case. John McMorris proved six days attendance as a Witness in this Case, Chas. Montgomery proved one day. and Wm. Bell two Days attendance in this Suit.

173

Moses Airs appeared in Court and took the Oaths prescribed by Law to the Office of Constable.

The Last Will and Testament of Elizabeth Austen was produced in Court and proved by the Oath of John Sloan a subscribing Witness, Whereupon Ordered that Letters of Administration with the Will annexed be granted unto Robert Rabb, and Davis Austen, Who appeared and were qualified as such, they proposed Adam Robison and James Robison Securities, to be bound in the sum of two hundred pounds.

John Robertson and Alexander Robertson Orphans appeared in Court and made Choice of Hugh McEwen, for their guardian, Whereupon Ordered that Letters of Guardianship be granted to the said Hugh McEwen on all and singular the Goods and Chattels of said Orphans. Who proposed James Blair and Thomas Poole and Stafford Curry as Securities, of whom the Court approved, to be bound in the Sum of three hundred and fifty pounds.

Margaret Agnes Robertson an Orphan appeared in Court and made Choice of Simeon Cameron for her Guardian, whereupon Ordered that Letters of Guardianship be granted to Simeon Cameron, Who proposed Thomas Fant as Security, to be bound in the sum of one hundred and fifty pounds.

Ordered that the Executors of the Estate of Alexander Robertson have Liberty to expose to Sale, such of the personal property thereof, as may not be specially disposed of by the Will of the deceased, and may be necessary to be sold in Order to make a Division among the Legatees.

Enoch James vs Basil Wheat. Debt. The same Jury were empannelled to try this Cause, who returned the following Verdict, Viz --- We find for Defendant with Costs of Suit.   John Brown foren

Robert Rabb vs Northrup Marple. Debt. The same Jury were empannelled to try this Cause, Who returned the following Verdict. Viz --- We find for the plaintiff twenty pounds with Costs of Suit. John Brown foren

Alexander Kincaid vs James Powell. Att. James McMorris proved eight days attendance as a Witness in this Cause.

Robert Rabb vs Northrup Marple. Debt. James McMorris proved Attendance two Days, Alexr. Kincaid proved three Days as Witnesses in this Cause. James Rabb also proved Six Days as Witness in this Case, John Wallace proved 3 Days.

James Robertson vs Huston McWaters. Appl. Judgt. of Magistrate reversed.

Adjourned till Tomorrow 9 O'Clock.   John Turner
                                               Aramanos Liles

Friday the 19th Day July 1799

Court met according to adjournment.

Judges Present. John Turner, Aromanos Liles & Gen. Richd Winn Esquires

Enoch James vs Basil Wheat. Debt. Samuel Mayfield proved four days attendance as a Witness in this Suit. William Rook also proved two Days attendance in this suit.

The Citation on the Estate of James Bishop was returned into Court, duly certified, Whereupon Ordered that Letters of Administration be granted to Sarah Bishop and Josiah Knighton who propose Elijah Hollis and Joseph Aldridge as Securities of whom the Court approved, to be bound in the Sum of one hundred pounds. the Administrators were qualified, and nominated Thomas Knighton, Musear Bolar, John King, Moses Knighton and Isaac Grimes as appraisers, a Dedimus Charles Picket Esqr. to qualify appraisers.

174

Robert Rabb   ) S. P.   This cause was committed to the Jury, Viz
   vs   ) John Brown, Ephraim Butler, Enoch Butler, James
Northrup Marple) Caldwell, Ezekiel Frazier, Richard Mansil, Saml.
              Fant, George Free, Edward Moberly, James Roseborough,
William Ederington, Gerard Duntze. Who, returned the following Verdict.
Viz. We find for the plaintiff five pounds and Costs of Suit.
                                      John Brown fore^{n}.

John Wallace proved nine days as a Witness in this Suit.

David James & Willm. Rayford, to have a Licence to keep a Tavern and
Retail Liquors for one year from the Date of their permit.

Richard Bolan vs David Thompson. Debt. The Same Jury were empannelled
to try this Cause, who returned the following Verdict. Viz. We find
for the plaintiff twenty pounds four shillings with interest according
to Specialty and Costs of Suit.   John Brown foreman.

Ordered that the Administratrix of the Estate of John Boykin deceased
have Liberty to expose to Sale the personal property thereof, on a
Credit of eighteen months for all Sums above ten shillings taking
bond and good Security, and for all Sums under ten shillings Cash,
giving twenty days previous Notice.

Mary McMullen vs James Gamble. Case. Nonsuit. Leonard Rhodon proved
8 days Attendance.

James Kincaid vs Saml. Park & Phillip Pearson. Debt. The same Jury
were empannelled to try this Cause who returned the following verdict.
We find for the plaintiff Sixteen pounds eighteen shillings and one
penny with Interest according to the Note.   John Brown foreman.

Ordered that Samuel Parke and Edward Carlisle have a Licence to keep a
Tavern and retail liquors for six months, from the 18th April last the
Date of his permit.

Thomas Fearis et Axor vs Sarah Penny. Slan^{r}. Nonsuit.

State vs William Evans. Asst. Bat. Noli prosequi.

On Application of John Brannon, Ordered that he have a Licence to keep
a Tavern and retail liquors for one year from the third of May last,
the Date of his permit.

John McDonald vs William Lowry. Debt. The same Jury, except James
Roseborough, in the Room of Whom David Wear, were empannelled to try
this Cause who returned the following Verdict (Viz). We find the
defendant Clear of said Note as also of Costs and Charges.
                                      John Brown foreman.

William Wood vs James Austen & John Neily. Case. Ordered that a
Commission do issue to the State of Georgia to take the Examination of
Clem Fennel, a Witness in this Cause.

Court adjourned until Tomorrow at 9 O'Clock.   John Turner
                                                  Richard Winn

                    Saturday 20th July 1799.

Court met according to adjournment.

Judges Present. Genl. Richard Winn & Aromanos Liles Esqrs.

Joshua Gossy vs Edmund Swinney & Wife. Slander.

Joshua Gossy vs Jacob Thorpe. Mal pro.

The above two Causes refered by the Parties to the arbitration of Thomas Means. William Woodard and Robert Coleman. they said Arbitrators to meet and Make their award in Writing and return the same at the next Court which award so made shall be a rule of this Court.

Admors of James Ward vs Minor Winn. Debt. Dismissed.

Joseph Laney vs James Phillips. S. P. Ordered that a new Trial be granted upon payment of Costs.

Henry Shrock vs Wm. Berry. Case. Abated by plaintiffs Death.

Henry Shrock vs Heze.^{h} Ford. Case. Abated by plaintiffs Death.

State vs Shadrick Jacobs. The Court have indulged the Deft. six months longer to pay his fine.

Jonathon Belton vs John Lewkes. Att. Ordered that a Rule do issue against William Pool the garnishee summoned in this Case to show Cause why Judgt. should not be entered against him.

Robert Ellison Jur. vs Martin Moon. S. P. Decree by Default.

James Berkley vs Littleton Rain. S. P. Decree by Default for four pounds eleven and seven pence.

James Kincaid vs Almon Yarborough & Rachael Lovan. S. P. Decree by Default according to Specialty.

Bird Owen vs John Jinkins. Debt. Judgement by Default.

Henry Dancer vs George Robertson. Att. Ordered that the Attachment in this Case be renewed.

State vs John Lee. Bench Warrant discharged.

State vs Charles McElewain. Recoges. to keep the peace. Discharged.

State vs Thomas Ferrel. Assault. Discharged.

State vs John Faughner. Recogee. to keep the peace. Discharged.

State vs William Smith. Assault. Discharged.

State vs Matthew Richmond. Assault. Discharged.

State vs James Phillips. Bast.^{d} Discharged.

State vs Alcey Strippling. Asst. Discharged.

Northrup Marple vs Michael Dailey. Appeal. Judgement of the Magistrate affirmed.

William Rabb Senr. vs Robert Phillips. Appeal. Judgement of the Magistrate affirmed.

Adjourned until Monday next 10 O'Clock.   Richard Winn
                                                 Aramanos Liles

Monday 22nd July 1799.
Court was opened agreeably to adjournment and Adjourned until Tomorrow at 10 O'Clock By   S. W. Yongue   C.C.

Tuesday 23rd July 1799.
Court was opened agreeably to adjournment, and adjourned until Tomorrow at 10 by   S. W. Yongue   C.C.

176

Thursday 25th July 1799.
Court was opened agreeably to adjournment and adjourned until tomorrow
at 10 O'Clock.   By   S. W. Yongue C.C.

Friday the 25th July 1799.
Court met according to adjournment.

Judges Present. John Turner, Genl. Richard Winn Esquires.

Ordered that the Administratrix of the Estate of Jesse Godboth have
Liberty to expose to Sale the personal property thereof on a Credit
of fourteen months for all sums above five shillings, for five and
under, Cash, taking Bond and Security, and giving twenty Days previous
Notice.

Ordered that the Administrattix of the Estate of Thomas Leshley, have
Liberty to expose to Sale the personal property thereof on a Credit
until January first for one half the Amount said sale, for the other
until January come a year --- Taking Bond and good security for all
sums above five shillings giving twenty days previous Notice.

Mr. John Bell, proposed William McMorris Senr. and William McMorris
Junr. as his Securities for the due discharge of his Office as Coroner,
for this County of whom the Court approved and they entered into Bond
accordingly.

Hugh Milling Esquire having been elected to the Office of Sheriff for
the County of Fairfield, now produced his Commission and took the
Oaths of Allegiance and Office prescribed by Law.

Adjourned till the next Court in Course.   John Turner
                                                Richard Winn

You as foreman of this grand inquest for the body of the District of
Fairfield shall diliquently enquire and true presentment make of all
such matters and things as shall be given you in charge, the states
council your fellows and your own, you shall keep secret. you shall
present no one for envy hatred or malice, neither shall you leave any
one unpresented for fear favour or affection reward or hope thereof,
but you shall present all things truly as they come to your knowledge
according to the best of your understanding, so help you God.

The same oath your foreman hath taken on his part you and each of you
shall truly observe and keep on your part, so help you God.

You shall well and truly attend this Jury as a Constable you shall
keep them together seperate and apart from all people you shall not go
into them yourself neither shall you suffer any other person unless
ordered by the Court neighter shall you suffer them to have drink or
fire light untill they shall have agreed in their verdict.

You shall well and truly

You as foreman of the Grand jury for the Body of the County of Fairfield shall well & truly enquire a true presentment make of all such
matters & things as shall be given you in charge or shall come to your
knowledge the states Council your Own & Your fellows you shall keep
secret you shall present no one through hatred or malice nor leave any
one unpresented through fear favour or Affection nor for any reward or
hope thereof.   So help you God

The same Oath your foreman hath taken on his part you & each of you do
Swear to keep & observe on you & each of your respective parts.
                                            So help you God

                                      Evangelist

Samuel Whorter Yongue   Evangelist

                          177

Beasely cont.
  George 126
Beasley, Adam 142, 144,
  145, 146, 171
Beasly, George 164
  see Beazely
Beatty, Saml. 1, 14
Beaty, James 171
  Saml. 11, 24
  see Baity
Beaumont, Henryh 16
Beazely, Adam 136
  George 71
  see Beasely
Becket, James 135
Bedford, Jonas 110, 130
Bell, George 30
  James 164
  John 6, 14, 24, 31, 45,
    56, 57, 59, 62, 63,
    67, 72, 73, 89, 106,
    108, 118, 119, 120,
    121, 124, 131, 135,
    136, 142, 146, 156,
    157, 160, 161, 162,
    168, 171, 172(2),
    177
  John Jr. 105, 118, 119,
    120, 147
  John Sr. 105, 106, 117,
    127, 131
  Mary 14
  Thomas 69, 157
  William 19, 157(2)
  William Jr. 147
Beltnen, Lewis 39
  see Boltner
Belton, ____ 36, 97, 105
  Jonathan 36(2), 37(2),
    39(6), 58(2), 59(3),
    69, 76, 77, 86, 87,
    99, 101, 105, 106,
    109(3), 110(6), 112
    (3), 113(2), 117(2),
    119(2), 124, 127,
    129(3), 131, 132(4),
    134(2), 137(3), 140,
    141, 144, 145(3),
    147, 148, 149(2),
    151, 152, 153, 154
    (2), 158, 159, 160,
    163(3), 166, 173,
    176
  Sarah 36
  see Bolton
Benner, William 99
Bennet, Sarah 168
Berkley, Hugh 168, 171
  James 167, 173, 176
  Robert 156, 163(2),
    164, 170(2)
  see Barkley
Berry, William 138, 176
Bethany, Jacob 63(2)
Bethna, Jacob 52, 66
Bethney, Jacob 7, 14, 16,
  17, 25
Betty, John 130
Billops, Richard 65
Bird, Michael 36
Bishop, Downy 135
  Drury 43, 48, 83, 93,
    124
  James 57, 109, 174
  John 57, 136
  Sarah 174
  Wiley 164
Black, James 5
Blain, Andrew 164
  see Blane
Blair, Adam 46, 106

Blair cont.
  Alexander 169
  Catherine 18
  James 141, 145, 174
  John 146
Blake, John 21, 137, 145
Blakeney, Thomas 134, 152
Blane, James 147
  see Blain
Boden, Andrew 144, 146(2)
Boilstone, ____ 70, 127
  George 119, 147
Bolan, Richard 57, 138,
  175
  see Bolen, Bowlen
Bolar, Muscar 160
  Musear 174
  see Boler
Bolen, Richard 160
  see Bolan, Bowlen
Boler, Christopher 100,
  137
  see Bolar
Boltnen, Lewis 42, 43(2),
  44, 45
Boltner, Lewis 38, 40, 44,
  50(2), 69, 74, 86,
  87, 90
  see Beltnen
Bolton, Sarah 37
  see Belton
Boner, William 136
  see Bonner
Boney, Jacob 137
  Sarah 137
  see Bonny
Bonner, John 94
  William 95, 96, 98(2),
    100, 106, 107, 105
  see Boner
Bonny, Jacob 137
  see Boney
Bookter, Alexr. 73, 143
Bosier, Susannah 39
Boughter, Alexr. 72
  Jacob 78
Bowdre, ____ 49, 64
  John 40, 64
Bowers, ____ 11
Bowlen, Richard 154
  see Bolan
Bowler, Chrisr. 129, 133
  Musco 109
  Nusse 101
  see Bolar
Bowles, James 23, 63, 72
  see Bawles
Boyd, ____ 103
  Andrew 127, 171
  Benjn. 36, 38(2), 40,
    42(2), 44, 45, 49,
    50(2), 52(2), 53(2),
    54, 55(2), 58(3),
    60(2), 61, 62, 65
    (5), 66, 68, 70(3),
    72, 76, 77, 80, 81
    (2), 82(2), 83(4),
    84(2), 85, 86, 89
    (2), 90(2), 148
  David 171
  Hugh 48
  John 109
  Robert 66, 132, 135
  William 1(2), 6(2),
    8, 14, 26, 28, 35,
    47, 66, 106, 109,
    118(3), 124, 125(2),
    127, 141, 171
  William Jr. 118
Boyde, Benjamin 168
Boykin, John 71, 107, 132,
  141, 142, 175

Boykin cont.
  Capt. John 136
Brack, Chrisr. 106, 156
  see Brock
Bradford, C.D. 8, 15, 29
  (2)
  C. Daniel 9
  Charles 140
  Charles D. 28, 45, 64
    (2), 67, 148, 167
  Charles Daniel 9
  Charles Darnel 37
  John 45, 50, 62, 65,
    79, 133
  John L. 55, 77(2), 78
    104, 133, 166
  Thomas 43(3), 45(3),
    52, 53(3), 54(3),
    57, 61(2), 66
Bradley, John 132
  S. 32
  William 97(2), 99
Bragg, Christopher 166
Brand, Andrew 147
  Samuel 147
Brannan, Thomas 52
Brannon, John 175
Bras, Chris. 165
Bratton, Jonathan 128
Brevard, ____ 50
  Joseph 66, 79, 80, 119,
    137, 152
Briant, Edward 171
  John 50, 82, 92, 171
  William 93, 106, 119
  see Bryant
Brice, Jas. 83
Briggs, ____ 104, 109
Bright, James 156
Brock, Christopher 42,
  168, 169
  Robert 109(2)
Brodie, John 109(2)
Broom, Firraby 14
  John 58, 72, 73, 77,80
  William 118, 135
Broome, John 106
  William 97
Brown, Agness 132, 152(2)
  D. 105
  Daniel 8, 16, 31, 41,
    53, 60, 64, 65, 104,
    118, 122, 138, 141,
    152, 159
  Jacob 7, 8, 23, 104
  James 8, 15, 22, 27,
    47, 88, 94, 106,
    118, 128, 146, 147,
    149, 156, 172
  John 16, 58, 129, 147,
    164, 172(4), 173,
    174(2), 175(4)
  Jonathan 109
  Joseph 58
  O. 35
  Richard 165
  Robert 171
  Stephen 38
  William 134(3), 135(2)
Brumet, Spencer 84
Brumcte, Spencer 56
Brumett, Spencer 56, 67,
  68, 77, 78, 80, 94,
  105
Brummette, Spencer 57
Brunnett, Spencer 53
Brunt, Alexander 135
  John 136, 162, 171
Bryant, ____ 13, 24
  William 23, 24
  see Briant
Buchanan, Creighton 80,
  82, 84, 85, 92,137

181

McGraw cont.
David 15, 29, 67, 82,
    89, 92, 157, 160
David Jr. 150
Edw. 3, 52(2), 73, 95,
    117, 135, 137(2),
    138, 139(2), 141
    147, 151, 152, 153,
    155
James 16
Patience 61(2), 102,
    159
Rachael 101
Reuben 89
Solomon 141
William 7, 16
McHale, _____ 37
McHenry, Alexander 146,
    168, 170
McKaihe, Alexander 18
McKaime, Alexr. 21, 22, 24
McKain, Alexander 170
McKaine, Alexr. 20(2)
McKaino, Alexr. 17
McKean, Alexr. 8
    see McCane
McKee, Saml. 46, 106, 122,
    149
    see McKey
McKemie, John 128, 151
McKenny, John 162
McKewn, John 79
McKey, Mariane 136
    William 136
    see McKee, Mackey
McKinney, Benj. 71
    Jane 71
    John 8, 17(2), 18, 20
    (2), 21, 22, 24, 26,
    27, 39, 58, 68, 108,
    136
    Mary 109
    Samuel 2, 58, 94, 172
McKinstry, Saml. 147, 152
    (2), 153, 155, 172
    (2)
McKown, Hugh 11, 19
    James 11
McLemore, Elizabeth 91
McMillin, James 1
McMorries, John 134
    William 128, 136
McMorris, James 154, 156,
    165, 174(2)
    John 173
    Joseph 106, 156, 165
    William 8, 13(2), 15,
    17, 25, 34, 40, 43,
    47, 48, 60, 64, 74,
    91, 112(2), 142,
    150, 157, 167, 172
    William Jr. 25, 57, 59,
    121, 154, 160, 177
    William Sr. 7, 16, 26,
    27, 82, 83, 94, 95,
    108, 112, 122, 147,
    150, 154, 160, 161,
    162, 167, 177
McMullen, Mary 175
McMullin, James 8, 16, 17,
    18, 20(2), 21, 22,
    24, 26, 127
    John 14
    Samuel 127, 164
McNeal, John 121
McQuiston, Andrew 128,
    129, 130, 131, 133,
    134, 171
    Archibald 108, 122,
    135, 153
    David 106

McQuiston cont.
    Hugh 135, 138, 139(2),
    141
    James 141
    William 135, 141, 148
    see Quiston
McShan, William 165, 167
McTannal, Jeremiah 139
    see McDaniel
McTeyrie, William 18, 23
McTyre, Frirrle 46, 49, 65
    Frizzle 67, 71(2), 75,
    78, 89(2), 95, 96,
    104, 105, 112, 135
    Robert 37, 65, 82, 94,
    109, 130
    William 75, 96, 109
McTyri, Frisell 27
McWane, Charles 109
McWaters, Huston 117(2),
    118, 122, 124, 174

Mabry, Adam 116, 117, 158,
    160
    Daniel 46, 50, 52, 54,
    58, 59, 60, 61, 71,
    118, 123, 131(2),
    157, 166
    see Mayberry
Mackenzie, _____ 13
Mackey, William 143
    see McKey
Macon, _____ 81
    Frank 139
    H. 105
    Hartwell 152, 164, 173
    Heartwell 37, 45, 49,
    53, 56, 57(4), 67,
    82, 130, 134, 139,
    144
    Heartwell Jr. 53, 56,
    65, 67, 68, 75, 77,
    80, 89, 93, 96(2),
    104, 116, 117, 124,
    127, 131, 132, 134,
    139, 149
    Heartwell Sr. 75, 77,
    78(2), 80, 81, 105
    J. Heartwell Jr. 132
    John 78, 139
Mainyard, _____ 149
    see Maynard
Major, Elijah 3, 97, 98,
    106, 171
    John 145
    Nathan 162(2)
    Nathaniel 43, 54, 55,
    57, 60, 109, 124,
    125(2), 127
Malone, Daniel 58
    Thomas 52, 54, 58, 72,
    73, 75, 77, 78, 79,
    80, 81, 116
    William 94, 135
Man, James 150(2)
Mann, James 42, 57
Manning, Robert 95
Mannion, Robert 102, 114,
    120
Mansel, John 135
    Richard 38, 42, 82, 89,
    92
Mansell, Robert 7
Mansil, Richard 164, 172,
    175
Maple, Thos. 16, 29
    see Marple
Mardough, Hugh 136
Marple, John 161, 167
    Northrup 161, 162,

Marple cont.
    Northrup cont. 166,
    167, 168, 169(2),
    174(2), 175, 176
    Thomas 28, 31, 32, 34,
    37, 161
    see Maple
Marr, James 162
Marshall, James 38, 59
    Robert 83
Marshaw, William 159
Martin, _____ 103
    Andrew 83
    David 135, 138, 139,
    140, 141, 149, 156,
    165(2), 166, 167,
    168(2), 169(3), 170
    Edward 8, 15(2), 29,
    44, 82, 83, 105(2),
    106, 108, 128, 166
    Capt. Edward 6
    George 170
    James 160
    Jesse 166
    John 41, 48, 52, 56(2),
    60, 64, 94, 96, 100,
    116, 122, 166
    Mary 158
    Phillip 48, 49
    Robert 7, 16, 17, 24,
    25, 36, 45, 107,
    156, 165
    Robert Jr. 15
    William 8, 89, 96(2),
    100, 103, 117(2),
    127, 131(2), 134(2),
    153, 173
Martyn, Robert Jr. 45
Maskall, Henry 99, 111
Mathews, John 36, 57, 108
    Phillip 75
Mathis, Chesley 167
    Samuel 131, 134
Mattocks, _____ 24
    McKenzie 12, 24
    Wm. Bryant 13
May, Benjamin 17, 27, 49,
    57(2), 68, 83, 92,
    102, 119, 130, 136,
    153, 160, 164
    John 171
    Philip 164
    Thomas 74, 89(2), 127,
    133, 134, 140
Mayberry, Adam 150
    Daniel 139, 150
    see Mabry
Maybin, John 1
Mayburn, John 16
Mayfield, Edmund 139
    Saml. 58, 174
Mayfird, Abraham 128
Maynard, Edward 9, 58, 79,
    115
    Ferabee 79
    see Mainyard
Meador, Job 113
    Thomas 113, 136, 142
Meadows, Job 123
    Thomas 110, 142, 144,
    145, 146, 157(2)
Means, _____ 95, 145, 149
    Hugh 11
    John 37, 40, 43(2), 45,
    49, 52, 53(2), 54,
    55, 57, 76, 77, 78,
    84, 94, 96, 98, 105,
    106, 132, 133, 139,
    166
    Thomas 37, 39(2), 42,
    45, 52(2), 58, 67,

189

Russell cont.
James Jr. 8, 15, 17,
27
James Sr. 43
Nathaniel 109
Rustick, Barrbary 40
Rutland, ____ 26
James 13, 17, 136, 137,
150, 158, 160
Ryley, Phillip 77
see Riley

Saine, Thos. 33
Saint, Thomas 124, 125(2),
127
Sandeford, William 135
Sanders, ____ 32
Henry 129(2)
John 129
Nathan 129
Sant, ____ 142
Thomas 108
Sarrowe, Peter 112
Saunders, Henry 117, 136
John 143, 146, 149
Nathan 90, 143, 146
Nathanl. 47
Sauney, ____ 162
Sawney, ____ 149
Scibel, Graaf 54
Scot, Benjamin 135
William 55, 56
Scott, Benjamin 135
George 95
James 74, 87
Nancy 87
William 10, 14, 95, 109,
110, 144, 159
Seal, Enoch 136 142(2),
144, 145, 146
James 102
Thomas 57
Seale, Antony 157
Seigler, George 16
Priscilla 39
Selby, George 149
Sent, Thomas 38, 39, 42,
121
Seymour, Judiah 105
Shane, John 57, 135
Shannon, Thomas 3, 27, 30,
56, 75, 83, 164
Sharer, Phillip 40
see Shirer
Shaver, ____ 6, 31
John 114
Philip 14
Phillip 14, 49, 64(2),
92
Simon 97
Shaw, James 115
Shed, George 42
Sheins, John 30
Shellhouse, Isaac 109
Shelton, ____ 103
David 40, 50(3), 59,
67, 82, 83, 89, 97,
98, 100, 102, 103,
106, 108, 119, 126,
127, 128, 148, 160,
171
Lucy 50
Thomas 134(2), 173
Shirer, ____ 3(2), 34,
129
see Sharer
Shirey, ____ 128, 145,
164
Shiries, ____ 148, 149(2)
Shirley, Robert 97, 165,
166

Shirley cont.
see Shurley
Shother, Richard 82
William 128
Shrock, Henry 176(2)
Shurlds, Benjamin 43
Shurley, Isham 152
John 153
Robert 46, 135, 153,
156, 168
see Shirley, Shurling
Shurling, Isham 132
Shuts, Jesse 73
Shutts, James 60
Sibley, Jesse 55, 86, 100,
104, 125
John 86, 104, 127, 150,
158, 160
William 12, 22, 76, 99,
102, 115
Simmons, Jesse 45, 46, 49,
83, 110
Randal 134
Saml. 12, 83, 92, 102,
110
Sims, ____ 35, 39
Edwd. 11, 155
John 48, 49, 97
William 104
William Jr. 129
Singleton, Joseph 117,
124, 130, 137
Slaves, Bess 23
Jacob 103
Phillip 141
Sloan, Joh. 153, 174
Slone, John 109, 125(2),
127
Smith, ____ 25, 27, 135
Aaron 143
Abner 147
Abraham 48
Alexr. 27, 71
Anne 101
Augustine 45
Austen 77, 150
Bartlee 110, 116(2),
145
Bartlee, D.C. 108
Bartet 127
Battee 135
Claton 122
Clator 48
David 172
George 66
Hugh 10, 27, 30, 36,
37, 38, 40, 79, 109,
J. 126
James 57, 115, 116,
131, 150, 169
Joel 57
John 21, 24, 40, 55(2),
81, 87, 88, 95, 97,
100(3), 102, 103,
108, 110, 116, 117,
124(2), 125(3), 126
(2), 127(4), 130,
132, 134, 135, 138
(3), 139(3), 140,
141(2), 143(2), 163
(2), 170
John Jr. 20, 21
John Sr. 21
Capt. John 139
Mary 20
Moses 113
Nathaniel 155
Nimrod 113
Patence 21
Robert 36, 38(2), 39,
42(2), 43, 56

Smith cont.
Samuel 80
Stephen 135
William 122, 130, 136,
147, 176
Smithwick, William 82
Smyth, Bartlee 159
Bartlett 156
George 150
William 151
Sorseby, Wm. 145
Splaun, Stephen 169, 170
Splawn, Margaret 38
Rosa 73
Sebara 73
Spradley, Andrew 13, 24
Spradling, ____ 24
Andrew 14, 22, 26
Charles 14
Charles Sr. 14
Spuries, ____ 148
Stanton, John 135, 138,
139(2), 144, 149
Johnston 163
Joseph 96, 166
Stark, ____ 8
Thos. 13, 33, 158,
171(2)
Starke, ____ 133, 135
John 152
Reuben 108, 150
Robert 104, 106
Thos. 24, 45, 107, 108,
124, 127, 129, 138
Turner 117
William 130, 133, 141,
143, 145
Starks, ____ 79
Robert 44
Samuel 61
Thomas 47
Turner 58
Stedman, Jno. 20
Steel, Joseph 134
Rebeccah 134
William 134
Stenson, John 137, 139(2),
141, 173
see Stinson
Steveman, John 19
Stevens, John 125
Stevenson, James 97
Steward, James 140, 155
John 135
Stewart, James 145
John 71, 143
Margaret 61
Mary 71
Stinson, John 1, 27, 89,
121, 135
Stip, John 48
Stokes, ____ 56
John 132
Stone, James 129(2), 133,
137
John 79, 80, 124
Thomas 3, 8, 20, 54,
118(2), 122, 129,
133, 137, 142, 158,
166
Stormond, John 5
Straisner, Ross 76
Strange, Edmund 21
Joseph 102, 145(2)
Street, Benjamin 10
William 110, 112, 132
(3), 137(3), 138,
144, 145(2), 148,
153, 154, 160
Stripberry, Alex 160
Strippling, Alcey 176

www.ingramcontent.com/pod-product-compliance
Lightning Source LLC
Chambersburg PA
CBHW021905020426
42334CB00013B/493